LIFE
MEETS
ART

ART
MEETS
LIFE

LIFE MEETS ART

Inside the Homes of the World's Most Creative People

Sam Lubell

ARTISTS IN RESIDENCE

Sam Lubell

The chief enemy of creativity is "good" sense.
—Pablo Picasso

Creativity is about voltage. It's an electricity that surges through us, willing us to mold the original, the beautiful, the powerfully artful. It's a force that can alter lives and even shift the currents of history. The world's most talented artists, designers, writers, musicians, and entertainers are the ultimate testament to this power. They're embodiments of the flowing, limitless creative spirit—the ability to chart bold new directions, even if it's the hardest thing to do.

If we want to learn from these creative geniuses, we should, of course, study their work and pore over what has been written and recorded about them. But an oft-overlooked, profound way to experience their power and legacy is to examine one of the most personal aspects of who they are: their homes. Their refuges. Their inner sanctums. The spaces that purely reflect their values, their wants, and their spirits, designed just for them and those they love.

In this book we explore living spaces belonging to extraordinary creative people, both past and present. From obscure furniture designers to Pulitzer Prize-winning novelists to international pop stars, they've each created inspiring, sometimes revolutionary homes, imbued with their inspired spirit, outsize skill, thirst for experiment, and passion for beauty. These intimate spaces, from waterside shacks to sprawling mansions, contain, like their creators, still more layers. Their interiors help us uncover hidden histories: who the artists lived and learned with, their triumphs and tragedies, their skills and inspirations, and their longings, failings, inner doubts, and turmoils. They also reveal not just how artists shape their spaces and their times, but also how they are in turn shaped by them.

Some of these locations can be visited; others can only be admired from afar. Each entry in the book includes either an eye symbol to denote that it can be viewed by the public (either as a museum or by appointment) or a padlock symbol to indicate that it is a private home. For a full list of the houses that are open to the public, see pages 288–93.

HOMES AS REVOLUTIONARIES

*The Revolution introduced me to art, and in turn,
art introduced me to the Revolution!*
—Albert Einstein

The cottages, villas, townhouses, apartments, and mansions in this book showcase their owners' creative visions, while also shedding light on the forces like culture, landscape, and technology that impacted their designs. Some of the homes are revolutionary: brave experiments that changed how we live altogether. While filtered through changing times (and of course wildly different personalities), their ability to channel the ever-evolving creative spirit in built form remains remarkably constant.

Mid-nineteenth-century English craftsman and designer William Morris had this spirit in droves, launching a countermovement to the grime, mundanity, and mass production of the Industrial Revolution with his hand-designed wallpaper, stained glass, furniture, and textiles. While the age of factories was pushing people toward conformity, he preached a different way: originality, beauty, and handmade craft. "Have nothing in your house that you do not know to be useful, or believe to be beautiful," said Morris, who also advocated for community in a time of stark anonymity.

In 1859 he and his wife, embroiderer Jane Morris, enlisted the help of architect Philip Webb to create Red House, a gable-and turret-filled, exposed-red-brick residence just outside London. It became the embodiment of William's emerging Arts and Crafts movement. The moment you walk through its heavy medieval wood door, you're captivated with the detailed creations by him and his fellow designers: mosaic stained-glass windows colorfully depicting the four seasons, built-in timber cabinets and furniture, hand-woven carpets, block-print willow-bough wallpaper, and sprawling English murals. Timber beams wrap around you, and hand-laid brick fireplaces take on strange, mind-bending shapes. William would host raucous, laughter-filled gatherings here—wine-fueled, almost mythical festivals of creativity, building a fervent community to broaden his ideas.

Red House's fine detailing and artful immersion, not to mention its elevated cultural status, not only helped prompt an explosion of Arts and Crafts homes throughout Europe and the United States, but also became an inspiration for endless residences to come, which would embrace its ideals of careful craft and the Gesamtkunstwerk, or total work of art. You can see its imprint surging through time, in the stained log walls and hooded copper fireplaces of Gustav Stickley's Craftsman Farms in New Jersey, or the colorful, geometric interiors of the Glasgow townhouse of Charles Rennie and Margaret Macdonald Mackintosh. It flows into the curving stonework and carved wood, stained glass, iron, and ceramic of Victor Horta's home in Brussels, and it continued to thrive well into the twentieth century. It shone inside the Cranbrook home of architect and designer Eliel Saarinen—with its simplified geometric motifs and sumptuous, perfectly balanced bespoke tapestries, furniture, and lighting—and in the sinuous, hand-carved interiors of master woodworkers like Wharton Esherick, Sam Maloof, and George Nakashima.

More than half a century after Morris set off a revolution in English living, Modern architects shifted the currents of design in a dramatically different direction, designing homes for themselves that embraced the new possibilities of the machine age. They employed cutting-edge materials and techniques that shifted residential norms from applied ornament and spatial hierarchy to a focus on function, structure, and seamless unity.

While leading the architecture program at Harvard's Graduate School of Design, Walter Gropius, founder of the Bauhaus, designed a home for his family in Lincoln, Massachusetts that modified and modernized the traditional New England vernacular, fusing wood, brick, and fieldstone with metal, chrome, glass block, and acoustical plaster. Inside, his residence opens radically to the wooded environment around it through wall-sized windows, clear view corridors, and outdoor rooms. Every detail, every structure, every view is carefully designed to maximize beauty, efficiency, and simplicity. Spaces are filled with experiment, including innovative art and furniture by Gropius's Bauhaus colleagues Marcel Breuer, László Moholy-Nagy, and Herbert Bayer.

HOMES AS CREATIVE CANVASES

*Architecture serves as an eloquent reminder
of our full potential.*
—Alain de Botton

In every realm of creativity in every era, imaginative thinkers have channeled their vision and skill into homes that mirror their artistic passion, forming works of art in themselves. Romantic painter Frederic, Lord Leighton, renowned for gauzy paintings filled with history, exoticism, and yearning, filled his London home with eclectic designs inspired by his faraway travels: a fretted tile dome, gilt Moorish friezes, gleaming silk-covered walls, and lavish oriental antiquities. This startling residence, like those of Leighton's contemporaries John Soane and Frederic Edwin Church, inspired those yearning to escape their rapidly urbanizing reality, prompting them to infuse their own homes with the mysterious wanderlust and elaborate escapism of the Victorian age.

Surrealist artists like Salvador Dalí, Carlos Páez Vilaró, and Niki de Saint Phalle created strange, life-size canvases for themselves, letting their fantastical visions take three-dimensional form. There's Dalí's house in Portlligat, with its winding hallways, rooms themed for pigeons, bears, and clocks, and tower topped by a giant egg; Páez Vilaró's gargantuan whitewashed seaside drip castle, Casapueblo, along the Uruguayan coast; and Saint Phalle's Tarot Garden on the west edge of Italy, filled with monster-shaped buildings, including her own residence, the sphinxlike "Empress." Visionary architect Konstantin Melnikov channeled the Russian Revolution's early (and short-lived) idealism and thirst for change into his avant-garde Moscow home's hexagonal windows, cylindrical form, and rooms colored according to his psychological theories. Designer, architect, and metalworker Jean Prouvé brought his dream of residential prefabrication—including panels, beams, and even the office from his failed factory nearby—to his own 1954 house on a clifftop in Nancy, France, a presage to the *Dwell*-famed prefab homes of the present.

Today's tastemakers continue to adapt their goals and their imaginations to their spaces. Fashion icon Ralph Lauren, taking a page from his preppy clothing empire, imported the trappings of patrician Britain—tartan carpets, mahogany walls, Old Masters' paintings, and icons from the hunt—to his Bedford, New York, home, serving as a prototype for the wealthy and those aspiring to be. London architect John Pawson delivered a similar level of refinement, but with a radically simplified palette: all the practical concerns of his London townhouse are imbedded into a spare, seamless finish of white plaster, warm wood, and elegant, smooth concrete. On the other end of the spectrum, artist Andrea Zittel's A–Z West, an "evolving test grounds for living" in the desert near Joshua Tree, California, has, with its plywood finishes and cheeky blasts of color and pattern, become a scrappy model for those wishing to escape the mundanity and overconsumption of our urban society. She simultaneously explores our society's obsession with self-regard; her lifestyle has become an integral part of her art.

HOMES AS STORYTELLERS

*And there were houses, he knew it, that breathed.
They carried in their wood and stone, their brick and mortar
a kind of ego that was nearly, very nearly, human.*
—Nora Roberts

Homes are, of course, much more than creative accomplishments. They're physical histories, embedded with our stories, with the stuff of our lives. We know the work of our favorite artists and thinkers intimately, but we're rarely cognizant of where they sat down to write or gathered themselves to paint. Where they chatted about new ideas with friends and fellow revolutionaries. Exploring the details of these spaces, in some cases in person, transports us into their lives in a way few experiences can. It opens up stories and revelations that bring them, and their art, to life in new ways.

Tale after tale is told in the walls, shelves, and floorboards of this book's residences. The exceptional Brontë sisters—Charlotte, Emily, and Anne—would gather around their dark wood drop-leaf table in the rose-wallpapered dining room of their father's drafty eighteenth-century parsonage home until late in the evening, hashing out plots and characters, and creating classics of literature, including *Jane Eyre*, *Wuthering Heights*, and *The Tenant of Wildfell Hall*. In the parlor of her family's clapboard farmhouse in Concord, Massachusetts, Louisa May Alcott would welcome her well-connected father's guests, including the leaders of the Transcendentalist movement, Ralph Waldo Emerson and Henry David Thoreau. (You can still walk the pathway from Emerson's nearby house to the site of Thoreau's famed cabin on Walden Pond.) In her bedroom upstairs, forced by circumstance to contribute to the family income, she would write at her semicircular timber half desk that was handmade by her father, creating, among other sensational novels, *Little Women*, based loosely on the lives of her and her sisters.

Physical details fill in needed gaps; they help flesh out the story. They bring distant figures closer to us, connected via a setting—home— that we're all intimately familiar with. They take on a life of their own, haunted by spirits that can feel surprisingly palpable. A lovely daybed in Russian poet Alexander Pushkin's St. Petersburg apartment speaks to his comfortable lifestyle, yes, but more importantly, it's where he lay dying, after having been shot in a duel for his beautiful wife's affection. Romantic English poet Samuel Taylor Coleridge lived with his family in relative poverty in Somerset, England, writing in his cold cottage by the light of a candle and fireplace, struggling with a deepening addiction to opium. Yet inspired by his glorious countryside walks, he created epic works that defined the Romantic movement.

HOMES AS CHARACTER PORTRAITS

An interior is a natural projection of the soul.
—Gabrielle "Coco" Chanel

Behind any good story is the depth of its characters. Exploring creatives' residences, like detectives we gather valuable clues, peel back layers, discover hidden dimensions about our heroes: their rare ability and incredible strength as well as their vulnerabilities and weaknesses. Sometimes our assumptions are proven, but invariably, new facets appear. Sometimes the clues are small, like a fedora hat or a bright painting on the wall. Other times they're larger than life, as when a painter or

sculptor builds an entire wing, or a garden, as a temple to their creative work.

This is one of the reasons people form lines around the block to see artist Frida Kahlo's La Casa Azul in Mexico City. The 1904 residence, which Kahlo shared with her husband, painter, muralist, and activist Diego Rivera, reveals Kahlo's heartbreaking complexity in physical form. Crutches and corsets nod to agonizing physical maladies; stockpiles of clothing, letters, and jewelry uncover tendencies toward hoarding and mental illness; gifts from famed artists like Isamu Noguchi talk to her lofty place in the cultural world; portraits of Lenin, Stalin, and Mao allude to her leftward political leanings. The home displays deeply personal artworks, like *Frida and the Caesarian Operation*, which she couldn't complete because of the pain of a miscarriage. Not far away, the luminous home of architect Luis Barragán uncovers the inner tensions of a gifted, urbane designer hailing from a small Mexican village. He shifts between and fuses tradition and modernity, a duality that makes his work all the more exceptional. Timber-beam ceilings, light wood walls, divided layouts, and volcanic-stone stairs merge with vibrant, simplified compositions of layered form, space, color, and light. Modern, sometimes radical art hangs on walls, adjacent to crucifixes and statues of saints. Art itself takes on a spiritual dimension, while spiritual pieces, perhaps paradoxically, ground the home in place and time.

Homes can also highlight their creative owners' indomitable will and resiliency, vital ingredients of their greatness. At the Villa Santo Sospir above the bay of Villefranche, near Nice, Jean Cocteau sketched beautiful murals of colorful gods and strange monsters onto walls, ceilings, lampshades, bookshelves, and tables, a testament to not only his wide-ranging talent and imagination, but also his sheer audacity to propose such an alteration to the home of his patron, Françine Weisweiller. Architect Jørn Utzon, stung from the fallout over his acrimonious exit from the Sydney Opera House project, fled with his family to Majorca, where he created a home that is revolutionary in its timelessness. Rooted in the faraway place's history and art, it provided a respite from his worries and the world.

Wandering through these spaces, in person or in our minds, we discover new genius, new dimension, in the people we thought we knew. The Mount, the eclectic home of iconic author Edith Wharton, reveals her exceptional talent for design: the residence is a stunning merger of European tradition and American ingenuity. She collaborated on the home's plans with architect Ogden Codman Jr., with whom she coauthored *The Decoration of Houses*, a book that prefigured her greatest novels and criticized her age's obsession with excessive ornament in favor of classical principles like symmetry and simplicity. Likewise, Victor Hugo, the acclaimed French author who created *Les Misérables* and *The Hunchback of Notre Dame*, worked with local carpenters, combining various elements of furniture—chair arms, table legs—to form his own surprisingly original creations in his homes in Paris and Guernsey, one of the Channel Islands.

Sometimes we meet entirely new talents, unfairly obscured by the arbitrary rules of society and taste, or the cruel injustices of history. In visiting the colorful, intricately sculpted townhouse of Charles Rennie Mackintosh in Glasgow, we encounter the work of his wife, Margaret Macdonald Mackintosh. She collaborated with her husband on almost every inch of the interior, and she herself authored their home's textiles and charismatic, highly dimensional gesso panels depicting mysterious female figures that seem to fuse with nature. "Margaret has genius; I have only talent," Charles is reported to have once said.

HOMES MAKE US WHO WE ARE

We shape our buildings, and afterwards our buildings shape us.
—Winston Churchill

Another lesson emerges from these living spaces: we form our environments, but they—like our art, our children, or any of our other creations—in time help form us. Expansive windows and skylights provide artists with soft, warm light, and enchanted landscapes and vibrant, effervescent cities inspire the work of composers and writers. But *every* piece of a home and its surroundings can alter the course of a creative's work and life. When you're inside, you can feel the forces that feed this creativity.

In visiting the Paris home and studio of the great French sculptor Émile-Antoine Bourdelle, you sense inspiration in every corner. Its neighborhood, Montparnasse, retains many reminders of what was once one of the world's most famous bohemian communities. Large-windowed ateliers, revealing colorful tilework, peek out from narrow streets. Light filters into Bourdelle's verdant courtyard, full of his magnificent bronze statues, and you proceed to a studio lit by a back alley that has been transformed into a mysterious secret garden. The layering of emotions is exquisite, a sensation that continues inside the workshop, which Bourdelle filled to bursting with completed work in plaster, bronze, and wood. The eyes of men, women, gods, monsters, owls, and foxes stare at you, beckoning you to create.

Winslow Homer converted a small carriage house on a craggy peninsula outside Portland, Maine, into a home that perfectly captured (as did his work) the ferocity and poetry of the crashing ocean surf outside. When here you feel the cool surf and hear the savage waves dash the rocks, it fills you, as it did Homer, with the place's wild spirit, a parallel to our often tumultuous inner lives. In Giverny, France, Claude Monet created luscious gardens—filled with arched bridges, bamboo clusters, ornamental trees, and every color of flower imaginable—that inspired hundreds of late-career *Nymphéas*. He also painted each room in his expanded farmhouse a unique bright color, instilling his life with his work's tonality and, in turn, his work with his life's tonality.

Creativity is not static. One doesn't possess it, like a bauble or a piece of clothing. Its current travels in all directions and takes all forms, following its own path and transcending any person or notion. It infuses our lives and haunts the world long after we're gone. When we harness it, we're harnessing our own genius and winning, even if only for a short time, the eternal battle against the established precepts within ourselves and our societies. The homes of creatives triumphantly reflect that drive to enhance our lives and find new methods of expression, new ideas, new beauty.

ART
MEETS
LIFE

LIFE
MEETS
ART

ALVAR AALTO

The Aalto House
Helsinki, Finland

Architect, furniture designer
👁

Located in Munkkiniemi, a quiet residential area at the west edge of Helsinki, the house of pioneering Finnish architect Alvar Aalto (1898–1976) is an excellent case study for what makes his work so special. Aalto and his first wife, Aino—a fellow architect and furniture designer—completed the project in 1936, very early in the timetable of Modernist architecture. It was initially both their home and office. Covered in climbing foliage and surrounded by trees, the flat-roofed building shows off its two original functions right away: its white brick studio and its dark-stained, timber-clad residential section. While the building appears to be a perfect cube, as you walk around, you discover that it's fragmented and shifted in places, not just providing formal variety, but also unlocking interior volumes,

and allowing for light and air to penetrate. The living and working areas below and bedrooms and terrace above flow into one another, and open to the private south garden, showing off the Aaltos' trademark blend of simplicity, functionality, and elegance. Wood, plaster, and brick surfaces work in harmony, and attention to detail is paramount in this complete work of art, from sinuous doorknobs to seamless built-in shelving. In fact, Aalto, who lived here until his death, designed virtually everything inside: lamps, tables, chairs, benches, shelves, sliding timber doors, even book brackets.

LOUISA MAY ALCOTT

Orchard House
Concord, Massachusetts, USA

Novelist, short-story writer,
poet, essayist
👁

Although writer Louisa May Alcott (1832–1888) was born in Germantown, Pennsylvania , she spent her childhood in Concord, Massachusetts. Thanks to the associations of her visionary father, Bronson, she often found herself in the company of leaders of the Transcendentalist movement, like Ralph Waldo Emerson, Henry David Thoreau, and Margaret Fuller. Early on she helped provide for her family by producing novels, short stories, and essays, the most famous of which was her novel *Little Women*, a loose account of the family's lives, which became a sensation and has since inspired countless movies and plays. Starting in 1857 the family moved to Orchard House, a two-story seventeenth-century clapboard farmhouse named for the property's apple orchard. The traditional home

(used in the filming of Greta Gerwig's 2019 film adaptation of *Little Women*) is brought to life by patterned, pearl- and earth-toned walls, family portraits (including one of Louisa by George Healy, who also painted Abraham Lincoln), water-color paintings by Louisa's sister Abigail, and her mother, Abba's family china. The formal parlor is decorated with a green patterned carpet that contrasts with the burgundy-themed study across the hall. Arched niches built by Bronson, whose portrait hangs in a corner, display busts of his favorite philosophers, Socrates and Plato. Louisa wrote *Little Women* in her bedroom upstairs, on a small rounded "shelf desk" that her father built for her.

ANNA AND MICHAEL ANCHER

Anchers Hus
Skagen, Denmark

Painters
👁

Michael Ancher (1849–1927) and Anna Ancher (1859–1935) were central figures of the Skagen Painters, a talented group of artists who gathered to work in the picturesque northern Danish village of Skagen, capturing its stunning seaside landscapes, documenting its hard-working people, and in many ways disrupting Denmark's stodgy academic traditions. In 1884 Anna and Michael (married in 1880) bought a typical country home here, following the birth of their daughter Helga (who would also become an acclaimed artist). The home's vivid exterior palette was quite standard in the region, but its interior was definitely not. The graceful, rustic rooms showcase the work of virtually all of the Skagen Painters, their walls filled with salon-style hangings that include clustered portraits of the artists themselves, softly lit landscapes capturing the "blue hour," in which sky and sea would seem to merge, and dramatic scenes of fishermen launching and sailing boats in the stormy ocean. The artworks, which include more than 250 painting, flow into the home's surfaces: raised panel doors are painted with wild birds, and moldings are decorated with dark green plants and geometric ornament. The artists also installed beautiful, eclectic furnishings, ceramics, decorative objects, and souvenirs from their travels. The crowded home was eventually extended by architect Ulrik Plesner to include a new wing for art studios and leisure spaces.

IRIS APFEL

Apfel Residence
New York, New York, USA

Fashion stylist, interior designer
⌂

A New York grande dame and fashion pioneer instantly recognizable by her oversize glasses, Iris Apfel (b. 1921) founded Old World Weavers with her husband, Carl, in 1950. Together they built up a luxury fabric company that took its inspiration from historical patterns, notably working for nine US presidents—from Truman to Clinton—on interior design projects at the White House. In 1978 the Apfels bought a three-bedroom apartment on Park Avenue in Manhattan and created a well-curated treasure trove of items picked up on shopping expeditions at markets in Europe and North Africa. Apfel combined these trinkets with French, English, and Italian antiques ("I don't care whether pieces are expensive or junk," she once said, although she has "a possible Velázquez" on

the wall). She both dresses and decorates with the same eccentric spirit, mixing colors, patterns, and textures that others would be too reticent to attempt. The hallway of the property is lined with nineteenth-century bookcases and dog paintings. The canine theme continues with a Bakelite carving of a French dog holding a large collection of jewelry in its paws; painted Genoese chests sit alongside antique woven paisley shawls draped over a Maison Jansen table. In the library, a Dutch painting is displayed above a Louis XVI daybed covered in fabric that Apfel reproduced from a seventeenth-century French pattern.

GIORGIO ARMANI

Chesa Orso Bianco
La Punt, Switzerland

Fashion designer
🔒

Born in Piacenza in northern Italy, Giorgio Armani (b. 1934) launched his own fashion house in 1975, and the company has grown to become one of the most recognizable global brands, a byword for luxury goods. The Engadine Valley in southeast Switzerland is best known for the resort of Saint Moritz, but this dramatic 60-mile-long (97-kilometer-long) valley is also home to La Punt, a peaceful village where Armani has a three-story winter house. As is typical in the region, Chesa Orso Bianco (Polar Bear House) has thick shutters and small windows to combat the alpine chill, but the property's interior is a world away from the carved-pine rooms one would normally expect to see. Instead, Japanese influences abound, injecting a luxurious formality that is a paean to the Milan designer's

obsessively high standards. There is a calm sense throughout, with no evidence of extremes in terms of colors, materials, or styles. A pair of open staircases leads to the home's six bedrooms, and mahogany beams contrast with the *marmorino veneziano*, a waterproof, ancient Roman mixture of lime putty and crushed marble that is polished to resemble limestone. The living room is overlooked by a stuffed polar bear, given to Armani in recognition of the house's name. The leather cube chair is Armani/Casa, and the sofa on the right is upholstered in one of the firm's fabrics.

LOUIS ARMSTRONG

Louis Armstrong House Museum
New York, New York, USA

Trumpeter, singer, composer, actor
👁

With his distinctive, gravelly voice and endless string of hits, jazz singer and composer Louis Armstrong (1901–1971) became one of the world's most recognized musicians. He was at the peak of his fame when he chose to live in the working-class neighborhood of Corona, Queens. "We don't need to move out in the suburbs to some big mansion with lots of servants and yardmen and things," he commented. Pure Satchmo. He and his wife Lucille Wilson lived here from 1943 until his death. Lucille recounted that she had to buy and furnish the house, because "Louis didn't live anywhere then and didn't want to." But the peripatetic talent fell in love with the 1910 three-story structure of red brick, designed by local architect R. W. Johnson. Inside, it's a time capsule of Armstrong's heyday. Lucille was

not shy with her design preferences, including vibrant mid-century touches like reflective floral wallpaper, Regency fixtures, laminated wooden cabinets, and a boldly lacquered blue kitchen. The couple's presence is everywhere: Armstrong's den, with its dark wood desk and walls, contains his scribbled notes and reel-to-reel tapes; the living room, with its textured, semi-circular satin couch, is full of the couple's travel mementos, along with a portrait of Armstrong by his friend Tony Bennett; the frilly bedroom, with its distinctive cane bed and crystal chandelier, is a touch of royalty and a lot of Queens.

JANE AUSTEN

Jane Austen's House
Chawton, Hampshire, England, UK

Novelist
👁

Beloved novelist Jane Austen (1775–1817), who fearlessly probed the hypocrisies and neuroses of eighteenth-century British gentry, lived and wrote in a few locations. But her career only flourished once she moved to what would be her final home in Chawton, England, southwest of London. It was in this seventeenth-century brick building, a former steward's cottage owned by her brother Edward, where Austen completed all of her major works, including *Sense and Sensibility*, *Pride and Prejudice*, *Mansfield Park*, *Emma*, *Northanger Abbey*, and *Persuasion*. She moved here in 1809 with her mother; sister, Cassandra; and friend Martha Lloyd. The home's intimate, well-preserved rooms contain a wealth of the family's fascinating possessions. Highlights include Austen's letters

(one to her niece Anna Lefroy is full of family gossip, and another to her sister describes the publication of *Pride and Prejudice*), her jewelry (such as a turquoise-and-gold ring and a topaz cross), clothing (such as a hand-woven white muslin shawl said to have been embroidered by her), first editions of her books (including a three-volume printing of *Sense and Sensibility*), and the spare, tiny walnut table by the window at which she wrote her novels daily. In 1817 she moved to Winchester for treatment for a short illness from which she died that year.

AGNÈS B

Le Coeur Volant
Louveciennes, France

Fashion designer
🔒

Born in Versailles, just yards from the former seat of French royalty, Agnès Troublé (b. 1941) grew up to establish a fashion empire inspired by all things French and based on chic simplicity. She registered the company name agnès b. (all lowercase) early in her career, as she didn't want to use her first husband's surname, Bourgois. Mixing the spirit of *liberté, égalité, fraternité* with the radical, hippie sensibilities of the 1968 Paris uprising, she built a global fashion empire, making her reputation with a series of classic pieces, including the emblematic snap cardigan. The fashion designer's elegant home in Louveciennes, in the western suburbs of Paris, is a stone's throw from her hometown and the very model of civilized French taste, where trends are ignored and history respected. Named Le Coeur

Volant ("The Flying Heart"), the house was commissioned by Louis XIV in 1710 and, due to its proximity to the royal palace, became the residence of the king's physician. Its rooms are filled with natural light, thanks to the window-dominated facade. The floors are Burgundy stone and Hungarian chevron parquet; the walls display ancestral oil paintings hanging next to candid Nan Goldin photography, a self-portrait by Jean-Michel Basquiat, and a Mappa by Alighiero e Boetti. The music room's acoustics are enhanced by eighteenth-century wood paneling, and handwritten letters and personal messages can be found throughout.

FRANCIS BACON

Francis Bacon's Studio
Dublin, Republic of Ireland

Painter
👁

The studio of Francis Bacon (1909–1992) is one of the world's great messes. The idiosyncratic painter, born in Ireland to English parents, was well known for his raw, emotionally charged (some would say depraved) artworks, presenting the human face and figure as expressively distorted, even grotesque. His studio at 7 Reece Mews in London was equally unruly; many would also call it grotesque. "I feel at home here in this chaos because the chaos suggests images to me," said Bacon, named for the sixteenth-century philosopher and statesman. For three decades he worked in the 13-by-20-foot (4-by-6-meter) second-floor atelier, surrounded by paint-splattered surfaces—walls, floors, doors, and shelves. Within these surroundings were slashed canvases, violently askew painting materials, empty boxes, books, personal snapshots, and folded and tattered newspapers and magazines and on every topic imaginable, from bullfighting to medicine. Sometimes all this stuff made it hard for Bacon to move in front of his canvases. But its contents would inevitably serve as inspiration and became a sort of crude artwork in itself, in many ways a reflection of Bacon's own life. His early years were marked by childhood illness, unaccepted homosexuality, and the alienation, violence, and suffering of two world wars. Later years brought carousing and tumultuous relationships. His studio was moved in its entirety to Dublin's Hugh Lane Gallery between 1998 and 2001.

JOHN
BALDESSARI

Baldessari Residence
Los Angeles, California, USA

Conceptual artist
🔒

John Baldessari (1931–2020) was a rare figure: he was a conceptual artist with a sense of humor, even achieving the high distinction of voicing his own character in *The Simpsons*. He was not afraid to break rules, notably in 1970 when he burned all of his own paintings at a local crematorium. He bought this rundown 1907 bungalow in Santa Monica, California, in the 1980s, but waited until the next decade before he started to renovate it. He asked husband-and-wife architects Ron Godfredsen and Danna Sigal to introduce some modern touches into the traditional Craftsman residence. They felt it important to add color, tying the project into Baldessari's own work: he was known for placing colorful dots on black-and-white photographs. Roy McMakin designed the dining table and white-enamel chairs, as well as the barstools in the kitchen. Much of the house and furniture were built oversize to accommodate Baldessari's 6-foot-7-inch (2-meter) frame, including his bed, the ceilings, and the stainless-steel bath. The increased height and volume of each room make the house feel bigger than it really is. The dining-room walls are lined with works by the artist's peers, including Sol LeWitt, Bruce Nauman, and Lawrence Weiner. Pamela Burton landscaped the garden, creating a courtyard of crushed red brick in the middle of an olive grove.

SHIGERU BAN

Ban Residence
Tokyo, Japan

Architect
🔒

Best known for his penchant for building with unorthodox materials, Japanese architect Shigeru Ban (b. 1957) was awarded the Pritzker Architecture Prize in 2014. Ban has created his unique structures around the world, often using cardboard or paper, as with the Cardboard Cathedral in Christchurch, New Zealand, following a devastating earthquake in 2011, and the Paper Log House he designed for people made homeless by the 1995 earthquake in Kobe, Japan. He built his own Tokyo home near Hanegi Park in 1997, with the aim of not removing any trees from the woodland. He envisaged the apartment building in this Tokyo suburb as being suitable for a Zen monk, with few furnishings and plenty of natural light through floor-to-ceiling windows and light wells.

He employed a grid of regular triangles, each side measuring 13 feet (4 meters) long, to create a stable structure. Ban's challenge was to provide well-proportioned living areas despite the intrusion of the resulting columns and beams. This triangular arrangement allows the floor slabs to be properly cantilevered, even when the spaces around the trees are hollowed out in circular or oval shapes. Each apartment unit is built in a terrace-house style across three floors, meaning no fireproofing is necessary between each story, and the building's structural workings can be revealed. This also allows inhabitants to view the natural setting at different heights.

LUIS BARRAGÁN

Casa Luis Barragán
Mexico City, Mexico

Architect, engineer
👁

Visiting the home of Mexico's most renowned architect, Luis Barragán (1902–1988), is about as close as you can get to walking into a three-dimensional painting. Every angle, every view, every shadow, every color, and every beam of light seem composed to alter, enhance, and challenge your senses. Located in Mexico City's Tacubaya neighborhood, the home presents a fairly uniform, austere facade, a nod to Barragán's introspective, private nature. Inside, he designed the residence as a purposeful mix of Modern and vernacular Mexican architecture. Spaces are planned in a cellular fashion, as if you were moving through a Mexican village, with tall walls and progressing plazas and fountains. Traditional elements like wood-beam ceilings, light wood walls, and volcanic stone

stairs merge with the architect's vibrant compositions of form, space, and light. The entrance stair, for instance, starts as a shadowy, compressed zone, but its height, dimensionality, and light explode at its landing, drawing you up, as if you were ascending to heaven. Throughout the house, you bounce from small, low-ceilinged hallways to light-filled double-height spaces to modest, almost monastic rooms, which hold a mix of religious icons, indigenous sculpture, gorgeous modern art, and ingenious plays of light. The wondrous roof terrace, which erupts in color and mass, as well as the wild, over-grown garden, typifies Barragan's conflicting characteristics of asceticism (he was a devout Franciscan Catholic) and expressive sensuality.

FREDERIC CLAY BARTLETT

Bonnet House Museum & Gardens
Fort Lauderdale, Florida, USA

Art collector, painter
👁

Wealthy Chicago native Frederic Clay Bartlett (1873–1953) made his name less with his lively modern paintings and murals than with his art collecting. "I am a collector," he once told a reporter. "It is a habit—a disease with me. I cannot help buying curios, antiquities, and works of art, even when I have no place to put them." His other habit was homes. In 1902 he decorated his first, Dorfred House, in Chicago, with his fantastical, flowery murals, frescoes, and painted beams, as well as fine furniture and decoration. After Bartlett's first wife, artist Dora Tripp, died, he married Helen Louise Birch, an accomplished poet and composer. In 1920, thanks to a land gift from Helen's father, they built Bonnet House on a barrier island outside Fort Lauderdale. The eclectic estate is Bartlett's

masterpiece. Using knowledge gleaned from interactions with Chicago architects, he designed the bright yellow home, with its broad veranda and sweeping roof, as an interpretation of a Caribbean plantation. Meandering around a courtyard, its radically diverse rooms are filled with art (by Bartlett and Bartlett's third wife, Evelyn Fortune Lilly, among others), mementos, wood paneling, decorative tile, and Bartlett's murals and frescoes. The living room's clam-inspired leatherette chairs speak to the sea; monkeys and birds grace pillows; colorful ceramic peacocks stand on the mantel, beneath a lush painting depicting a pair of white and black swans.

GEOFFREY BAWA

Number 11
Colombo, Sri Lanka

Architect
👁

One of the most influential Asian architects of his time, Sri Lankan architect Geoffrey Bawa (1919–2003) was a pioneer of what is now known as Tropical Modernism, blending nature, architecture, and serene sensuality with the functional tenets of Walter Gropius and Le Corbusier. He achieved international recognition while remaining a regional architect, designing details and spaces that reflected traditional building and sensitivity to the local topography and climate. Bawa's own home, at the end of a narrow suburban lane in Colombo, intricately blends indoor and outdoor living areas through a sequence of porches and planted courtyards, and the incorporation of textured natural materials like stone, wood, and clay. Textiles and artwork infuse rooms with seductive

energy, and the modulation of bright light and restful shade is artfully orchestrated throughout the subtly conceived, and often surprising, series of views and experiences. The central space echoes both a type of pillared hall found in ancient Sri Lankan Buddhist temples and the impluvium, or courtyard pool, of a Roman villa. (Bawa also cited sources as diverse as Italian hill towns and the Alhambra in Granada, Spain.) The architect's original residence was the third in a row of four small bungalows. Eventually, Bawa acquired all four buildings, creating a tapestry of structures; he converted the first in the row into a glass-brick-clad tower with an open viewing deck.

VANESSA BELL AND DUNCAN GRANT

Charleston
Firle, East Sussex, England, UK

Painter, interior designer, book-cover designer (Bell); painter, textile designer, pottery designer, set designer (Grant)
👁

"The house is most lovely, very solid and simple, with flat walls in that lovely mixture of brick and flint that they use about here, and perfectly flat windows in the walls and wonderful tiled roofs.... The rooms are very large.... One I shall make into a studio," wrote boldly expressive British painter Vanessa Bell (1879–1961) to the critic and painter Roger Fry in 1916. The artist, perfectly describing Charleston, her future farmhouse in East Sussex, moved in the same year, along with serenely sculptural painter Duncan Grant (1885–1978), his friend and lover, David Garnett, and Bell's two sons. Over sixty-four years the property became a living canvas for the painters and a refuge for the unconventional relationships now synonymous with the Bloomsbury group, whose early twentieth-century members included Bell's husband, art critic Clive Bell, and her sister, author Virginia Woolf. Each room was decorated and transformed by both Bell and Grant, including the painting of walls and furniture. As Garnett wrote, "One after another, the rooms were decorated and altered almost out of recognition, as bodies of the saved are said to be glorified after the resurrection." The studio (used predominantly by Grant) embodies the house's unfussy, liberated aesthetic: its decor includes painting ephemera, a Dutch walnut cabinet once owned by novelist W. M. Thackeray, a decorated fireplace featuring two caryatids, and Stephen Tomlin's unfinished bust of Woolf.

MARIO BELLINI

Bellini Residence
Milan, Italy

Furniture designer, product designer,
architect
🔒

Equally comfortable working on buildings like the Milano
Convention Centre and on products for Olivetti, Cassina,
and Vitra, Mario Bellini (b. 1935) has been a fixture of contemporary design for more than half a century. The magnificent
nineteenth-century palazzo where he lives and works was
originally reworked by another renowned Milanese architect,
Piero Portaluppi, during the 1930s. Bellini began making his
own interventions in the 1980s, mixing different periods of art,
colorful murals, tapestries, and furniture by himself, Alvar
Aalto, and Norman Cherner, among others. The home's centerpiece is its mezzanine library, which can be glimpsed from
the foyer. Accessed via a monolithic double stair, its wooden
shelves are navigated using a scaffold-like system of sliding

metal ladders, their aquamarine color popping against the
Portaluppi fresco paintings that adorn the surrounding walls.
Standing 30 feet (9 meters) tall, the bookshelves extend
beyond the mezzanine and down three levels, lending their
cerebral presence to several interior spaces and comple-
menting the encyclopedia of objects they contain: works by
Charles and Ray Eames, Aalto, Gio Ponti, and Ettore Sottsass.
When it was featured in the 2014 Milan exhibition *Where
Architects Live*, Bellini likened his house to "one huge, tall, tall
bookcase which I walk around, touching my books: sometimes
I tidy them up and every now and then I leave them in a terrible
mess so that I have difficulty finding them again—but it's
really the heart of my home."

WARD BENNETT

Dakota Apartment
New York, New York, USA

Furniture designer, interior designer,
textile designer, sculptor
🔒

Design legend Ward Bennett (1917–2003) gracefully walked the tightrope between edgy and corporate, pared down and sumptuous. He was at his best when making contemporary refinements to historical standards. This was exactly the scenario for his own attic duplex, carved out of a warren of gables and maids' rooms inside the Dakota, Henry Janeway Hardenbergh's famed Gothic Revival masterpiece overlooking Central Park. The unit's sloping walls, formed by the building's angled roof, simultaneously create a feeling of embrace and uplift, and frame an open, uncluttered space that fills the old building with a sense of modernity. Spare beige tones accentuate the layout's simplicity but add warmth and nobility. As usual, Bennett was able to turn potential liabilities into

assets: a central airshaft becomes the outline for a sculptural focal point; the building's flagpole anchors a circular center-piece table in his office. Bennett-designed furniture is spare but luxurious, like black leather sofas, which dialogue with a sophisticated selection of art and antiques. High-tech components are a stealthy surprise—a steel spiral stair elegantly links floors, and double-story sloping windows provide unique views. George O'Brien, a design reporter for the *New York Times Magazine*, aptly called it "perhaps the most exciting modern apartment in New York."

ALEXANDRE DE BETAK

Betak Residence
New York, New York, USA

Fashion designer, furniture designer
🔒

The New York apartment that Alexandre de Betak (b. 1968) calls home is a testament to the fun side of his personality. The French fashion designer and events producer is best known for his spectacular runway shows, working with the likes of John Galliano and Dior Couture. When Betak bought the 4,000-square-foot (372-square-meter) SoHo loft in 2013, his skills and experience were important tools in creating a space he and his wife, Sofía, describe as "playful, warm, versatile, Europeanish." A white-planked, sun-bleached floor reclaimed from the walls of a barn acts as a base for Betak's flourishes. He drew inspiration from traditional Japanese architecture, Minimalism, and 1980s New York loft living. The most-used space is the tatami room, which is built on an oak

platform. It is the spot where the couple practice Pilates, watch movies, eat from a motorized table, and enjoy sake on tap. A bookshelf acts as a secret entrance to a mirror-paneled party room, complete with stripper pole. The kitchen is dominated by a large stainless-steel island, and nearby are a swing and a Vespa scooter. The living area contains a Louis Durot chair shaped like a woman's upturned torso and legs; it shares the space with a Galerie Berger sofa and André Cazenave pyramid lamps.

ANTONIO BLANCO

Blanco Renaissance Museum
Ubud, Bali, Indonesia

Painter
👁

Born to Spanish parents in Manila, Antonio Blanco (1912–1999) became one of the most famous, not to mention eccentric, artists to live in the region. His dreamlike paintings, unabashedly focusing on the female form, merged realism and Surrealism, as well as a healthy dose of eroticism. After receiving a block of land from the king of Ubud, Bali (who actively recruited artists and collectors), he built his mansion and studio in Campuan, on top of a mountain overlooking the Campuan River. Blanco and his Balinese wife, the celebrated dancer Ni Ronji, lived with their children here, barely leaving, while receiving guests from around the world. Before his death Blanco worked to turn his property into a museum for his work. The lavish building, a somewhat bawdy blend of Balinese and European architectural elements, contains more than three hundred Blanco paintings from different periods of his career, as well as his illustrated poetry and erotica. The art is accompanied by ornate pillars, colorful walls, marble floors, elaborate wrought-iron staircases, and a glass dome. The building also contains Blanco's studio, which has been preserved exactly as he left it, with brushes, paints, and canvases scattered, and paintings covering the walls. A green marble archway, guarded by two massive stone dragons, frames the museum's entrance. The 215,000-square-foot (19,974-square-meter) grounds contain lush tropical gardens filled with pavilions, sculptures, ornaments, temples, shrines, and endless exotic birds.

BILL BLASS

Sutton Place Apartment
New York, New York, USA

Fashion designer
🔒

Iconic American fashion designer Bill Blass (1922–2002) dressed the likes of Jacqueline Kennedy, Nancy Reagan, Gloria Vanderbilt, and Marlene Dietrich. Spread across the top floor of Sutton Place's 444 East 57th Street (the same building where Marilyn Monroe once resided with Arthur Miller), Blass's expansive 2,200-square-foot (204-square-meter), two-bedroom residence boasts 3,000 square feet (279 square meters) of private terraces and views over the East River and the 59th Street Bridge. With its tonal palette and warm yet restrained aesthetic, the masculine, traditional interior is refined and neatly tailored—like Blass himself. "There is a sense of dignity, a simplicity, and a classicism in my clothes which can be read into the apartment," the designer remarked.

Designed by Blass with Mica Ertegun and Chessy Rayner of New York–based MAC II studio, the residence has high-ceilinged, perfectly orthogonal rooms. "I work in fashion. I don't want to live somewhere that looks fashionable," he explained. The quiet interior design places a controlled mix of substantial, sculptural antiques, classical male nudes, continental furniture (in shades of black, white, brown, or beige), and architectural drawings against a spare backdrop of ivory walls, wood and marble floors, and classical moldings. "What I have here is the result of a lifetime of collecting," Blass said. "There is no relationship between the things themselves—except that I like them."

KAREN BLIXEN

Karen Blixen Museet
Rungsted Kyst, Denmark

Novelist, short-story writer,
autobiographer, essayist
👁

Danish author Karen Blixen (1885–1962) created seminal works that include *Out of Africa* and *Seven Gothic Tales*. She's unknown to many, in part because she wrote under several pen names, including Isak Dinesen, her nom de plume for *Out of Africa*. Born into a wealthy noble family in Rungsted, north of Copenhagen, Blixen followed her future husband, Baron Bror Blixen-Finecke, to Kenya, where they established a coffee plantation and became big-game hunters. She divorced Bror Blixen in 1925 and subsequently ran the farm with thousands of employees singlehandedly. Her turbulent years in the country were recorded in *Out of Africa*, her memoir that decades later would become an Oscar-winning film. In 1931, after the failure of the farm, Blixen reluctantly moved back to her family home,

Rungstedlund, where she would develop her writing career. The whitewashed seventeenth-century property features a broad tile roof and interiors that marry rustic and aristocratic aesthetics. Classically inspired rooms, their colorful walls outlined in gold trim and layered with fine antiquities, complement locally wrought timber furniture. Blixen's study, known as Ewald's room (for Danish writer Johannes Ewald), is a testament to her time in Kenya and her loved ones: African spears and shields are hung on the wall behind the desk, animal-skin drums sit on the floor beneath the bookcases, carved masks and wooden boxes inlaid with shells and animal bone cover tabletops. A bust of Ewald stands atop the gun cabinet of her father, Wilhelm Dinesen.

LINA BO BARDI

Casa de Vidro
São Paulo, Brazil

Architect, furniture designer,
illustrator, set designer
👁

While Philip Johnson's mythical Connecticut residence has monopolized the moniker of Glass House, you might get a second opinion if you ask someone in Brazil. There the title goes to Casa de Vidro, the home of renowned Italian-born architect Lina Bo Bardi (1914–1992). Located on São Paulo's southern outskirts, the house, its walls clad in glass sheets, was completed just two years later than Johnson's abode. But while Johnson's home sits easily on a rolling site, Bo Bardi's is propped above a sharp slope on tall, thin columns. The home is divided into two portions: the exposed living and dining rooms, their internal courtyard popping up from below, and modest bedrooms and staff quarters at ground level. Entered from below, via a floating stair, the residence is filled with

color—from light blue glass floor tiles to an emerald green kitchen—and a mix of styles, from Bo Bardi's iconic Bola chairs to an immense collection of Italian Baroque art and furnishings. Bo Bardi, born in Rome, worked with renowned Italian Modernists like Carlo Pagani and Gio Ponti, and married famed art critic Pietro Maria Bardi. They moved to Brazil in 1946. Their home is now the headquarters of the Instituto Bardi/Casa de Vidro and hosts exhibitions promoting Brazilian architecture and culture.

RICARDO BOFILL

La Fábrica
Sant Just Desvern, Spain

Architect
⌂

Known for his prolific output and his ever-changing aesthetic, full of expression, innovation, and chutzpah, Ricardo Bofill (b. 1939) is one of Spain's most influential architects. A perfect symbol of, and influence on, the Catalan designer's spirit is his office and home, La Fábrica ("The Factory"), located in a former Sansón cement factory on the outskirts of Barcelona. The behemoth space, partially in ruins, presented Bofill with a surrealist palette that included stairs climbing to nowhere, concrete columns supporting nothing, and vast empty spaces. Taking three years to renovate (although work on the space continues to this day), his office demolished some elements, renovated others, teased out unique details, and heavily planted the roof, walls, and grounds. They converted the factory's production floors and cylindrical silos into offices, archives, living quarters, exhibition spaces, and a cavernous concert hall known as "the cathedral." The building, its Brutalist concrete walls marked by age and industrial use, resembles an ancient castle or overgrown fortress. Inside, giant halls, enlarged through the removal of interior walls, bleed from one to the next, and to the lush exterior. Other rooms, like the library and living spaces, are more intimate; their finished walls and oversized windows make them feel like well-lit caves. More industrial elements, like smokestacks and underground tunnels, provide constant surprises and contrast poetically with Mediterranean vegetation that includes cypress, olive, and palm trees, and flourishing climbing vines.

ROSA BONHEUR

Château de By
Thomery, France

Painter, sculptor
👁

One of France's greatest Realist painters, Rosa Bonheur (1822–1899) was also one of its first renowned female artists. In 1865 she became the first female artist to be awarded the Grand Cross of the Legion of Honor. Bonheur was lauded across Europe for her masterful paintings and sculptures of animals; she gained intimate knowledge of animal anatomy from her studies at farms, stockyards, horse fairs, and slaughterhouses. Bonheur's magnificent fifteenth-century estate, Château de By, is on the edge of the Fontainebleau forest, far from the hubbub of her former home, Paris. She moved here in 1859, at the height of her popularity, remaining until her death. Bonheur renovated the property and added a major addition, a multistory neo-Gothic workshop that now

stands as its centerpiece. The light-bathed space is an eccentric time capsule, filled with animal heads and taxidermy (mostly former pets of Bonheur's), a stately hooded fireplace, and several salon-hung paintings. Personal elements include her embroidered blouse, hat, boots, palettes, brushes, colors, sketchbooks, notes, and even cigarette butts. Other rooms contain a similar mix of antique grandeur and quirky detail. The grounds outside, which still contain a greenhouse built by Gustave Eiffel's workshop, are where Bonheur set up pens for her "models," including sheep, deer, horses, and even lions.

ÉMILE-ANTOINE BOURDELLE

Musée Bourdelle
Paris, France

Sculptor
👁

An apprentice and later colleague of Auguste Rodin, Émile-Antoine Bourdelle (1861–1929) is considered one of France's finest turn-of-the century sculptors. In 1885 the ambitious artist and his parents moved to 16, impasse du Maine (now 18, rue Antoine Bourdelle), in Paris's thriving Montparnasse district, where artists, he noted, were "as numerous as blades of grass among the paving stones." He remained for about forty-five years. Determined to create a studio-museum for his work, "as Rodin did," Bourdelle later drew up several building plans. But the museum didn't come to fruition until 1949, long after his death. The complex encompasses several interconnected pieces: Bourdelle's intimate apartment and painting studio; the voluminous Great Hall,

filled with hefty, breathtaking plaster pieces and friezes; and a modern 1993 addition by Christian de Portzamparc, hosting temporary exhibitions. Bourdelle's intimate workshop, its tall windows and skylights drawing in soft light from above, exudes the sculptor's presence. The timber-beamed space is heated by a quirky iron stove and filled with exquisitely wrought wood, plaster, and bronze figures and busts that seem like they're staring at you. A mezzanine allowed the sculptor to see the pieces from above. An upstairs terrace is filled with haunting bronze busts, including those of Gustave Eiffel, Anatole France, and Auguste Perret. All of these spaces flow around a front courtyard and narrow rear garden, both filled with the sculptor's evocative bronze works.

DAVID BOWIE

David Bowie and Iman Residence
Mustique, St. Vincent and the
Grenadines

Singer, songwriter, actor
👁

While enigmatic rock star David Bowie (1947–2016) spent most of his time in big cities like New York, London, and Los Angeles, his favorite getaway was the hilltop home he built with architect Arne Hasselqvist on the island of Mustique in the Grenadines. The area is a famed retreat for celebrities, including Mick Jagger, Tommy Hilfiger, and Bryan Adams. In response, the iconoclastic artist captured an island spirit, but that of Indonesia, not Mustique itself. "I wanted something as unlike the Caribbean as possible, because it's a fantasy island, Mustique," he told *Architectural Digest*. The five-bedroom house, which he shared with his wife, fashion model Iman, unfolds in a series of thatched, hardwood-framed Balinese temple pavilions and verandas, arranged around a two-tiered

ornamental pool that leads down to a seafront infinity pool. The airy "parlor," as Bowie called it, remains as he left it. The ceiling is painted with a trompe l'oeil of tropical foliage, and an eighteenth-century Murano-crystal oil chandelier hangs from the ceiling. Antique Venetian mirrors, nineteenth-century settees, and colonial-style leather armchairs, topped with zebra- and leopard-patterned pillows, complete the exotic/luxurious look. A square threshold frames magnificent views of the ocean and sky, reflecting off the pools and the polished hardwood floor. After five years Bowie sold the property to eccentric publisher and poet Felix Dennis, who renamed the house Mandalay and lived here from 1995 to 2014.

ROBIN BOYD

Boyd House II
Melbourne, Victoria, Australia

Architect
👁

Architect, writer, and critic Robin Boyd (1919–1971) was one of just a small handful of Australian Modernists to ascend to international fame. It's a wonder, because his most influential buildings were not major commissions, but small houses. None is more acclaimed than his own, Boyd House II, in South Yarra, an upscale suburb of Melbourne. Boyd, an outspoken critic of the unimaginative buildings proliferating in his country (discussed in his book *The Australian Ugliness*), challenged the traditional suburban model with a home that embraced artistry, modernity, and the Australian climate and landscape. This 1957 family home, his second, consists of a main structure and a separate three-bedroom children's pavilion, centered around a modest, green-dappled internal courtyard and linked by a sloping, steel-cable-supported timber roof. The home maximizes its modest footprint with interlinked, multifunctional rooms and enlivens it with texture, color, and natural light. Luminous paintings are by local artists Asher Bilu, Donald Laycock, and Tony Woods, while the furniture is by Boyd himself, Australian Modernist Grant Featherson, and Harry Bertoia. Movement from the entrance to the courtyard is enhanced by clear vistas to a large window wall, as well as a loose arrangement of spaces that feel informally connected. The residence, now the home of the Robin Boyd Foundation, is open via public and private tours.

ROBERT BRADY

Museo Robert Brady
Cuernavaca, Mexico

Art collector, artist
👁

Charismatic art collector and artist Robert Brady (1928–1986) lived a charmed life, traveling the world and collecting beautiful works of art to create a transdisciplinary dialogue. Born in Iowa, Brady received a staggering inheritance and, taking to art from a young age, rigorously studied fine arts. His artistic eye and passionate art collection helped make Casa de la Torre, his effervescent house in Cuernavaca, Mexico—originally part of a sixteenth-century Franciscan monastery adjacent to the city's cathedral—such an astonishing place. Brady, who equally loved the tasteful and the quirky, curated every room, paying attention to how art, shape, color, and light worked together. He showcased a 1,200-piece collection spanning myriad countries and epochs, from Mexican fine art to Indian silks,

Oriental rugs, and tribal pieces from Africa, Oceania, and the Americas. Clearly influenced by his mentor, Barnes Foundation founder Albert C. Barnes, he placed them side by side, often in unpredictable clusters. He installed his own work, including a lively portrait of his good friend Peggy Guggenheim; painted the home in bright yellows, oranges, and greens; and covered it in carved wood and elaborate tile. Brady, who moved to Cuernavaca in 1961, made his home available to his many friends, including Josephine Baker (who had her own bedroom in the house), David Hockney, and John Cage.

REMO BRINDISI

Casa Museo Remo Brindisi
Lido di Spina, Italy

Painter
👁

Remo Brindisi (1918–1996) vigorously applied his training in graphic design and wood carving to fine art, creating intensely rendered, violently colorful works that incorporated both political protest and hallucinatory escapism. His unreal home in Lido di Spina, about 60 miles (100 kilometers) east of Bologna, reflects this type of churning unpredictability. Created between 1971 and 1973 by Brindisi in collaboration with radical architect and designer Nanda Vigo, the plaster-clad residence—now a museum of twentieth-century international art, with many works by Brindisi—is highlighted by a cylinder-shaped atrium that connects all floors and living spaces. Within this unified, skylit frame, covered almost completely in rectangular white glazed tiles, emerges a spiral stair, edged with a tubular, stainless-steel rail, interior mirrors, and tall apertures. This merger of many arts, accompanied by bold furnishings from the likes of Achille Castiglioni, Pio Manzù, and Vico Magistretti, could be likened to a 1970s Guggenheim, but don't tell Frank Lloyd Wright that. The museum's collection, which contains more than two thousand pieces, fills most areas, including living spaces, Brindisi's former bedroom (which still displays his Art Nouveau bed), his paint-filled studio, and dedicated exhibition galleries. Vivid artworks from every stage of modern art pop up wherever you look: there are bright green plastic trees, a hanging sunburst, and vertebrae-like sculptures, as well as works from legends like Pablo Picasso and Marc Chagall.

CHARLOTTE, EMILY, AND ANNE BRONTË

Brontë Parsonage Museum
Haworth, West Yorkshire, England, UK

Novelists, poets
👁

Growing up in a clergy house in Haworth, a tiny industrial town in the north of England, the sisters Charlotte Brontë (1816–1855), Emily Brontë (1818–1848), and Anne Brontë (1820–1849) were one of the most talented groups of siblings in history. They created groundbreaking novels of powerful imagination and fearsome passion, including Charlotte's *Jane Eyre*, Emily's *Wuthering Heights*, and Anne's *The Tenant of Wildfell Hall*. In 1820 their father, Patrick, an Anglican priest, and his wife, Maria, (who died the following year) moved their family into a two-story brick-faced home, now the Brontë Parsonage Museum, set against the damp, brooding moors of West Yorkshire. The sisters created most of their work in this 1779 building, which Charlotte's friend Elizabeth Gaskell described

as "exquisitely clean . . . Everything fits into, and is in harmony with, the idea of a country parsonage, possessed by people of very moderate means." Indeed, the tidy home reflected the simple tastes of an Irish-born minister living in a village of around four thousand. Nonetheless, Patrick keenly fostered his children's interest in art, literature, politics, and music here. Before Emily and Anne's early deaths, the three sisters did most of their writing in the crimson-on-white wallpapered dining room, where they would walk around the mahogany table discussing their writing plans. An engraving of Charlotte hangs over the classical-style mantel, which is flanked by period books of all hues and sizes.

OLE BULL

Ole Bull Museum Lysøen
Lysøen, Norway

Composer, violinist
👁

Norwegian virtuoso violinist and composer Ole Bull (1810–1880) was both a charismatic innovator and a traditionalist. Trained in classical as well as folk techniques, he played in ways people had never seen or heard, becoming a true star of his time. His charm and good looks (and tender, languorous songs) prompted smelling salts to be on hand for concerts, since it was said women inevitably swooned for him. He used his magnetism and influence to campaign for the preservation of Norwegian culture, founding Norway's national theater in Bergen and even attempting (unsuccessfully) to found a utopian community in the United States called New Norway. Bull's fairy-tale hilltop summer villa, on the island of Lysøen, near Bergen, typifies his dual nature. He referred to the residence as his "little Alhambra," and it is considered the high point of Norwegian historicism. Its Norwegian pine frame reveals the country's austere, understated rural style. But its ornately carved and filigreed facade reflects a plethora of foreign influences, including Swiss, Moorish, and (with its giant onion dome) Russian. Bull drew the plans for the villa himself, under the supervision of Norwegian architect Conrad Fredrik von der Lippe. Rooms also mix regimentation and ebullience, with exposed wood planks and extravagant colors and patterns. The most spectacular is the high-ceilinged timber concert hall, with its profusion of crystal chandeliers, cusped arches, twisted columns, and abstract symbols.

GORDON BUNSHAFT

Travertine House
East Hampton, New York, USA

Architect
🔒

Although located on the undulating edge of a coastal lagoon, the East Hampton weekend home of Gordon Bunshaft (1909–1990), a crucial partner at Skidmore, Owings & Merrill for more than forty years, largely eschewed the glass curtain walls for which his practice was renowned. Bunshaft designed the home for himself and his wife, Nina Wayler, crafting solid walls clad in travertine that could perform another function: hanging space for the couple's superb collection of modern art, encompassing Joan Miró, Fernand Léger, Pablo Picasso, and Henry Moore. An exception was made for the water-facing living room, positioned at the center of the rectangular, single-story structure—its long plate-glass windows meet the outside terrace. The seamless white travertine floor mirrored in the tones of the Modernist furniture (some designed by Bunshaft himself) helped focus attention on the couple's exquisite sculptures. A line of repeating clerestory windows was created just under the ceiling by the exposed concrete beams that ran across the room and skimmed freestanding walls that added to the space's gallery feel. Travertine House, as the home became known, was later owned by celebrity chef Martha Stewart, who enlisted John Pawson to renovate the interior. Sadly, that job was never completed. The subject of various disputes, the house fell into disrepair before being demolished in 2004.

ROBERTO BURLE MARX

Sítio Roberto Burle Marx
Rio de Janeiro, Brazil

Landscape architect, painter, sculptor, fabric designer, set designer, costume designer, jewelry designer
👁

Producing hundreds of pulsating, painterly landscapes, Brazilian landscape architect Roberto Burle Marx (1909–1994) gloriously channeled the bold, hedonistic spirit of his country and the abstract palette of modern art. His most famous designs include the sinuous mosaic walkways of Rio de Janeiro's Copacabana Beach, and the jagged, spiraling, pastel-hued rooftop garden at Banco Safra in São Paulo. His estate in Barra de Guaratiba, west of Rio de Janeiro, is now the Sítio Roberto Burle Marx. The artist, who lived here from 1973 until his death in 1994, designed spectacular gardens featuring more than 3,500 species of tropical and subtropical plants, as well as waterfalls, terraces, reflecting pools, and ruin-like stone structures. He also applied his textured, jubilant approach to his home and studio, a former nineteenth-century plantation house. The whitewashed stone residence's sweeping verandas are filled with still more greenery and embellished with brightly colored, surprisingly friendly gargoyles. Loggia framing the courtyard come alive with Burle Marx's blue- and violet-toned Cubist tiles. Inside, white walls edge colorful moldings and textured, playful polychrome ceilings, and are ornamented with hundreds of the artist's colorful paintings, ceramics, sculptures, tapestries, and prints. Burle Marx's personal art collection, which numbers more than three thousand pieces, stresses vernacular craft: brooding pre-Columbian sculptures, flashy yellow-and-red colonial altarpieces, carved wood creatures, and infinitely more.

GEORGE, LORD BYRON

Newstead Abbey
Ravenshead, Nottinghamshire,
England, UK

Poet
👁

Romantic poet and playwright George Gordon Byron (1788–1824), a.k.a. Lord Byron, was one of the more enigmatic figures in British history. Simultaneously cynical and idealistic, hilarious and melancholy, stubborn and pliant, he was famously described by one critic as "mad, bad and dangerous to know." His chameleonlike character was in many ways echoed by Newstead Abbey, an inherited home within the fabled Sherwood Forest and surrounded by immaculate gardens, where he lived from 1808 to 1814. Established by King Henry II as a twelfth-century Augustinian monastery, Newstead steadily accrued and lost components over the centuries. Byron's ancestor John Byron converted it into a sixteenth-century country house, reusing stone from the monastery to merge

Gothic and Tudor. In 1808, when Byron moved in, the poet, barely twenty-one, did little to restore a place that had long been suffering from decay. He used the baronial great hall for fencing and pistol shooting, decorated his study with skulls found on the estate's grounds, and restored the former prior's lodging as his bedchamber. The sumptuous room, its canopy bed adorned with floral textiles and wrought brass, hints at the home's extensive restoration at the hands of its next owner, Byron's childhood friend Thomas Wildman. Later additions and renovations encompass Renaissance Revival, Victorian, and neo-Gothic. In the garden, a monument to Byron's dog Boatswain, inscribed with the poet's famous "Epitaph to a Dog," is larger than Byron's own.

GUSTAVE CAILLEBOTTE

Maison Caillebotte
Yerres, France

Painter, art collector
👁

Located just southeast of Paris in Yerres, the Palladian estate of Gustave Caillebotte (1848–1894) was an incubator for one of the key talents of the Impressionist movement. Caillebotte began coming here with his wealthy family in 1860, at age twelve, and quickly benefited from his father's efforts to embellish its extensive grounds (edging the Yerres River) with pathways, fountains, buildings, follies, and piers. As a teenager he reveled in its surroundings. Once in his twenties, he began painting its landscapes, plants, boats, and visitors, developing a distinctive realist style that was influenced in part by early photography. More than eighty of the artist's works depict what is now known as the Parc Caillebotte. He continued expanding on these early explorations long after he had moved away in

1879. His home's twelve rooms are ideal examples of lavish Second Empire bourgeois life, showcasing classical murals, crystal chandeliers, gilded fireplaces, and ornate wood detailing. The family room, created by former owner Madame Biennais, contains original First Empire furniture upholstered in emerald-colored silk, embroidered with golden symbols of empire, echoed by silk wallpaper and a print of Napoleon Bonaparte. Caillebotte's studio has been turned into an exhibition hall displaying work by him and his Impressionist contemporaries. Thanks to his wealth, Caillebotte became their vital champion, collecting their paintings and funding their workshops and salons. This role ironically caused him to long be overlooked as a painter.

PIERRE CARDIN

Palais Bulles
Cote d'Azur, France

Fashion designer
🔒

In 1992 revolutionary French couturier Pierre Cardin (b. 1922) acquired the perfect vacation home to match his space-age, geometric fashions (which expanded into industrial designs like automobiles and pens) and edgy image: Palais Bulles ("Palace of Bubbles"). Nestled on a hillside overlooking the bay of Cannes, the residence was originally designed by avant-garde Hungarian architect Antti Lovag for French industrialist Pierre Bernard. It was built between 1975 and 1989 and remains one of the world's most distinctive examples of retrofuturism. Lovag, who devised a new typology that he called bubble housing, described his approach as *habitology*, or how architecture works in relation to the human body. Considering the straight line to be "an aggression against nature," he improvised a framework of interconnected spherical modules, rendered in ocher-colored concrete, interspersed with terraces and pools. The ultraorganic house includes ten carved, undulating bedroom suites, a reception hall, and a panoramic lounge, each lit by curved windows and bulging skylights. Though Cardin was the second owner, the mazelike Palais Bulles could easily have been custom built for him, since his fashion collections have incorporated space helmets and his iconic 1954 bubble dress. Inside, furnishings echo the building's curves. Signature pieces include round beds, undulating bookcases, and built-in circular seating. Some rooms feature specially commissioned pieces by Pierre Paulin, Gae Aulenti, and Claude Prevost, among others.

PAUL CAUCHIE

Maison Cauchie
Brussels, Belgium

Painter, interior designer, architect
👁

Unfairly overshadowed by Belgian luminaries like Victor Horta, Paul Cauchie (1875–1952) was one of the country's leading architectural talents, not to mention a gifted painter and interior designer. Cauchie's 1905 townhouse, on the upper end of Brussels's rue des Francs, is one of the world's great remaining examples of Art Nouveau. Implementing all of their talents, Cauchie and his wife Caroline (Lina) Voets, herself a noted painter, designed the tall, narrow home's facade as a sort of billboard for their business. (At the center it says, "Par Nous—Pour Nous," meaning "By Us—For Us"). It shows off a stunning combination of integrated geometric forms— round and tightly rectangular windows, wavy metal balconies, tree-like columns, and overlapping moldings. These are coupled with flowing pictorial frescoes of classically robed women in shades of gold and ivory, which Cauchie and Voets created using the sgraffito technique; a process, dating back to antiquity, of scratching a thin surface layer to expose a different colored background. Inside, tightly arranged rooms are full of the couple's art, like paintings, sculptures, murals, lamps, cabinets, tables, chairs, stained-glass windows, and embroideries, as well as sgraffito frescoes in ivory, green, and purple, lavishly filled with voluptuous sirens, white doves and swans, and abstracted organic forms. The home, where the couple both lived and worked, now contains exhibition spaces on the ground floor and in their former basement workshop.

PAUL CÉZANNE

Atelier de Cézanne
Aix-en-Provence, France

Painter
👁

Whether or not you agree that Paul Cézanne (1839–1906) was, as many proclaim, the father of Modern painting, a visit to Atelier de Cézanne—his studio from 1902 until his death—is a must. The artist, who lived with his housekeeper Madame Brémond in an apartment on Aix-en-Provence's rue Boulegon, bought some nearby land on which to build a studio in 1901. Kissed by dappled sunlight and buffered by its garden, the hilltop studio, with its views of the magnificent Mount Sainte-Victoire, exudes refuge; Cézanne let no one but himself inside. "I'm better here than in the city," he wrote to his art dealer Ambroise Vollard in 1903. "In every corner, the canvases pile up, still on their stretchers or rolled up." They piled up indeed. Cézanne, working both in the studio and the surrounding countryside, created his final works here, including the last of his bathers scenes, *Les Grandes Baigneuses*, as well as famed still-lifes, portraits, and landscapes. The modest studio, flooded with soft natural light, thanks to an outsize main window, contains models for his still-lifes, clustered on shelfs and in drawers, including bottles, vases, porcelain objects, and even skulls; and his equipment and furniture, like paints, brushes, ladders, easels, stools, and chairs. Visitors can tour other nearby Cézanne sites, including the Bastide du Jas de Bouffan and Carrières de Bibémus, the quarry of jagged red stones where he received endless abstracted inspiration.

MARC CHAGALL

Marc Chagall House
Saint-Paul de Vence, France

Painter, illustrator, printmaker,
ceramicist, stained-glass painter,
set designer, tapestry weaver
🔒

Injecting folklore, mysticism, and a powerful sense of his
own psychic world into abstract painting, sculpture, and stained
glass, Marc Chagall (1887–1985) created colorful, vivid dreamscapes that would inspire and confound artists for generations.
"I don't know where he gets those images from," his friend
Pablo Picasso once said. "He must have an angel in his head."
Much of Chagall's inspiration came from Vitebsk, the small
town on the western edge of the Russian Empire where he grew
up. Playing an active role in his imagery were its domes,
cobbled streets, houses, shops, wooden fences, and horse-cab
drivers. At the other bookend of his life, Chagall and his wife,
Vava, built a larger but still modest home out of local stone in
the lovely Provençal village of Saint-Paul de Vence. His mystical

mural *The Large Sun* adorns one of the whitewashed walls.
Inside, spaces reveal Chagall's amalgamation of simple humility
and extravagant intellect. Bathed in warm natural light,
the living room is furnished sparely, with leather-upholstered
chairs, floor lamps by Diego Giacometti, and geometric rugs
partially covering stone tile flooring. Above the stone mantel is
Chagall's *The Bride and Groom of the Eiffel Tower*. The artist's
bronzes, ceramics, and drawings fill the home, as do works by
Georges Braque, Henri Matisse, and Pierre-Auguste Renoir,
and a collection of ancient pottery.

GABRIELLE CHANEL

31, rue Cambon
Paris, France

Fashion designer
🔒

The residence of French fashion designer Gabrielle "Coco" Chanel (1883–1971) was above her boutique and haute couture salons at 31, rue Cambon, a stern classicist structure a short, chic walk from place Vendôme and the Faubourg Saint-Honoré. The residence was accessed via a curved, mirror-lined staircase, where Chanel could sit unseen on the steps, observing people's reactions to fashion shows below. The decor of Chanel's intimate apartment, where she entertained the likes of Elizabeth Taylor, Salvador Dalí, Igor Stravinsky, Diego Giacometti, Jean Cocteau, and Pablo Picasso, remains unchanged since her death. The living room communicates Chanel's exceptional sense of style: classical, luxurious, with exquisitely made furniture and objets d'art. But unlike her unadorned designs, it showcases both simple lines and ornate, nature-inspired details. The couch, her own design, is in suede. Handmade Chinese screens with camellia motifs are used throughout. Intricate animal sculptures provide a sense of exoticism, and the golden Venetian lion reflects her astrological sign of Leo. The chandelier was custom-made; she attested to the healing power of crystal, and number fives (the superstitious Chanel's favorite numeral) are incorporated into the chandelier's design. Shelves are filled with leather-bound books. Chanel did not sleep in the apartment; at night she would cross the road to her suite at the Ritz. Chanel's apartment was listed by the Ministry of Culture as a historical monument in 2013, in recognition of its national significance.

CHARLIE
CHAPLIN

Manoir de Ban
Corsier-sur-Vevey, Switzerland

Actor, film director, film producer,
composer
👁

English-born Charlie Chaplin (1889–1977) was not just the most famous actor of the silent film era—he was one of the most important figures in all of film history. His film career, launched by *Kid Auto Races at Venice*, spanned over seventy-five years and more than eighty films, as an actor, director, and producer. But while Chaplin is undoubtedly an international icon, his home for the last twenty-five years of his life, the Manoir de Ban in Corsier-sur-Vevey, Switzerland, is not. Perched above Lake Geneva, 55 miles (89 kilometers) northeast of the city of Geneva, the property, which includes parks, gardens, and outbuildings spreading across 33 acres (13 hectares), gave Chaplin—exiled from the United States due to, among other charges, supposed links with the Communist Party—and his

family the privacy they sorely needed. Once the home of nobles, military captains, and industrialists, Manoir de Ban boasts stunning views of the lake and the Swiss Alps. The 1841 neoclassical residence, graced with fluted pilasters and pedimented windows, has nineteen rooms, some still holding the family's furnishings and possessions. The sumptuous salon centers around a Rococo-style fireplace and mirror, a French Empire beaded crystal chandelier, and a Jacquard-print sofa. Manoir de Ban is part of Chaplin's World, a large-scale museum dedicated to Chaplin that contains reconstructed film sets, a multimedia theater, and lots of wax figures.

HAN CHONG

Chong Residence
London, England, UK

Fashion designer
🔒

Malaysian-born designer Han Chong (b. 1979) made a serious impact on the world of fashion relatively late, at the age of thirty-four, with the launch of Self-Portrait, his accessibly priced womenswear brand. The company rose rapidly to global status, with fans including Meghan Markle, Reese Witherspoon, and Beyoncé. Chong studied at Central Saint Martins in London, the city he now calls home. His concrete retreat in Shoreditch is a calming haven that is a shrine to minimalism. The five-and-a-half-story stand-alone property was built in the 1990s by architect William Russell, and Chong lived in it for a year before deciding on the changes he wanted to make. He commissioned architecture firm Casper Mueller Kneer, which also designed Self-Portrait's flagship store in London,

to remove some interior walls to increase the feeling of airiness, and turned a bedroom into an art-book library with a metal balcony and a cream modular sofa. Other relaxation areas include a sunken bath where he catches up on emails. Chong keeps it simple in his choice of interior pieces, sticking to a neutral palette and elegant midcentury shapes, partly to accentuate the residence's space, and partly because he doesn't feel the need for many possessions. A Cornelia Baltes painting hangs above the entrance to the rooftop level, where Chong can view the city from his black Jean Prouvé daybed.

AGATHA CHRISTIE

Greenway
Galmpton, Devon, England, UK

Novelist, short-story writer, playwright
👁

Beloved worldwide for her detective novels and short stories, Agatha Christie (1890–1976) is still the best-selling novelist of all time. Many of her characters, like Hercule Poirot and Miss Marple, are celebrities in their own right. Christie's vacation home, nestled in a subtropical garden overlooking the River Dart in Devon, is as tranquil and lovely as her stories are dark and suspenseful. The writer, who grew up nearby, called it the "loveliest place in the world." The snow-white Georgian residence, which remains as the family used it, feels like an escape from the world; life slows down, and you're immersed in beauty, stillness, and nature. In the drawing room, dominoes and card games are laid out in front of the fire. Cupboards in the dining room are filled with the family's immense collection of china. The library, with its frieze painted by a US Coast Guard lieutenant during World War II, is stacked with the family's many books, not to mention dolls and knickknacks. Highlighting the property are its bountiful gardens, which course down the hillside, with their lawns, hydrangea bushes, vegetable plots, and a vinery. A light-dappled fernery contains a cemetery for the family's dogs, and the Top Garden affords sweeping views of the River Dart and Dartmouth beyond. Several Christie novels are set in and around Greenway, including *Dead Man's Folly* and *Five Little Pigs*.

FREDERIC EDWIN CHURCH

Olana State Historic Site
Hudson, New York, USA

Painter, architect, landscape designer
👁

Thanks in part to his family's wealth and status, Hudson River School painter Frederic Edwin Church (1826–1900) from an early age was able to pursue his shimmering art, infused with atmospheric light and earnest spirituality. But his greatest masterpiece was Olana, his 250-acre (100-hectare) hilltop estate overlooking the Hudson River, just south of the town of Hudson, New York. Inspired by their extensive travels to both Europe and the Middle East, Church and his wife, Isabel, consulted with architect and landscape architect Calvert Vaux to create a house that mixes Victorian architectural elements with Middle Eastern decoration. Church called it "Persian, adapted to the Occident." The home's ebulliently irregular silhouette is punctuated by mismatched towers and fanciful

windows, balconies, and porches. Within this framework is an eclectic mix of Middle Eastern details: decorative brick and tile; slate, wood, rough stone, and ceramic surfaces; Moorish arches; and a trapezoidal turret. Inside, a more regular rhythm of rooms is arranged around a stunning central hall. A breathtaking layering of architecture and ornament includes intricate stencils, Asian tiles, carved Indian woodwork (by Ahmadabad-based Lockwood de Forest), exotic objects from the Churches' travels, and artworks by Church and his mentor, Thomas Cole, among others. Arched windows and doors frame views, some bordered with amber glass to give the appearance of a frame. Others are overlaid by cut-paper patterns, creating a soft glow.

FRANCESCO CLEMENTE

Clemente Residence
New York, New York, USA

Painter
🔒

Italian artist Francesco Clemente (b. 1952) is known for his dreamlike paintings innocently (or at least they appear that way) exploring sexuality and spirituality. He specializes in what he calls "cultural contamination," creating simultaneously placeless and deeply rooted art that exudes easy sensuality and a sense that all is in flux. A relentless traveler, and a collaborator with the likes of Andy Warhol, Jean-Michel Basquiat, and Alex Katz, Clemente divides his time between homes in places like Chennai in India, Rome, and New York. His townhouse in Greenwich Village is pervaded with art and a color palette that expresses his wandering interests and inspirations. "Objects and friends are really how I get my education. I have no interest in history; I am interested in human experience," he told *W* magazine. The tall, light-filled living spaces feature soft, fragrant colors that seem borrowed from an Indian spice market. Furniture includes tables and chairs by Isamu Noguchi and Frank Lloyd Wright. On one mantel sits a scribbled drawing by Cy Twombly, and on another is a crude Joseph Beuys sculpture, above which hangs Henry Fuseli's *Head of Satan*, from 1790. Other exquisite paintings, drawings, and sculptures include a tall, glowering Oceanic wooden sculpture; ceremonial statuary from India; Basquiat's portrait of Clemente, a Christmas gift from the artist; and Clemente's own *Tree of Life*, weaving folklore, sex, and abstract mysticism into the most natural of all symbols.

JEAN COCTEAU

Villa Santo Sospir
Saint-Jean-Cap-Ferrat, France

Poet, painter, sculptor, novelist, essayist, playwright, librettist, screenwriter, film director, actor
👁

Perched on a cliff above the bay of Villefranche, just outside Nice, Villa Santo Sospir is the perfect embodiment of the writer/poet/playwright/painter/muralist's staggering array of talents and his fluid ability to flaunt norms. The red-tiled Mediterranean villa belonged to Parisian socialite and arts patron Françine Weisweiller, who in 1950 invited Jean Cocteau (1889–1963) and his adopted son to stay for a week's vacation. Soon the home, which became a regular part of their lives (their other refuge was Cocteau's remarkably eclectic home in Milly-la-Forêt, outside Paris), became known as la villa tatouée, or the tattooed house, due to Cocteau's astonishing creative work inside. The site's crystal blue waters and rocky outcroppings reminded Cocteau of the Aegean, and he

(with Weisweiller's permission) began his elegant graffiti by illustrating Apollo on a wall over the fireplace, sketching first with charcoal, then enhancing with pigmented tempera. Soon the home's walls and ceilings were adorned with playful, often erotic depictions of Dionysus, Narcissus, Echo, Diana, Actaeon, and others. He sketched local fishermen, sea life, and foods, and later began painting on lampshades, bookshelves, and tables. He even designed wall hangings to drape over uncovered surfaces. "Tattooed" just a few years after World War II, the house became a literal and symbolic haven. "We have tried to vanquish the spirit of destruction that has dominated our era," Cocteau said. "We have decorated surfaces that men dream of destroying."

GRACE CODDINGTON

Coddington Residence
East Hampton, New York, USA

Photographer, fashion stylist,
fashion editor
🔒

As longtime creative editor of *Vogue*, Grace Coddington (b. 1941) is responsible for some of the most iconic fashion imagery ever published. She was born in a remote part of Wales, but became famous as a model in the London of the swinging sixties, particularly for her flame-colored hair. In 1968 she crossed the creative threshold to take up an editorial role at *Vogue*, and her work since then, particularly in partnership with editor Anna Wintour, has had a profound influence on fashion publishing. She bought her weekend retreat in East Hampton, Long Island, in 1988, a light-filled, homely, relaxing place to escape the world of high fashion. Her desire for beauty in richly detailed design elements is evident in the property: the walls are filled with a vast collection of prints by famous photographers she has worked with, as well as dozens of framed personal messages between Coddington and her partner, and there is an extensive collection of cat paraphernalia. Native American rugs are scattered on the floors, and the George Sherlock sofas in the sitting room are built for comfort. Coddington has invited friends to add their own touches down the years, resulting in columns on the front porch made of railroad ties, and bookshelves held up by a raw tree trunk. The decor is deliberately neutral and restrained to allow the plethora of items space to breathe.

THOMAS COLE

Thomas Cole National Historic Site
Catskill, New York, USA

Painter
👁

Painter and essayist Thomas Cole (1801–1848) is widely considered the founder of the Hudson River School, the United States' first major art movement. Hailing from industrial Lancashire, England, in 1825 he discovered and fell in love with the landscapes of the Hudson River Valley, immortalizing them through paintings of epic scale and intensity. Infusing his work with historical and religious allegory—particularly in series like *The Course of Empire*—he also became a committed proto-environmentalist, and his paintings would influence the likes of Frederic Edwin Church, Albert Bierstadt, and Daniel Chester French. In 1836 Cole and Maria Bartow married and moved into Maria's uncle's property, historically known as Cedar Grove. The yellow Federal-style Main House,

its western rooms and porches framing breathtaking views of the Catskill Mountains, was structurally restored in 2001. Cole, who had once worked in decorative arts factories, crafted the interiors, shifting hues in each room and creating colorful ornamental borders (recently rediscovered behind coats of paint) on the tops of walls. The hall's floor cloth adopts ancient Roman motifs. Two first-floor parlors are opulently appointed with a carpet featuring red peacocks, period furnishings, and replicas of Cole's paintings. Original paintings are on display on the second floor. The Old Studio, a tall, brick-walled space containing Cole's easels and materials, exudes little fuss; all defers to the art and the natural world outside. The rebuilt New Studio contains exhibition spaces.

SAMUEL TAYLOR COLERIDGE

Coleridge Cottage
Nether Stowey, Somerset, England, UK

Poet, literary critic, philosopher
👁

The author of sweeping, penetrating poetry and prose, Samuel Taylor Coleridge (1772–1834) was a key figure in the English Romantic movement. Yet his two-story seventeenth-century cottage on a curving street in the village of Nether Stowey, in rural Somerset, reveals that despite his charisma, profundity, and eloquence, he and his young family then lived a humble life, dogged by debts and doubters. They stayed here for three years, starting in 1797, viewed with suspicion and incomprehension by a populace not ready for Coleridge's radical politics and eccentricities. Their "lowly cottage," or "hovel," as the Cambridge-educated Coleridge put it, was quite spare, with bare walls, dirt floors, and leaky sash windows. Its small parlor (where Coleridge wrote by the large fireplace), primitive

kitchen, and bedchambers contain period furniture as well as the family's paintings, engravings, and handwritten poems and letters. Coleridge's marriage to his wife Sara began to founder here, and his poor physical and mental health and noted addiction to opium seemed to worsen. Yet Coleridge, inspired by his fruitful collaborations with nearby friend William Wordsworth, was as productive here as anywhere else in his life, producing *The Rime of the Ancient Mariner* (tellingly, a tale of psychological obsession and remorse), "Kubla Khan" (theorized to be inspired by an opium-laced fever dream), and "Frost at Midnight" (inspired by the windows and hearth of his cottage).

JASPER CONRAN

New Wardour Castle
Wiltshire, England, UK

Fashion designer, product designer,
costume designer, set designer
🔒

Jasper Conran (b. 1959) founded his own artfully wearable fashion brand at age nineteen. In 2010 he made his home in an eighteenth-century mansion, New Wardour Castle, in Wiltshire. Architect John Pawson converted the mansion into apartments in 2004; Conran took up residence in Apartment 1, which spreads across two main floors of its central building's column-filled Palladian expanse. Conran describes eighteenth-century architect James Paine's dramatic rotunda staircase as a piece of pure theater. "It's one of the great beauties of this country, that staircase," he said. "It looks quite over the top, but at the same time quite simple." While the scale and ambition of the stairs are not matched in the living spaces (which reflect idyllic country house as much as regal

palace), Conran's interior design emulates the staircase's mixture of minimal forms and elaborate detail. The white, high-ceilinged rooms, crystal chandeliers and all, have been dressed with antique furniture and art that subtly show the patina of age—the story of the object's history, as the designer terms it. Tables, Conran's preferred piece of furniture for both working and relaxing, are a common theme throughout the apartment, and in the White Room, one dominates the end of the space, while large houseplants blur the transition between the interior and the views across the countryside.

TERENCE CONRAN

Barton Court
Berkshire, England

Furniture designer, product designer,
restaurateur, writer

In the 1960s British design icon Terence Conran (b. 1931) created Habitat, an affordable, Modernist-inspired home furnishing empire that has been emulated worldwide, by companies from IKEA to Pottery Barn. Conran didn't rest on his laurels, thriving as a groundbreaking designer, restaurateur, and hotelier, among other roles. After living in Barton Court, a 145-acre (59-hectare) seventeenth-century estate in Berkshire, for over thirty years, he took on yet another intrepid project: a complete overhaul, intended to salvage its rotting bones and usher it into the twenty-first century, with larger, more open, modern spaces. Running along the front of the house, a new 80-foot-long (24-meter-long) living area was formed by knocking down two walls. Evoking the cluttered minimalism of his early Habitat stores (simple, painted white to let the furniture and objects take prominence), the space is dressed with a mixture of old furnishings—either inherited or bought in antique shops or flea markets—and new furniture. A sofa and rug of Conran's own design, and coffee and chess tables by Benchmark are paired with a Thonet bentwood chaise longue, Achille Castiglioni's Arco floor lamps, and Ingo Maurer table lamps. Together with Conran's collection of ceramics, glass, butterflies, and moths presented on shelves that run the length of the back wall, the effect is of a modern environment set harmoniously within the classical, elevated proportions of a Georgian home.

MADISON COX

The Gardener's House
Tangier, Morocco

Landscape architect
🔒

Madison Cox (b. 1958), renowned garden designer and widower of Pierre Bergé (Yves Saint Laurent's former lover and business partner), transformed this two-bedroom residence in a quiet part of Tangier. It has been his home for over a decade, a place to recover from a hectic lifestyle managing Marrakech's Jardin Majorelle, directing the Saint Laurent museums in France, and serving as president of the Fondation Pierre Bergé - Yves Saint Laurent. He also designs graceful, exuberantly naturalistic gardens for clients such as Sting, Lauren Santo Domingo, and Michael Bloomberg. Cox's modest Moorish structure offers stunning views of the dark blue Strait of Gibraltar, its beguiling gardens stretching half a mile along a clifftop. The house had been abandoned for twenty years prior to his purchase,

disintegrating in the heat and sea air. Cox shored up and decorated the structure, with its arabesque traces, as well as its grounds, blending Modernism with rougher, hand-built forms. In the open-plan living/dining room, eighteenth-century botanical prints by Robert Thornton create a focal point and place Cox's beloved plants (more than three hundred luscious varieties) in constant view. White-linen-draped banquettes line the walls. On the minimalist fireplace—also Cox's design— are personal objects: pieces of coral, photographs, some simple copper candlesticks. Above hangs a mirror in a brutish, gnarled stone frame. White keeps everything cool and simple, with the odd splash of organic color.

SALVADOR DALÍ

Casa Salvador Dalí
Portlligat, Girona, Spain

Painter, printmaker, film director,
screenwriter, set designer, costume
designer, jewelry designer, actor

👁

If you love the work of Surrealist artist Salvador Dalí (1904–1989), you won't be disappointed by his home in Portlligat, a village on Spain's Costa Brava. Setting up in a small beachside fishing hut ("the smaller the more womblike," he once wrote) in 1930, he and his wife, Gala, bought a slightly larger hut nearby in 1932, and they kept adding spaces, indoors and out, from there. "Each new pulse in our life had its own new cell, its room," explained Dalí. The labyrinthine, and, yes surreal whitewashed structure spreads out in a succession of chambers (with varied windows, framing the Portlligat bay so often included in Dalí's work) linked by narrow corridors and filled with small level changes and blind passages. Spaces are filled with peculiar objects, artworks, and memorabilia, coupled with antique

furniture. The first "cell" begins with the Bear Lobby, highlighted by a stuffed, necklace-wearing polar bear, along with a tiger rug, lip-shaped couch, and wall-mounted crossbow. Next come the dining room, living room, workshop, and bedroom. Cells after that contain Dalí's bedroom, kitchen, library, and his final studio, completed in 1950. Then comes the Pigeon Loft, Clock Hut, Oval Room, towers topped by large eggs, several courtyards, a pool, and an outdoor dining room. The couple kept adding until Gala died in 1982 and the artist moved to the Dalí Castle in Púbol.

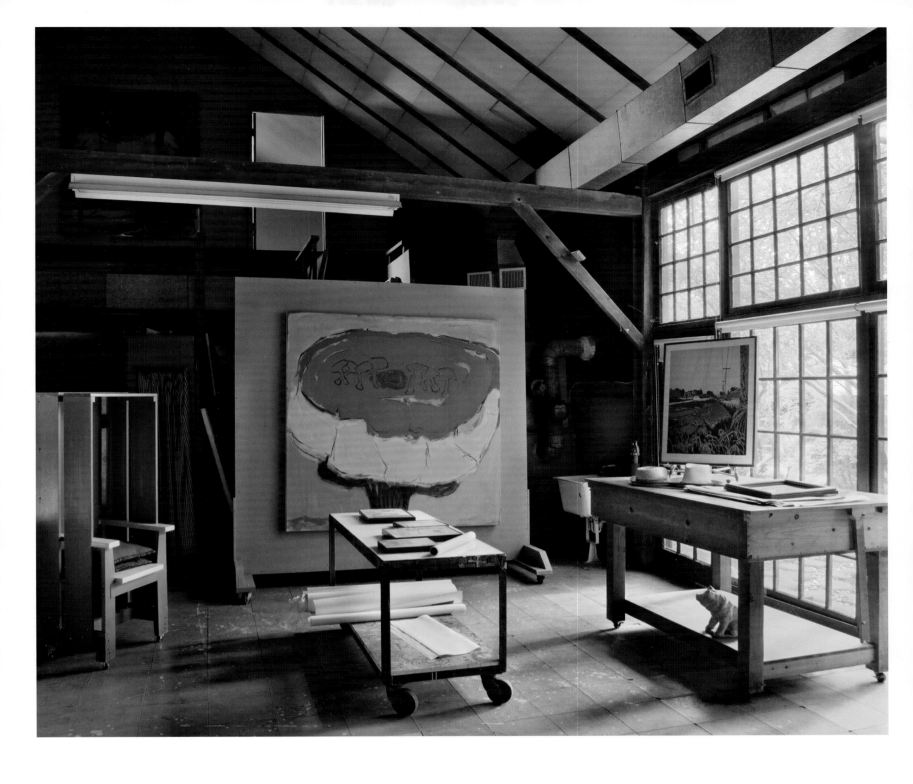

ROBERT DASH

Madoo
Sagaponack, New York, USA

Painter, poet
👁

"What brought me here was the light and the soil," Robert Dash (1931–2013) said. "It winked at me." Dash, a distinguished poet, painter, and gardener, called his property Madoo (an old Scottish word meaning "my dove"). He purchased the 2-acre (0.8-hectare) farm, on Long Island's South Fork, in 1967 and renovated its eighteenth- and nineteenth-century barn buildings, transforming them into a home and a studio. Depending on the season, he alternated between the two. In the summer he worked on the garden; in the winter he would paint. The property's luxuriant and expressive garden is an extension of Dash's creative labors. As Dash wrote, "All good garden paths lead to loitering with fine intent, and if they don't, then something is wrong indeed. Loitering is horticulturally permissible behavior." With its worn blue floors, high windows, and magnetic views, his studio, too, allowed for imaginative loitering. It is very much an artist's interior, carrying itself assuredly, without fuss. (An apt description of Dash's art.) Speaking of his garden, with its ranging variety of plants, Dash wrote, "I have gone about it as I would a painting, searching for form rather than prefiguring it, putting it through a process more intuitive than intellectual." This could extend to his interiors. The Madoo Conservancy, which is dedicated to the preservation, enhancement, and study of this site, was established in 1993. Dash continued to lived at Madoo under a lifetime tenancy until his death.

LUCIENNE AND ROBIN DAY

Day Residence
London, England, UK

Furniture designer (Robin);
textile designer (Lucienne)

In 1951 the Festival of Britain put Modernist designers Lucienne Day (1917–2010) and Robin Day (1915–2010) on the map: Lucienne for her textiles, Robin for his furniture. The following year the couple, often compared to Charles and Ray Eames for their outsize influence and optimistic designs, moved to a four-story Victorian house on Cheyne Walk in Chelsea. They stayed for nearly fifty years. The first floor was converted to studio space, the second to a huge, open-plan living area with windows at either end. There was no clutter. Quiet brick walls, with intermittent textured surfaces, were painted art gallery white to emphasize furniture forms and splashes of color and pattern. Arrayed around the fireplace is a suite of leather Forum seating with walnut surrounds and chrome frames, epitomizing Robin's rigorous, functional design. While more of his work—such as a glass-topped table, cube-shaped lamp, and benchlike dining table—revolved into the couple's surroundings, Lucienne was less eager to be surrounded by her output. "It is wonderfully restful in the evening, after leaving the studio, where one has been wrestling with patterns for curtains, patterns for wallpapers, or patterns for dress fabrics all day, to go into this un-patterned room," she said. Plants, always a major inspiration for Lucienne—whose botanical Calyx fabric is a seminal design—also added a sense of well-being.

GIORGIO DE CHIRICO

Casa Museo di Giorgio de Chirico
Rome, Italy

Painter, illustrator, sculptor, set designer,
costume designer, autobiographer,
essayist, novelist, poet, playwright
👁

Italian artist Giorgio de Chirico (1888–1978) once declared, "What is especially needed is great sensitivity: to look upon everything in the world as enigma. . . .To live in the world as in an immense museum of strange things." His distorted dreamscapes, with their atmosphere of uneasy menace and childlike imagination, captivated a generation of avant-garde artists, from the Surrealists to the Situationists. With his second wife, Isabella, the artist lived and worked for the last thirty years of his life in a third-floor apartment-studio inside Rome's seventeenth-century Palazzetto dei Borgognoni. The location at the base of the Spanish Steps was supremely central, and the artist knowingly called it "the apogee of anti-eccentricity." On the apartment's first floor, living and dining spaces are

an uneasy amalgam of Italian Baroque and spare modern. Textured white brick walls and simple 1950s furniture seem to contradict red damask curtains, gold frames, marble tables, and Louis XVI-style armchairs. De Chirico's eccentric paintings and sculptures coexist with wooden cherub sculptures and paintings by grand masters. The artist's upstairs studio is humble and intimate, a single bulb hanging from its ceiling, paintbrushes, tubes of paint, frames, and an original palette placed casually. A bluish wicker chair is draped with a blue smock. Plaster busts and horses rest atop De Chirico's art-book library. The artist's beloved terrace boasts views of the two-towered Trinità dei Monti church and the Villa Medici.

CHARLES DEATON

Sculptured House
Genesee Mountain, Colorado, USA

Architect
🔒

"People aren't angular, so why should they live in rectangles?" Charles Deaton (1921–1996), the architect and intended inhabitant of the Sculptured House, reportedly said when asked about the remarkable curves of the elevated, clam-shaped residence perched on Genesee Mountain, near Denver. Deaton ran out of money, so the three-level interior, united by sweeping window walls, elliptical shapes, and a concrete and steel stair, was never finished during his lifetime. The home, which appeared in Woody Allen's 1973 sci-fi comedy *Sleeper* (and instantly became nicknamed the "Sleeper House"), fell into disrepair, and it wasn't until 1999 that it received an interior befitting its famed Structural Expressionist exterior. The new owners enlisted the help of the architect's daughter, Charlee

Deaton, to honor the design preferences of her father, who was troubled by descriptions of the house as a "futuristic" UFO. In his view, it was a natural outgrowth of its surroundings. (The owners also hired architect Nicholas Antonopoulos, who was Deaton's architectural partner, to build a curving addition.) In the sunken space on the second level, the younger Deaton expressed her father's fascination with organic forms through similarly curving pieces of design: Eero Saarinen's 1948 Womb Chair, Arne Jacobsen's 1958 Swan chair, and Warren Platner's 1966 armchair. Completing the space is a patterned carpet based on sketches by the architect.

CHARLOTTE OLYMPIA DELLAL

Dellal Residence
London, England, UK

Fashion designer
🔒

The shoe designer Charlotte Olympia Dellal (b. 1981) has a hectic life running her eponymous business as well as being a mother of four sons. However, that domestic juggling does not prevent her from ensuring her house has touches of old-school glamour—in similar fashion, she has her hair set weekly in the style of a 1940s Hollywood starlet. Home is a four-story Georgian house in North Kensington, west London. Dellal shows off her love of color, and that extends beyond the dozens of pairs of shoes she keeps in her leopard-print-decorated boudoir. Carpets are bright green, mustard, and rose, and a neon sign spells out the fun question, "What would Prince Charles wear?" Her art collection includes works by Paulina Olowska and Lawrence Owen, and photography is an important component too, with pictures by Shirin Neshat, Guy Bourdin, and Alex Prager, along with shots of pinup girls, rescued from Portobello Market. Teddy bears from childhood are framed, and a vintage Versace outfit is on display that belonged to her mother, the Brazilian model Andrea Dellal. The lounge is full of eclectic items, including framed copies of Diana Vreeland's advice columns for *Harper's Bazaar*; a ceramic leopard next to the cocktail bar; and a silver coffee table by Mattia Bonetti. Dellal is eternally practical and has an IKEA sofa in the kitchen and artificial turf in the garden. "The only way forward with four boys," she said.

JOHN DERIAN

Derian Residence
New York, New York, USA

Decoupagist
🔒

John Derian started making decoupage art in New York in 1989, when he set up his eponymous company. Since then, he has built an empire of home goods and art with a seemingly authentic vintage look. In 2011 he acquired a whole floor of an 1850s East Village apartment building: a former artist's studio and, purportedly, a factory that made shrouds. Its historic aura fascinated and inspired him. He gave it a minimal makeover; the *New York Times* called it a "nonrenovation renovation" and quoted Derian saying, "I wish I had spray dust or spray dirt in a can. I don't want to lose the look of the place—I want that patina." The living/dining room is divided by the only major intervention: a worn, pale blue eighteenth-century dividing wall from Sweden. The space continues the style of the whole apartment: bohemian but utterly stripped back. Floors and ceilings are in their original warped wood board, simply given a coat of white paint. The upholstered pieces are a mixture of eclectic antiques—tables, chairs, sofas, and dishware—and Derian's own customizations of eighteenth- and nineteenth-century furniture. Touches of rich red and orange, such as the oriental-design needlepoint-covered table, warm up the space, and the room is decorated with characteristically eclectic objects that have caught Derian's eye. "I create a room naturally," he said, "being attracted to the things I love."

ES DEVLIN

Devlin Residence
London, England, UK

Set designer, sculptor
🔒

British designer Es Devlin (b. 1971) creates electric, utterly contemporary art pieces and performance sets, ranging from production designs for *Hamlet*, *Faust*, and *Orphée* to stage sculptures for Kanye West, Beyoncé, and U2. At its essence, her highly psychological work is about phase change: from digital to physical, physical to ethereal, and back again. Devlin and her husband, costume designer Jack Galloway, gutted an 1895 home in the southeast London suburb of Dulwich, pervading it with the edgy elegance and expert sleight of hand that Devlin specializes in. The couple enlarged rooms, enhanced interior and exterior connections, and inserted furniture and contents largely made by Devlin and her design team, as well as famed friends, local artisans, and students.

The biggest reveal is the vast glass rear wall, complemented by a skylight, that showcases the bucolic garden like a movie screen or a stage set. Another proscenium of sorts is the switchback floating stair, set back and lit from above like one of Devlin's cube-shaped sculptures. Yellow sandstone bricks —which feel real and fake at the same time—have been retouched by a painter at the National Theatre. Jewel-like niches are cut into walls. Mirrored doors separate the living and working areas, which include a studio for each spouse. Flanking a studio window are two giant hands, replicas of those made for Devlin's production of *Carmen*.

CHARLES DICKENS

Charles Dickens Museum
London, England, UK

Novelist, short-story writer,
essayist, journalist
👁

Full of tales, the home of Charles Dickens (1812–1870), a modest Georgian townhouse just around the corner from the British Museum in London's Bloomsbury neighborhood, gives visitors a better understanding of one of the world's most acclaimed authors. Dickens moved here in 1837 with his wife, Catherine. (The author called it a "frightfully first-class family mansion.") In the three years they lived there, the couple had two daughters, and Dickens wrote the books that launched his career, including *The Pickwick Papers*, *Oliver Twist*, and *Nicholas Nickleby*. The home, which contains an extensive archive, is full of the family's possessions, including furniture, porcelain, art, family portraits, clothing, jewelry, and even Dickens's walking stick and calling card, as well as numerous original books and letters.

Delicate spaces—some painted in solid colors, others wallpapered—include the ground-floor dining room, the basement kitchen, and the upstairs drawing room and bedrooms. The room of Catherine's sister Mary tells the story of her tragic death from a sudden illness. And in Dickens's book-filled study, you can peer at his desk, with its slight incline for writing, as well as handwritten drafts (he usually wrote by candlelight with a quill pen) of his work. As he grew more famous, Dickens moved his family into grander homes, but this is the author's only surviving London house.

CHRISTIAN DIOR

Château de la Colle Noire
Montauroux, France

Fashion designer
🔒

The status of Christian Dior (1905–1957) as one of the twentieth century's most important couturiers originated with his first collection. Launched in 1947, just two years after the gloom of World War II, it featured soft shoulders, cinched waists, and full skirts. Termed the "New Look," its designs celebrated femininity and helped revive France's ailing fashion industry. In 1951, at the height of his career, Dior purchased the Château de la Colle Noire, a stone manor house dating back to the fifteenth century overlooking the Provençal village of Montauroux. Inspired by the profound peace of its setting—recalling his idyllic childhood in rural Normandy—he fully reconfigured the building's layout and decorated its rooms in a sophisticated manner that he described as "simple, ancient, and dignified."

Simple is debatable (considering its gilded mirrors, shimmering chandeliers, and fine fabric furnishings), but dignified is not. For a few months each year, the château, its timeless gardens inspiring several perfumes, became Dior's haven—his true home—although he didn't get to see it completed. After his death, it passed through several owners and was eventually acquired by Parfums Dior in 2013. It has since been restored to a mix of authentic rooms—some include Dior's original, seamlessly coordinated furniture—and reimagined suites in the styles of Pablo Picasso, Marc Chagall, and Salvador Dalí, all of whom were guests at the château.

KARL DULDIG

Duldig Studio – Museum and
Sculpture Garden
Melbourne, Victoria, Australia

Sculptor
👁

Much has been written about the flood of modern artists who fled Nazi-occupied Europe for places like Britain and America, where they helped fortify those countries' cultural scenes for decades to come. While few made it all the way to Australia, an important exception was Karl Duldig (1902–1986), a talented Jewish sculptor who studied at both the University of Applied Arts and Academy of Fine Arts in Vienna before fleeing Austria in 1938. After arriving (via Switzerland and Singapore) in Australia in 1940, Duldig and his wife Slawa, also a talented artist, settled in Malvern, an eastern suburb of Melbourne. Their brick California bungalow appears unassuming from the exterior. But within, they re-created their extraordinary Vienna apartment, whose possessions had been hidden in a cellar

during the war by Slawa's sister, Rella. Extraordinary Modern originals encompass latticed leather chairs, Bauhaus-inspired metallic floor lamps, wood-paneled modular cabinets, and colorful abstract textiles. The couple also filled the spaces with their own art: Slawa's *Portrait of an Old Lady*, Duldig's thrilling sculptures in marble, bronze, and ceramic. Duldig's studio is even more saturated with his playful terra-cotta pieces, which showcase classical training and a willingness to break free from it: is that ancient or modern art? Is that a dog or a human? The pieces spill out, to an enthralling degree, into the sculpture garden, raised on tree-trunk bases in a theatrical group display.

ALBRECHT DÜRER

Albrecht-Dürer-Haus
Nuremberg, Germany

Painter, printmaker, writer
👁

Germany's most famous Renaissance artist, Albrecht Dürer (1471–1528), gained international renown for his painting, drafting, and writing. But above all, he stood out for print-making, which he revolutionized and elevated to the level of fine art. Deeply influenced by his travels to Italy, Dürer became a master of classical detail and of human anatomy, typified by his haunting *Apocalypse* series. From 1509 until his death, Dürer lived in a five-story, red-and-white, half-timbered burgher house in Nuremberg, a city that was at the time one of the world's economic capitals, and a center of humanism and culture. Originally built around 1420, the home, kept intact for centuries (it was bought by the city in 1826), survived an intense air raid during World War II. It was repaired

by 1949 and opened as a museum in 1971, Dürer's five hundredth birthday. With the exception of its museum-like exhibition spaces, which present a substantial collection of high-quality copies of the artist's work, the residence ushers you into the sixteenth century, with its timber floors and ceilings, patterned stained-glass windows, and ornate wood furnishings. Spaces include Renaissance-era living rooms (re-created in the 1880s), a stone hearth kitchen, and workshops for both printing (including a working large-relief printing press) and painting. The home is located at the end of what is now called Albrecht-Dürer-Strasse, near the Tiergarten gate and Nuremberg's Imperial Castle.

CHARLES AND RAY EAMES

Eames House
Los Angeles, California, USA

Industrial designer, furniture designer, architect (Charles); industrial designer, furniture designer, textile designer, architect (Ray)

The Eames House, also known as Case Study House #8, is as delightfully quirky, magical, and transformative as its creators, Charles Eames (1907–1978) and Ray Eames (1912–1988). Sited on a pastoral bluff, dappled with light through peppertrees and eucalyptus and acacia trees, the home was one of the most famed examples of *Arts & Architecture* magazine's Case Study House Program. Its minimal design features prefabricated, off-the-shelf materials, promoting the program's ideals of affordability and mass production. Large glass expanses overlap with gridded windows, diagonal braces, and white, black, and colored stucco walls, like a Mondrian painting. Inside, lofted, double-height spaces—living areas below and sleeping above—flow without interruption, showing off the Eames'

furniture, lighting, and small sculptures, among other things. Walking the dirt-and-stone path around the house, whose living and studio sections are divided by a small courtyard, feels like a Los Angeles rite of passage, and it's the best way to take in the home's energy. The meadow around it is a healing spot, particularly if you choose to sit in the grass, on a stump overlooking the Pacific, or on the swing hanging from one of the trees. There is a colony of Case Study homes around the Eames House, including Charles Eames and Eero Saarinen's Case Study House #9 (also known as the Entenza House), Richard Neutra's Case Study House #20, and Rodney Walker's Case Study House #18.

JIM EDE

Kettle's Yard
Cambridge, Cambridgeshire,
England, UK

Art collector, curator, painter
👁

Welsh-born Jim Ede (1895–1990) began his career as a painter, attending the renowned Slade School of Fine Art in London. But after working as an assistant at the Tate Gallery, he gave up the artist's path to become a curator, writer, and supporter of modern artists. After living in London, Morocco, and France, Ede and his wife, Helen, moved to Cambridge, England, renovating four derelict nineteenth-century stone cottages (and later commissioning a sleek, skylit extension) to create what they would call Kettle's Yard, a beautiful complex filled with beautiful objects. Thanks largely to Ede's friendships with artists, the home—with its exposed-wood beams and floors, light-enhancing bay windows, and brick fireplaces— is essentially an art museum minus the labels, with art in every nook, edging up to antique furniture and items like ceramics, and natural objects. The collection includes splendidly selected (and refreshingly original) paintings by, among many others, Joan Miró, Alfred Wallis, and Ben and Winifried Nicholson, and sculptures by Constantin Brancusi, Henry Moore, and Barbara Hepworth. Ede held an open house every school term, during which he took Cambridge students and locals alike through his house's collections. Calling the home a "way of life," Ede wrote an illustrated book about his home of the same name, which reads like a guided tour.

STEVEN EHRLICH

700 Palms
Los Angeles, California, USA

Architect
🔒

Los Angeles architect Steven Ehrlich (b. 1946) has carved out a place for himself in Southern California with his multilayered approach employing detailed refinement, embrace of climate and landscape, and attunement to local culture. Ehrlich's own house, on a narrow lot in Venice, puts a modern spin on traditional courtyard housing. The two-story residence is broken into two layered volumes built around an outdoor configuration of courtyard, desert garden, and lap pool. A wall along the sidewalk encloses these outdoor spaces, and a seven-legged steel frame projects from the house to suspend sunshades. The larger volume, with its bedroom mezzanine level wrapping a double-height living space, feels like it's outdoors, thanks to an open plan and multiple glass walls,

including a 16-by-16-foot (5-by-5-meter) sliding aperture that pours in light and ocean breezes, eliminating the need for air-conditioning. "I wanted the glass to go away," Ehrlich explained. The project couples Ehrlich's usual finesse with durable, raw materials like Corten steel, copper, Trex, and stucco outside, and chocolate brown concrete floors and textured, unfinished concrete block and waxed steel walls inside. A floating timber stair doubles as a bookshelf, adding, along with modern furniture and orange and red accents, pinpointed warmth. The compound's smaller structure contains Ehrlich's studio and extensive African art collection below and guest quarters above.

RALPH WALDO EMERSON

Ralph Waldo Emerson Memorial House
Concord, Massachusetts, USA

Poet, essayist, philosopher
👁

Ralph Waldo Emerson (1803–1882) was one of the most prominent figures of the Transcendental movement of the mid-nineteenth century. He championed personal freedoms, criticized his young country's inflexible political and religious institutions, and espoused the essential goodness and unity of humans and nature. Emerson and his family called their colonial American Foursquare-style house "Bush." They planted dozens of flowers and trees after arriving in 1835. "In the woods, we return to reason and faith," wrote Emerson in his seminal essay "Nature." His plan for his home was to "crowd so many books and papers, and, if possible, wise friends into it, that it shall have as much wit as it can carry." Indeed, the high-ceilinged, gracefully proportioned house became a destination for groundbreaking intellectuals, including Louisa May Alcott (whose residence, Orchard House, is down the street); Margaret Fuller; Nathaniel Hawthorne; and Henry David Thoreau, who lived with the family for several months and built his famed hut on Emerson land, a couple of miles away. Emerson's study, which has been re-created with its original furnishings in the nearby Concord Museum (pictured above), sat to the right of the entry in its original location. Its tall, dark bookshelves, containing hundreds of volumes, dominate one wall, while gold-on-white wallpaper and carpeting depict abstractions of nature. Emerson wrote many of his best-known works at the round center table, and conversed there with his many visitors.

WHARTON ESHERICK

Wharton Esherick Museum
Malvern, Pennsylvania, USA

Furniture designer, sculptor,
painter, printmaker
👁

Located atop Valley Forge Mountain in Malvern, about 25 miles (40 kilometers) west of Philadelphia, the Wharton Esherick Museum spotlights one of the most enigmatic furniture designers of the twentieth century. The complex, constructed over a forty-year period beginning in 1926, includes the home and studio of Wharton Esherick (1887–1970), a 1956 workshop, which he designed with famed Philadelphia architect Louis Kahn, and a log garage, which now serves as the museum visitor center. The fairy-tale home and studio, which Esherick built by hand with the help of a local mason and cabinetmaker, reveals—with its staggered, off-kilter ceilings, its sinuous, tactile doorknobs, and its three-level spiral staircase, built from oddly angular pieces of red oak—Esherick's astonishingly

eclectic approach, influenced by Arts and Crafts, Organic Modernism, Cubism, and Expressionism, among other movements. His studio contains more than three hundred of his works, including sculpture, furniture, paintings, and prints. Esherick often merged these art forms and was equally free-spirited in his private life, known to walk (and often dance) nude around the house with his wife, progressive educator Letty Nofer Esherick. The Kahn workshop, only viewable on special tours, features a zigzag roof and abstract-patterned concrete walls. New additions to the museum complex include the farmhouse where Esherick first lived on the site and a one-room schoolhouse that he used as an early painting studio.

WILLIAM FAULKNER

Rowan Oak
Oxford, Mississippi, USA

Novelist, short-story writer, screenwriter,
poet, playwright, essayist

👁

Author William Faulkner (1897–1962) started as a poet, which helped infuse his novels—radical, epic, and socially charged works like *The Sound and the Fury*, *As I Lay Dying*, and *Light in August*—with finely honed language and experimental form and voice. His 1844 white-clapboard Greek Revival home, ensconced in the woods south of the picturesque town square in Oxford, Mississippi, was a steady inspiration and the perfect place to craft his work away from the drama and distraction of larger cities. He and his family would spend more than forty years in the residence, which Faulkner named Rowan Oak, after the rowan tree, a mythical symbol of peace. Reached via a canopied allée of ancient cedar trees, the home and surrounding grounds were in a sorry state when the author

purchased them in 1930. Still earning a modest living, he did much of the repair work himself. The rooms, each with its own brick fireplace, are simple and staid: light-toned walls are differentiated only by slight shifts in color or pattern. In the library a portrait of the writer (painted by his mother, Maud) hangs over the mantel. Faulkner built the bookshelves himself, and on the table sits an incongruously modern sculpture, a gift from Brazilian artist Marnarz. In the study the writer's ramshackle typewriter sits on a tiny table. The scribbled outline for his Pulitzer-winning novel *A Fable* remains in graphite and red grease on the wall.

FEDERICO FORQUET

Forquet Residence
Cetona, Italy

Fashion designer
🔒

Federico Forquet (b. 1931) seemed destined to become a concert pianist until a chance encounter with his future mentor Cristóbal Balenciaga in the summer of 1954. Abandoning music, Forquet went to work for the revolutionary couturier in Paris and then Russian princess Irene Galitzine in Rome (a partnership that created the iconic wide-legged "palazzo pyjama" lounge pants) before establishing his atelier in 1962. The expansion of prêt-à-porter made it difficult for Forquet to continue, and a decade later he closed his label. Hoping to find escape from their busy lives in Rome, Forquet and his partner, film publicist Matteo Spinola, bought a farm with two rustic stone houses near Cetona, Tuscany, in the 1960s. Forquet poured his creativity into transforming the interiors,

recycling old doors and windows, creating custom furniture, and commissioning Gustav Zumsteg in Zurich (who had made fabric for his fashion collections) to produce textiles for the interior. Terraced gardens filled with scented plants unite the two buildings. Generous windows, floral patterns, flashes of lily green, and organic art all complement the omnipresent natural surrounds. Friends soon asked Forquet to design their homes, and what began as a hobby morphed into a serious business. He has since redecorated numerous villas, palazzos, and hotels, including the Royal Palace of Brussels and the Belmond Hotel Caruso in Ravello, Italy.

NORMAN FOSTER

La Voile
Cap Ferrat, France

Architect
🔒

Pritzker Prize-winning architect Norman Foster (b. 1935) has made a career of creating high-tech solutions to challenging problems. A perfect example is La Voile, his personal residence between 2002 and 2006, which he created with his wife Elena in Cap Ferrat, France, on the Côte d'Azur. Somehow the resourceful architect transformed a glum five-story 1950s tower into a light-filled seven-story retreat. Getting there wasn't easy. "Any sane person looking at the house would have said, 'You are absolutely mad!'" Foster told writer Michael Webb. His team carved out the stacked building using cranes, diggers, and a lot of stressful patience. Design team member Juan Vieira described the demolition process as "keyhole surgery." "We would demolish then rebuild, bit by bit, and carve the openings out while keeping the line of the wall." The home is now lofty, luminous, and vertically open, necessitating the final element—a cable-supported stretched canvas, which shades both the home and its pool, and helps give the residence its name (along with the residence's clarity of form and function, Foster claims). Balconies rise through the heart of the villa like terraces and incorporate a library and seating and dining areas. White, reflective surfaces, and light-colored furniture and art, animate the space through the changing patterns of sunlight. A towering mud work by artist Richard Long adds a textured contrast to all this cool, futuristic white.

DANIEL CHESTER FRENCH

Chesterwood
Stockbridge, Massachusetts, USA

Sculptor
👁

One of the central figures of the American Renaissance, an era celebrated for its grand public buildings and monuments, sculptor Daniel Chester French (1850–1931) designed noble, lifelike statues of artists, philosophers, industrialists, war heroes, and most famously, Abraham Lincoln as the centerpiece of the Lincoln Memorial in Washington, DC. French split his time between New York City and Chesterwood, his home and studio in Massachusetts, which endlessly inspired him with views of the surrounding Berkshire Hills. French and his wife, Mary, bought the property in 1896. Shortly thereafter French worked with architect Henry Bacon to design a new studio and later a larger residence to replace the original clapboard farmhouse. Friends who visited Chesterwood included author

Henry James and Berkshires neighbor Edith Wharton. Brushed with painterly rays of natural light, the residence is filled with antique family furnishings. The studio and barn gallery display a wealth of French's works in plaster, marble, and bronze, including working models, bas-reliefs, and portrait busts such as those of Bronson Alcott and Ralph Waldo Emerson. French would paint portraits of family and friends in the studio reception room, and the workroom's 26-foot-high (8-meter-high) ceiling allowed plenty of space for large works. To enable outdoor work, French and Bacon designed a railroad track hidden below the studio floor. When the floorboards are lifted, a flatcar could be pushed outdoors along the tracks.

LUCIAN FREUD

Lucian Freud Home and Studio
London, England, UK

Painter

One of the twentieth century's most affecting portraitists, Lucian Freud (1922–2011) created haunting works of piercing psychic intensity. His confident, expressive art showed keen insights and a tense, slightly altered vision of reality, leading many to compare Freud with his grandfather, Sigmund Freud. (His long sessions with sitters, from David Hockney to Kate Moss, have also been paralleled with Sigmund's.) Freud's unsparing scrutiny of subjects' bodies and inner lives led to a distinctive, controversial oeuvre, while his charm and self-absorption led to a busy, though tumultuous personal life. The exterior of his tall terraced home in London's posh Kensington neighborhood conveys a sense of bourgeois traditionalism that belies Freud's energetic tumult. But inside, the home reveals varying levels of his intensity. Rooms maintain their original fireplaces, wide paneled doors, and voile curtains, and artworks from the likes of Auguste Rodin, Edgar Degas, and Jean-Baptiste-Camille Corot. But the painter stripped back the walls to reveal the original lime plaster, and paraphernalia are scattered in corners. His full ferment is on display in his first-floor studio (a separate garden studio provided more natural light), its walls painted umber to absorb any reflected light. Everything is strewn about: easels, paints, brushes, scissors, and an old iron bed and mattress. Paint splotches the floor, messages are scrawled on the walls, and rags are piled up like a mountain.

ALBERT FREY

Frey House II
Palm Springs, California, USA

Architect
👁

Swiss-born architect Albert Frey (1903–1998) produced many of Palm Springs's most essential icons, including its City Hall and Aerial Tramway station. His own house, perched on a concrete platform at the edge of a cliff above the city, is far less accessible, but every bit as remarkable. The tiny glass, steel and cinder block residence—typical of Frey's preference for simple, industrial materials—blurs the line between indoor and outdoor, and between man-made and natural in profound ways. The large glass walls, which open to a small pool, are protected by the long overhang of a corrugated-aluminum roof. More protection comes from bright yellow curtains, whose color matches the desert's vivid brittlebush flowers. Inside, the home is built around a massive boulder, which protrudes into its heart, dividing the bedroom and living room. The bedroom, cantilevering off the cliff, contains one of the most remarkable desert views you'll ever see. Frey reportedly took five years to select the site, then spent another year tracking the movement of the sun. Obviously, it was worth it. There is no home in the world quite like this one. Since the home is part of a gated community, the best way to visit is on a rare public tour. Or you can peek up from South Tahquitz Drive, appreciating how the blond rectangle blends into the landscape like modernist camouflage.

JAMES GALLIER, JR.

Gallier Historic House
New Orleans, Louisiana, USA

Architect
👁

You probably don't recognize the name James Gallier, Jr. (1827–1868). But the Irish immigrant (he was born James Gallagher), who settled in New Orleans at age thirty-six, became not only one of most prolific architects in that city, but also one of a group of architects who created the concept of professional architectural practice. The French Opera House and Luling Mansion, both in New Orleans, are among his many projects, as is his own family home, a local masterpiece now known as the Gallier Historic House. Built in 1861 on Royal Street in the city's French Quarter, the refined Victorian townhouse, combining classical and Italianate details, has a stone and stucco facade fronted by one of the city's trademark wrought-iron balconies. Inside, the home reveals an opulent era in New Orleans history, with copious fine art, Victorian and Rococo furniture, and restaged decorative elements that were drawn directly from the original household inventory. Being the home of an architect, it naturally showed off the technological innovations of its day, including indoor plumbing, hot and cold running water, an air-ventilation system, and a double skylight in the upstairs library. Varied rooms comprise two parlors, a dining room, a modern kitchen, and slave quarters (sadly common in the antebellum South) downstairs, with bedrooms upstairs. Most rooms face a large, grassy courtyard, which leads to a road.

ELIZABETH GASKELL

Elizabeth Gaskell's House
Manchester, Greater Manchester,
England, UK

Novelist, biographer, short-story writer
👁

English writer Elizabeth Gaskell (1810–1865) created astute, socially responsive novels and short stories that charted the uneasy transformations of Victorian society and the brutal world wrought by the Industrial Revolution. From 1850 until her death in 1865, Gaskell and her husband, William, a Unitarian minister, and their four daughters lived at 84 Plymouth Grove, a Regency-style villa on the new outskirts of Manchester, which was then a fast-growing manufacturing city. While the residence is austere, even vault-like outside, the interior showcases Victorian exuberance, cheered by floral patterns adorning its floors, walls, curtains, and furniture. Rooms are filled with realist landscape paintings and portraits, while leather-bound books, letters, fine china, silver, and miniatures ennoble period tables, shelves, and mantles. This is where Gaskell wrote *Cranford*, *North and South*, and *Wives and Daughters*, as well as a biography of her friend Charlotte Brontë. "It certainly is a beauty," Gaskell once wrote of the stone-faced residence. "I must try and make the house give as much pleasure to others as I can." And so she did, frequently welcoming Charles Dickens, who happened to be her publisher, as well as Brontë, John Ruskin, and Harriet Beecher Stowe, among others. Brontë described it as "a large, cheerful, airy house, quite out of the Manchester smoke." The home reopened to the public in 2014 after a £2.5 million restoration.

FRANK GEHRY

Gehry Residence
Los Angeles, California, USA

Architect, furniture designer
🔒

The first major project of Frank Gehry (b. 1929)—one of the world's most famous living architects—was the design of a house for himself and his wife Berta in Santa Monica, California, in the late 1970s. He simultaneously enlarged and deconstructed an existing bungalow using unconventional materials like chain link, corrugated steel, and plywood. Almost forty years later, Gehry, now past ninety, and his son Sam, an architect at Gehry Partners, designed a new Santa Monica home overlooking both Santa Monica Canyon and the ocean. This residence is less scrappy, more luxurious, but it still very much showcases Gehry's frenetic, subversive energy. From above tall hedges, its pitched roof cracks open, revealing splinters of glass and steel. The tall-ceilinged living spaces,

fronted in glass, are framed with exposed Douglas fir structure and boxy plywood protrusions. In the dining room, beams are inset with fragmented, Gehry-designed fish lamps, which float above a long plywood table and purplish leather benches. Marshmallow-like Arflex sofas in the living room surround a Gehry-designed glass table. Splashes of color arrive via amorphous Ken Price sculptures and art by Ed Ruscha, Cecily Brown, and Alejandro Gehry (Gehry's other son). The family room is accented with twisting Gehry Knoll chairs, the plywood kitchen is floored with bright patterned Granada tile, and a large music room, on the other side of an interior garden, is anchored by a glossy green piano.

GESELLIUS, LINDGREN, & SAARINEN

Hvitträsk
Luoma, Finland

Architect (Gesellius); architect, painter
(Lindgren); architect, painter (Saarinen)
👁

Finnish architecture firm Gesellius, Lindgren, & Saarinen, founded in 1896, helped pioneer architecture's transition into the modern era. Designing innovative structures melding old and new like the National Museum of Finland, the Helsinki Railway Station, and the Finnish pavilion at the 1900 Paris world's fair, its partners Herman Gesellius (1874–1916), Armas Lindgren (1874–1929), and (particularly) Eliel Saarinen (1873–1950) each had a profound impact on the country's development. In 1901 the firm began work on Hvitträsk, a home and studio on the shores of Lake Vitträsk, about thirty minutes west of Helsinki. Completed in 1903, the residence, divided into private living quarters, is a splendid example of the National Romantic style, a Nordic movement that simultaneously looked to medieval and prehistoric precedents while using technology and new ideas to fill spaces with light, space, and a sense of equality. Comprising a main structure with two wings, Hvitträsk was built of logs and stone, like an ancient fort, with a pitched shingle roof evoking a Nordic cottage. The south wing, which contained Saarinen's living spaces (and now houses the museum) is dominated by a high, wide living room, opening onto a vaulted dining room, tattooed with Nordic-themed frescoes. Timber beams, wide fireplaces, and colorful decoration evoke old European country manors and castles. Saarinen designed much of the furniture, while local artists and craftspeople created textiles, metalwork, tiles, and more.

GILBERT & GEORGE

8 Fournier Street
London, England, UK

Performance artists, photographers
⌂

London's Spitalfields district is the center of the Gilbert & George (a.k.a. Gilbert Proesch, b. 1943, and George Passmore, b. 1942) universe. According to the latter, "Nothing happens in the world that doesn't happen in the East End." Inside 8 Fournier Street, the Georgian townhouse they have called home for over fifty years, the artistic couple—who make no separation between their practice and everyday life—have lovingly staged an eighteenth-century ensemble to serve as their domestic canvas. Throughout the property, period building techniques have been paired with nineteenth-century furniture, vases, and books they've amassed since the 1970s. "We've used the same paint as they used originally, the same plaster, everything is as it would've been originally," George said.

Items salvaged from London's streets pair with furniture owned by Gothic Revival architect Augustus Pugin and a cast-iron table created by Napoleon's furniture designer, George Bullock. The interior is kept meticulously neat, which, the artists say, allows them to instead channel chaos and filth into works such as their infamous *The Pictures* series. "It has to be immaculate in order for us to make all these unpleasant pictures," George remarked. This in part explains why Gilbert & George have never used the house's kitchen or dining room for their intended functions, maintaining their tradition of eating at an East End café every single day.

BOB GILL

Gill Residence
New York, New York, USA

Graphic designer, illustrator
🔒

Graphic designer and illustrator Bob Gill (b. 1931) was a founding partner of Pentagram, a global design agency set up in 1972. At that stage, Brooklyn-born Gill had lived in England for twelve years, his distinctive illustrative style in the advertising industry helping him become one of the more fashionable names in the London scene. He added writing, teaching, and film directing to his set of skills and returned to his native New York in 1975 to launch the musical *Beatlemania* on Broadway. His effortlessly relaxed apartment sits seven floors above Fifth Avenue and boasts a bohemian feel that gives a nod to Gill's own work. White walls offer a blank canvas for the open-plan living area, with colorful touches from pieces throughout the apartment, such as the red accessories and

equipment that sit above the long desk that acts as his work-space. There are mismatched armchairs and Eames lounge chairs to sit on, and books abound on shelves, including a unit that runs the length of one wall. A piano hints at Gill's passion for music; in his early years in London, he played jazz with a young work colleague who was a keen drummer. The drummer soon quit his job working as a graphic designer to join a rock band. The drummer? Charlie Watts. The band? The Rolling Stones.

HUBERT DE GIVENCHY

Manoir du Jonchet
Cloyes-les-Trois Rivières, France

Fashion designer
🔒

Born in Beauvais, France, Hubert de Givenchy (1927–2018) left his hometown for Paris at the age of seventeen and established his own atelier in 1952, at the age of just twenty-five. A celebrated couturier, Givenchy set the benchmark for flawless French chic, dressing the likes of Audrey Hepburn, Jacqueline Kennedy, and Gloria Guinness in beautifully proportioned clothes that married elegance with a certain insouciance. Givenchy had an eye for interior decoration as much as fashion. He owned several homes across France, including a sixteenth-century château, Manoir du Jonchet, which he shared with fellow couturier Philippe Venet. Surrounded by a moat and formal gardens, it looks like a fairy-tale castle. The salon, with its lofty beamed ceiling and

limestone walls, is an easy space of air and light. Soft furnishings are in restful whites or grays; furniture is earthy and masculine, in wood, metal, and leather—the oak and bronze octagonal table is by Diego Giacometti, as are the four stools. Although the room has a spare, slightly monastic feel, there is nothing austere about the quality or expense of each individual piece. Each space hits a perfect, effortless note, even when you might think it wouldn't. The dining room, with its antique Chinese wallpaper and custom engraved goblets; Venet's vaulted atelier, with its own Giacometti coupled with wicker furniture. Some people just know.

JOHANN WOLFGANG GOETHE

Goethes Wohnhaus
Weimar, Germany

Novelist, poet, playwright
👁

Although Johann Wolfgang Goethe (1749–1832) inhabited eighteenth- and nineteenth-century Germany, he was really a Renaissance man. Considered the greatest German literary figure of the modern era, Goethe was also a scientist, statesman, lawyer, theater director, critic, gardener, designer, and artist. Born into bourgeois wealth in Frankfurt, he quickly earned praise for his poetry, written in a lyrical style and exploring the maddening, painful complexities of love. While itinerant in his youth, Goethe lived the last fifty years of his long life in a Baroque house on Weimar's Frauenplan, deeded him by his ally, Grand Duke Charles Augustus. Goethe himself redesigned its many rooms, which reflect the classical ideals of his time— geometric motifs, mythical friezes, long axes,

expressionless busts, and austere geometries. But in his personal spaces, he inserted a warm, understated palette that suited a man who spent his days looking inside himself. The soft, rustic furnishings of his study exhibit exquisite attention to handcraft and color. Rear rooms look out to the lovely garden, with its rich flowerbeds and vegetable patches. The home became a center for intellectual dialogue in what was the cultural center of Germany, and Goethe used it to store and display his incredible collection of over twenty-six thousand artworks and twenty-three thousand scientific specimens. Many are on display here, but most are stored in the adjacent Goethe National Museum and the nearby Klassik Stiftung Weimar.

ERNÖ GOLDFINGER

2 Willow Road
London, England, UK

Architect, furniture designer
👁

Hungarian-born architect Ernö Goldfinger (1902–1987), an acolyte of Le Corbusier and a member of the Modern Architectural Research Group, became one of Britain's most influential Modernists, equally lauded and reviled for his Brutalist social housing estates erected after World War II. Just prior to the war's outbreak, Goldfinger completed a home for his family in Hampstead, London, a neighborhood that became a gathering place for progressive artists, writers, and other Hampstead intellectuals in the 1930s. The residence was one of three apartments, all clad in red brick, with exposed columns and stretched white-edged horizontal windows. The complex drew protest before it was built, based on the mistaken belief that it would be a white concrete block,

out of context in historic Hampstead. In fact, these apartments featured a successful integration of the traditional Georgian terrace, its contextual brickwork and proportions executed with a clearly Modernist approach. Spaces inside are full of creative innovation. The windows, which fold to open, feature Goldfinger's first use of a "photobolic screen," an upper horizontal plane that bounces light into a room. Open-plan spaces flow freely along varying levels and surfaces, filled with ebullient art from the likes of Henry Moore and Max Ernst, as well as built-in cabinets, folding walls, sliding doors, and unconventional custom furniture (much of it designed by Goldfinger himself, like cupboards shaped like picture frames and a table made from industrial machinery).

EILEEN GRAY

Villa E-1027
Roquebrune-Cap-Martin, France

Architect, furniture designer,
interior designer
👁

A free spirit and artistic genius, Eileen Gray (1878–1976) mastered every medium she took on—including painting, cabinetmaking, lighting, textiles, furniture, interior design, and architecture—becoming one of the most revolutionary figures of Modernism. Born in Ireland, Gray made her name in London, Paris, and the South of France, working with luminaries like Le Corbusier, Adrienne Gorská, Seizo Sugawara, and Romanian architect and critic Jean Badovici, who was to become her lover. The couple collaborated on a "little refuge" in Cap Martin, France, on the French Riviera, which they would name E-1027, a cryptic interlinking of their initials and their alphabetical order (including E for Eileen and 10 for J). Its design is a splendid amalgam of Gray's talents. Perched on thin pilotis atop a cliff, the long, telescoping structure has white walls, a flat roof, floor-to-ceiling windows, a thin, ship-like deck, and a central spiral staircase. Inside, floating and built-in furniture and clever subspaces are designed to ensure that inhabitants "remain free and independent." (The circular glass-and-steel E-1027 chair would become world-famous.) Architecture critic Rowan Moore noted E-1027 "grows from furniture into a building." After Gray and Badovici parted ways, Le Corbusier notoriously defaced (or he would likely have said graced) the home with several vivid murals of amorphous naked women. Malicious or not, the act helped immortalize what has become a legendary location.

EDVARD GRIEG

Edvard Grieg Museum Troldhaugen
Bergen, Norway

Composer
👁

Nineteenth-century Romantic composer and pianist Edvard Grieg (1843–1907) created a lively, somewhat bohemian style of music, informed by Norwegian folk tradition, that would color classical music for years to come. He created most of his best-known works at Troldhaugen, in the picturesque lakeside villa just south of Bergen, Norway, where he lived with his wife, Nina. The musician called it his "best opus so far," and it's easy to see why. Sited on a lush promontory jutting into Lake Nordås, the residence resembles a tall Swiss chalet, blending with the folds of greenery and earth around it. Inside, Grieg, working with architect Schack Bull (his cousin), devised a balance of pastoral and sophisticated. The lofty sitting room's timber-paneled walls and floors reveal their knots and

imperfections, while expansive windows fill the space with natural light and lake views. The room's centerpieces are its ornate brass chandelier and Grieg's black Steinway grand piano. It's then layered with furniture upholstered in patterned textiles, framed artworks, and collectibles from the couple's extensive touring. Despite the home's beauty, Grieg would amble down to his tiny red composer's hut every day, locking himself inside to get work done. Upon leaving he would always place the following note on his desk: "If anyone should break in here, please leave the musical scores, since they have no value to anyone except Edvard Grieg."

WALTER GROPIUS

Gropius House
Lincoln, Massachusetts, USA

Architect, furniture designer
👁

Although Bauhaus founder Walter Gropius (1883–1969) is a Modernist icon, a visit to his house in Lincoln, Massachusetts, is even more exceptional and revelatory than you might expect. Gropius, who in 1937 became chair of the Architecture Department of the Harvard Graduate School of Design (he had fled Nazi Germany in 1934), hoped to create a new type of living experience, still steeped in the tradition of New England cottages, but infused with new forms, spaces, and materials. He was joined by his wife Ise, his daughter Alma, and his longtime colleague Marcel Breuer, who built a house next door. From outside, the home is simple and stylish: a white cube with thin ribbon windows fronted by an off-center portico. Traditional wood, brick, and fieldstone fuse with glass blocks, acoustical

plaster, and chrome. Inside, every detail maximizes both efficiency and beauty. Rooms flow from one to the next, opening dramatically to the natural landscape: large windows, view corridors, and porches lead your eye first to the manicured perimeter, then to the more savage landscape beyond. The home contains an exceptional collection of Bauhaus furnishings and art, much of it designed by Breuer, László Maholy-Nagy, and Gropius himself, and the family's possessions, from Gropius's typewriter and travel mementos to Isa's elegant dresses and coats, provide you with an intimate view into their lives.

CHAIM GROSS

The Renee & Chaim Gross Foundation
New York, New York, USA

Sculptor
👁

Hidden behind a yellow-trimmed storefront along Greenwich Village's LaGuardia Place is the townhouse of Chaim Gross (1902–1991), a talented Eastern European émigré who created highly animated, semiabstract drawings and sculptures exploring the sensuousness of the human form. The son of a lumber merchant, Gross was especially talented as a wood carver, but he developed an equally powerful body of bronze and stonework. His large public pieces can be found in gardens and plazas around New York, New Jersey, and Connecticut. Gross and his wife, Renee, purchased 526 LaGuardia Place in 1962, after raising their two children. They converted the four-story industrial building, dating from 1873, into a residence, adding a studio and sculpture gallery on the ground floor.

The glorious studio, with its vast, sloping skylight, exhibits about one hundred of Gross's major wood, stone, and bronze sculptures. The dense forest of finished and unfinished figures, tools, worktables, and vertical files was designed by Gross himself, with architects Arthur Malsin and Don Reiman. The third floor houses the couple's living and dining areas, relatively traditional spaces infinitely enlivened with salon-style installations of their superb art collection. Work from Europe, the Americas, and Africa include a whirling portrait of Gross by Milton Avery; work by Louise Nevelson, who was Gross's student; a selection of cast bronze Ashanti brass weights; and paintings by Moses Soyer, Willem de Kooning, and John D. Graham.

PATRICK GWYNNE

The Homewood
Esher, Surrey, England, UK

Architect
👁

Early Modernist architect Patrick Gwynne (1913–2003) specialized in designing houses that meshed with their sites through varied plans, raised profiles, fluid interiors, and other adaptations. His most famed project was his own home, the Homewood, a Modernist icon in Esher, a wealthy town southwest of London. Gwynne, who had briefly worked for Wells Coates, a member of the Modernist think tank MARS (Modern Architectural Research) Group, designed the residence for his family when he was only twenty-four. He replaced their sprawling Victorian house, situated on a wooded site, with the polar opposite: a reinforced-concrete structure raised on concrete piloti and brick piers, like the work of his early-Modernist role model Le Corbusier.

The pearl-white edifice is essentially in an H form. It is made up of three volumes: a large open-plan first-floor living and dining space with floor-to-ceiling glazing on two elevations (and kitchen behind); a bedroom wing; and staff quarters. The ground floor comprises the study, garaging, services, and an outdoor living room terrace. Extravagant details inside include a large spiral stairway, and walls and floors of terrazzo, marble, mahogany, and glass brick. Bisected by a stream, the lovely woodland garden offers a series of layered vistas and varied plantings. The stream flows into several more water features, including a pond that reflects the house, a colorful bog garden, and a series of cascades.

ZAHA HADID

Hadid Residence
London, England, UK

Architect, product designer,
furniture designer, fashion designer
🔒

Known for the gravity-defying forms of buildings such as
Rome's MAXXI museum and the London Aquatics Centre,
Zaha Hadid (1950–2016) had her own home in the penthouse
of an otherwise nondescript (from the outside, at least)
three-story apartment building in London's Clerkenwell neighborhood. The loft's skylit, white-cube interior formed the
perfect backdrop for an extraordinary array of art and design
pieces, all of which Hadid designed herself. The only exceptions
were her Murano glass vases and kinetic creations by Shiro
Kuramata. Hadid's 1977 painting *Malevich's Tektonik*, originally
presented as part of her AA thesis project, adorned one
wall, while her fluid and tectonic 3-D design works, such as her
Stalagmite & Stalactite Table, Iceberg Bench, Acqua Table,

Moraine Sofa, and Crevasse Vase added further to the
gallery feel. Like the rest of the apartment, the bedroom was
a minimalist space, complete with white floor and blinds, so
colors and shapes screamed. Any personal effects that were
on show echoed the sculptural qualities of the furniture upon
which they were placed. Her dressing table, for example, was
covered in an array of colorful perfume bottles, brushes,
tchotchkes, and mirrors, lined up in orderly fashion as though
they were tools on an architect's desk.

GEORGE FRIDERIC HANDEL

Handel House
London, England, UK

Composer
👁

It's fair to say that Baroque composer George Frideric Handel (1685–1759) never imagined he would have to share the spotlight with Jimi Hendrix. The German-born composer lived in a three-story Georgian townhouse at 25 Brook Street in London from 1723 until his death. About two hundred years later, Hendrix rented an apartment on the top floor of the adjacent building, 23 Brook Street. The two lodgings have since been merged into Handel & Hendrix in London, creating one of the most unusual house museums in the world. Handel, a virtuoso composer in the frilly era of harpsichords, clavichords, and chamber organs, was the first occupant of his house, part of a new extension of Brook Street. The location was perfect, in a good upper-middle-class area, close to both of his places

of work: the St. James's Palace and the Theatre in the Haymarket. Its stacked rooms included a basement kitchen, first-floor entertaining and composing spaces, a second-floor bedroom, and garret servants' chambers. The Georgian-style interiors were restored using paintwork samples and real estate inventories. Their spartan gray walls and simple plank floors are enlivened with rich, colorful possessions like eighteenth-century oil paintings, a complexly decorated wooden harpsichord (patterned with birds, flowers, and arabesques, it has three sets of strings per note), an organ, and sinuous baroque furniture.

WILLIAM S. HART

William S. Hart Museum
Newhall, California, USA

Actor, film director, screenwriter,
film producer
👁

You may have never heard of William S. Hart (1864–1946) or Newhall, California. But that makes Hart's estate north of Los Angeles more special: it's a hidden California treasure. Hart, a successful New York stage actor, transitioned into silent film at around age fifty, going on to become one of the most successful actors and directors in the world. Known as "Two-Gun Bill," Hart starred in about seventy features between 1914 and 1925, nearly all of them Westerns with dusty, sweeping scenes, like *Tumbleweeds* and *The Money Corral*. Exalted with the likes of Charlie Chaplin, Mary Pickford, and Douglas Fairbanks, Hart left his house to the county of Los Angeles. "When I was making pictures, the people gave me their nickels, dimes, and quarters," he said. "When I am gone, I want

them to have my home." Visiting his ranch is like walking into the Wild West of Hart's films, albeit more luxurious. The rocky grounds are full of cacti, chaparral, hillocks, gullies, and even a herd of bison. The Spanish Colonial mansion contains twenty-two rooms (including one for his two Great Danes), and almost all of its original contents are intact: Western art by friends like Charles M. Russell, James Montgomery Flagg, and Joe De Yong; Native American beadwork and textiles; and stage and film costume and props displayed in Hart's Southwestern-inspired interior with its hand-painted exposed ceiling beams, wrought iron railings, walls painted to mimic stucco, built-in bookcases filled with volumes pertaining to the art and history of the West, and much more.

ERNEST HEMINGWAY

Ernest Hemingway Home and Museum
Key West, Florida, USA

Novelist, short-story writer, journalist
👁

Author Ernest Hemingway (1899–1961), mythologized for his understated yet vivid writing, adventurous lifestyle, and stormy personal life, famously lived around the world, becoming the face of the so-called Lost Generation of American expatriates in the early twentieth century. Raised in Oak Park, Illinois, Hemingway served in the American military in Italy and Spain, and resided in Paris, London, and Havana, among other locales. On the advice of fellow expat writer John Dos Passos, Hemingway visited Key West, Florida, in 1928, living there with his wife Pauline from 1931 to 1940, an eternity for this restless soul. Their 1851 home, abandoned before Hemingway bought and renovated it, is a stunning eclectic colonial built of native limestone, with two-story wooden verandas; a deeply overhanging, slightly canted roof; and French doors with large yellow shutters. Inside, interiors have been re-created to resemble those in Hemingway's time. Not every item is original, but you can gaze at Hemingway's seventeenth- and eighteenth-century Spanish furniture, including his bed and writing desk, as well as built-in details like an ornate marble fireplace, glass chandeliers, Art Deco tiling, and turn-of-the-century fixtures. Spaces stocked with knickknacks and art from his travels (not to mention cat sculptures, taxidermy, and other evidence of his love of animals) are filled with natural light and surrounded by an explosion of tropical plants in the garden.

JIMI HENDRIX

Hendrix Flat
London, England, UK

Singer, songwriter, guitarist
👁

Although he died at just twenty-seven, American guitarist Jimi Hendrix (1942–1970) remains immortal; he's still one of the most influential, electric musicians of our time. The London apartment where Hendrix spent some of the last months of his life, from July 1968 to March 1969, adds even more mystique: it's located on the top floor of 23 Brook Street, an eighteenth-century townhouse adjacent to 25 Brook Street, where German composer George Frideric Handel lived more than two hundred years before. (Hendrix claimed to have seen Handel's ghost one night.) Both residences are part of a house museum called Handel & Hendrix in London. The rock star's upper-floor apartment, which he shared with girlfriend Kathy Etchingham, was opened to the public in 2016 after a significant restoration.

Hendrix hosted friends, wrote songs, rehearsed for shows, and gave interviews in the eclectic space, crowded with items from London's department stores and antiques markets. The bedroom is opulent and exotic, with its bright red carpet, Persian throw rugs, silk canopy, hippie-quilt cushions, and royal blue curtains. Replicated belongings include Hendrix's Epiphone FT79 acoustic guitar, wide fedora, turntable, cassette recorder, retro TV, and B&H cigarettes. Plenty of oddities include knickknacks from the Portobello Road Market, colorful ostrich feathers, and his hybrid stuffed animal, aptly named "Dog Bear."

BARBARA HEPWORTH

Barbara Hepworth Museum and
Sculpture Garden
St. Ives, Cornwall, England, UK

Sculptor
👁

British sculptor Barbara Hepworth (1903–1975) used nature as her muse, employing the shapes of hills, fields, bluffs, roads, and people to inspire her amorphous, abstract pieces in bronze, stone, plaster, and wood. "I was born with the ideas of certain shapes in my mind, as far back as seven," the always well-spoken artist recalled. At the outbreak of World War II, Hepworth and her husband Ben Nicholson moved their family from London to St. Ives in Cornwall, on the western edge of England. A few years later they acquired a simple fieldstone and stucco home and studio, providing Hepworth much-needed breathing room to further develop her work. "Finding Trewyn Studio was a sort of magic," she wrote. "Here was a studio, a yard and garden where I could work in open air and space." The heart of her world was her stone-carving and plaster studios: white, fairly unkempt spaces adjoining a lushly planted yard. Light pours in through skylights, and the overflowing rooms, still full of tools and work, flow in and out of the family's crowded home. The adjacent sunroom, with its tin roof and red tile floor, has a similar palette. Odd sculptures add punctuation, and exotic plants press up against the windows. The garden outside is a scraggly wonderland of artworks—from hand sized to story tall—layered and terraced within the grounds every which way.

TOMMY HILFIGER

Hilfiger Residence
Golden Beach, Florida, USA

Fashion designer
🔒

World-renowned fashion designer Tommy Hilfiger (b. 1951) launched his eponymous brand in 1985, inspired by pop culture and classic Americana. His name is now one of the world's most recognized lifestyle brands, appearing on all manner of clothes and accessories, from denim to sportswear, fragrance, and watches. Hilfiger and his wife, Dee, bought this seven-bedroom home in Golden Beach, Florida, in 2013 and embarked on a spectacular makeover. They asked Los Angeles-based interior designer Martyn Lawrence Bullard, a favorite of the Kardashians and Elton John, to create a beachside mansion that would exude fun and fantasy, as well as housing Hilfiger's impressive Pop art collection. The result draws on the ocean setting's natural light, set off by a bold use of color and design quirks, such as a lifelike sculpture of a security guard by Marc Sijan that makes guests do a double take. A black marble staircase, with a 23-foot (7-meter) custom chandelier, rises through the center of the mansion. The walls are canvases for bright splashes of color: one bedroom is decorated with red-and-white diagonal stripes, an ideal backdrop for Andy Warhol's Mickey Mouse artwork; bathrooms have scratch-and-sniff wallpapers, giving off the smells of oranges and bananas. The media room, bathed in psychedelic red, is inspired by the *Austin Powers* films, and an infinity pool looks out on to a palm-tree-fringed beach.

WINSLOW HOMER

Winslow Homer Studio
Prouts Neck, Maine, USA

Painter, printmaker, illustrator
👁

A pivotal figure in nineteenth-century American art, oil painter and watercolorist Winslow Homer (1836–1910) had a singular ability to make his landscapes and, more famously, his seascapes come forcefully to life. His studio in Prouts Neck, Maine, a jutting peninsula about 12 miles (19 kilometers) south of Portland, can be visited via tours coordinated by the Portland Museum of Art. In 1884 Homer, who had lived in New York for over twenty years, hired local architect John Calvin Stevens to convert a wood-sided carriage house overlooking the coast into a 2,200-square-foot (204-square-meter) residence and studio. Homer lived here, taking advantage of its sweeping views of the Atlantic, until his death. Inspired by Maine's turbulent surf and ever-changing weather, he painted (both inside, or along the nearby cliff walk) his late marine paintings here, vividly capturing the raw power of waves crashing against the rocky shore in all seasons. The two-story building, to which Homer added a second-story porch, pergola, and, later, painting room, is filled with his furniture, artworks, and photographs. Homer, who had a reputation as a "hermit with a brush," once posted a sign (now displayed in the house) on his yard exclaiming, "Snakes Snakes Mice!" to deter potential unwanted visitors. But he was very much a country gentleman, not a true Mainer, and spaces inside, dominated by timber, brick, and a mint green palette, suggest a slightly softened cosmopolitanism.

MICHAEL AND PATTY HOPKINS

Hopkins House
London, England, UK

Architects
🔒

The husband-and-wife architect team of Michael Hopkins (b. 1935) and Patty Hopkins (b. 1942) built their own home in 1976, creating a modern structure quite out of step with its Regency villa neighbors in Hampstead, north London. The two-story home and office is a lightweight steel-and-glass structure with a 33-by-39-foot (10-by-12-meter) footprint on each floor. It appears single story from the front, as the site lies beneath the road, with a footbridge providing a second-floor entrance. Engineer Tony Hunt used construction techniques normally seen on larger commercial buildings. A small structural steel grid of 7 by 13 feet (2 by 4 meters) was chosen, which meant the components could be small and light. Inside, the house has few divisions, with venetian blinds acting as

demarcation lines, although no distinction was made between the office and living areas (the practice moved out to offices in Marylebone eight years later when it outgrew the space in Hampstead). An open, blue spiral staircase leads down to the ground floor, which contains the kitchen, and living and dining areas, along with three bedrooms. Wall-to-wall carpeting is gray throughout. The master bedroom is on the upper floor, overlooking the garden, and overall the couple (now Sir Michael and Lady Hopkins) have created a feeling of restraint and refinement. The house won a RIBA award in 1977 and was granted Grade II* listing in 2018, which means it is considered to be of national importance and worth protecting.

VICTOR HORTA

Horta Museum
Brussels, Belgium

Architect, furniture designer
👁

One of the founders of the Art Nouveau movement, with its stylized, vegetal forms and curving, whiplash forms, Belgian architect Victor Horta (1861–1947) ushered its marriage of fine arts and applied arts to a new level of sophistication, deftly employing open floor plans and new materials like iron, steel, and glass. He created several spectacular buildings in Brussels: his four major townhouses are together a UNESCO World Heritage site, and his breathtaking Hôtel Tassel is generally considered the world's first Art Nouveau building. But none is as valued as his own house and studio, the only Horta property fully open to the public. Built between 1898 and 1901, the two buildings on rue Américaine are slightly more restrained and mature than Horta's earlier work (a precursor to

his late work, which moved even further from Art Nouveau). But their facades still employ Horta's signature bending stonework and columns, and twisting and knotted iron balconies. Inside are sun-filled spaces, permeated with sensuous flourishes in iron, wood, stained glass, and ceramic tile. The home's dining room, perhaps its most elaborate area, shows off structural metal arches, white-enameled brickwork, a geometric parquet floor, snake-like mosaic details, carved bas-reliefs, and endless Nouveau furnishings. Its spaces are united by a spiraling stair, decorated by painted motifs, mirrors, and sinuous balustrades, leading to a glowing skylight.

ELBERT HUBBARD

Roycroft Campus
East Aurora, New York, USA

Essayist, publisher, philosopher
👁

In 1895 former soap salesman Elbert Hubbard (1856–1915), inspired by Arts and Crafts icon William Morris's Kelmscott Press in England, launched the Roycroft Press in East Aurora, New York. Creating whimsical, inspirational illustrated publications like the *Fra* and the *Philistine*, it soon grew into an American Arts and Crafts community, becoming a destination for artists, writers, and philosophers. Hubbard himself (who would die with his wife aboard the *Lusitania*) became a popular writer and orator. His most famous essay, "A Message to Garcia," sold more than forty million copies, and with its proceeds he built what became known as the Roycroft Campus, still the best-preserved of America's turn-of-the-century guild properties. Begun in 1897, it consists of fourteen buildings constructed with natural materials, such as wood and stone, including an inn, chapel, print shop, furniture shop, and copper studio. The thirty-eight-room inn, created from the original print shop, was designed by Hubbard in a country Gothic style; its exterior merges medieval stone castle with half-timbered guild hall. The light-filled reception hall, entered via a heavy wooden door carved with Roycroft mottoes, contrasts a light fretwork of exposed oak rafters with heavy arched brick fireplaces. Aside from the colorful Navajo rugs, Roycroft artisans created most components, from handmade Arts and Crafts furniture to geometric gold-and-amber stained glass and copper lighting fixtures.

VICTOR HUGO

Maison Victor Hugo
Paris, France

Novelist, poet, playwright
👁

Acclaimed French writer Victor Hugo (1802–1885) created fantastical, culture-defining novels, poems, and plays, drawing on classical form and political reality. The son of a general in Napoleon's army, Hugo spent his youth as a loyalist but, as his work suggests, his views moved sharply left. He spent a twenty-year exile mostly on Guernsey, one of Britain's Channel Islands, before returning to France in 1870 after the founding of the Third Republic. Hugo's second-floor Paris apartment, which he rented from 1832 to 1848 on place des Vosges (then place Royale), reveals his surprisingly keen talent for design and decoration. The splendid Regency abode, where he wrote the start of *Les Misérables*, is layered with bold decoration: deep-colored, finely patterned damask walls, traditional wood

molding, carved monograms, and quirky furniture, much of it created by Hugo himself, working with carpenters to combine disparate pieces into complex new creations. Reproductions of Hugo's drawings, letters, and first-edition books are on display throughout. Due to sparse documentation and original artifacts, the home today is, intentionally, not true to life. Instead, it draws from several of Hugo's living spaces and reflects his lifestyle before, during, and after exile. The Chinese Lounge displays the original decor from Hugo's home in Guernsey, including intricate Asian-style panels designed by Hugo (painted by a craftsman); fine porcelain blanketing the walls and shelves; and the table on which he wrote *The Legend of the Ages* in 1859.

CLEMENTINE HUNTER

Melrose Plantation
Melrose, Louisiana, USA

Painter
👁

After living and laboring for seventy-five years on the Melrose cotton plantation near Natchitoches, Louisiana, Clementine Hunter (1886/1887–1988) began, late in life, to teach herself to paint. Working from memory and disregarding formal perspective and scale, she created scenes of life on the plantation on any surface she could find, including canvas, wood, gourds, paper, cutting boards, and milk jugs. Hunter slept and painted, by the light of a kerosene lamp, in a white clapboard shack, topped with a rusted-red-tin roof. The cramped space left room for very little: a wood stove, a steel-tube-framed twin bed, a small wooden painting table. But she was able to create more than five thousand paintings here before she died at age 101, charging visitors fifty cents to have a look. Next door to Hunter's

shack is the plantation's African House, a top-heavy structure with a small brick base and a wide top floor, its cypress shingles projecting more than 12 feet (4 meters). On the building's unique second floor, Hunter covered the walls in murals, depicting life for workers on the plantation: picking cotton, gathering pecans, washing clothes, and performing funerals and baptisms. Other buildings on the plantation include Yucca House, a French Creole cottage that served as its first residence, and the Big House, an 1833 Creole mansion belonging to the plantation's owners, the Henry family.

HENRIK IBSEN

Ibsenmuseet
Oslo, Norway

Playwright, theater director, poet
👁

Norwegian playwright Henrik Ibsen (1828–1906) transformed European theater with his rigorous dialogue and unsparing moral analysis. The restless writer, his work poorly received in traditional nineteenth-century Norwegian society, spent much of his mature life self-exiled in Italy and Germany. But for his last eleven years, he and his wife, Suzannah, lived in an apartment right across from Oslo's royal palace, at what is now Henrik Ibsensgate 26. After his death, the home was gradually dismantled, with furnishings and entire rooms scattering to other museums and residences. In 2006 the apartment was carefully restored, with floors, walls, ceilings, and surfaces reconstructed according to building studies and other documents. Tablecloths, curtains, and drapes were rewoven as exact replicas, and many original artworks and furnishings were returned. The apartment neighboring Ibsen's is filled with displays about his life, including personal items like his hat, coat, diploma, medals of honor, and writing paraphernalia. Spaces in his home exude an effete sumptuousness fitting for late nineteenth-century European bourgeois life, but a decided contrast to Ibsen's spare prose and withering social criticism. From floor to ceiling are plush geometric carpets, quilted Baroque furniture, patterned tile fireplaces, colorful walls, framed paintings, gilded mirrors, silk curtains, porcelain vases, and crystal chandeliers, to name just a few elements of the decor.

MARC JACOBS

Jacobs Residence
New York, New York, USA

Fashion designer
🔒

One of the best-known names in the world of fashion, Marc Jacobs (b. 1963) runs his own fashion label, as well as having served as creative director of Louis Vuitton from 1997 to 2014. He is associated with outrageous fashion statements, wearing a black lace dress for a gala at the Metropolitan Museum of Art and promoting clothes that pay no attention to gender. However, this approach is not reflected in the interior of his Manhattan home; instead, the four-story West Village property is a model of restrained, impeccable taste and old-school style. He bought the three-bedroom townhouse in 2009 and instructed interior designer Thad Hayes to carry out its decoration. The result combines 1970s pieces, Art Deco furniture, and contemporary art, although Jacobs was happy to disrupt any aspect that felt too ordered. For instance, once the television room was complete, Jacobs installed a giant sculpture of Dopey from Paul McCarthy's *White Snow* series, his justification being that the room was too perfect without it. Women feature strongly in Jacobs's art collection: a classic Andy Warhol silkscreen of Jacqueline Kennedy hangs in the living room, with works by Elizabeth Peyton and Lisa Yuskavage among those on display. Jacobs put the townhouse up for sale in 2019, following his purchase of a Frank Lloyd Wright-designed property in Rye, New York.

THOMAS JEFFERSON

Monticello
Charlottesville, Virginia, USA

Architect
👁

One of the greatest autodidacts in history, Thomas Jefferson (1743–1826) essentially taught himself architecture. His vision for a new (read: not colonial) architecture based on classical and Enlightenment ideals had a profound impact on his young country. He not only helped design Virginia's state capitol and (later) the University of Virginia, but also influenced decisions on the US Capitol, the White House, and the layout of Washington, DC, itself. Jefferson called his home Monticello his "essay in architecture," laboring on its design and construction for about forty years (1769–1809). Located on a hill (Monticello means "little mountain" in Italian) just outside Charlottesville, Virginia, the Palladian-inspired mansion is built in red brick and trimmed in cream wood. Its layout includes an octagonal dome flanked by sunken wings that wrap around a U-shaped rear lawn. At first quite modest, the plantation's main house grew to include thirty-three rooms, most showcasing jaw-dropping art and artifacts. The spectacular double-height entrance hall, for instance, includes explorers' maps, busts of French philosophers, scientific specimens, an engraving of John Trumbull's painting *The Declaration of Independence*, and more evidence of Jefferson's belief "that knolege [sic] is power, that knolege is safety, and that knolege is happiness." Visitors can also discover Monticello's lovely gardens and forests.

PHILIP JOHNSON

The Glass House
New Canaan, Connecticut, USA

Architect
👁

One of the enduring symbols of the midcentury, the Glass House is a must-see for any architecture enthusiast. But even for those who know it well, the legendary domicile of Philip Johnson (1906–2005) is full of surprises. The home has become—along with Mies van der Rohe's Farnsworth House near Chicago—a residential embodiment of the pared-down simplicity of the International Style. The steel-framed, glass-clad rectangle contains a bedroom, a kitchen, and areas for dining and entertaining. Spaces flow from one to the next, interrupted only by a brick column containing a bathroom and utilities. The highlight of the space, besides its breathtaking furniture and art, is its collection of ever-changing, elegantly framed vistas, including a lovely wooded pond below and

rolling fields and forests above. Johnson quipped that the large glass walls were basically expensive wallpaper and claimed the home was "the only house in the world where you can see the sunset and the moonrise at the same time, standing in the same place." Johnson lived here (much of the time with his partner, David Whitney) from 1949 until his death. The Glass House's 49-acre (20-hectare) site contains thirteen other buildings, including Johnson's one-room studio, a bunker-like painting gallery (with works by Andy Warhol, Frank Stella, Julian Schnabel, and many more), an intricately terraced sculpture gallery, the Brick House (for both Johnson and his guests), and abstract sculptures and spaces.

DONALD JUDD

101 Spring Street
New York, New York, USA

Sculptor, painter, printmaker,
furniture designer
👁

Groundbreaking sculptor Donald Judd (1928–1994) transformed art, using compositions and industrial materials like steel, concrete, and plywood to stress the physical experience—scale, materiality, physicality— of three-dimensional objects over their symbolic impact. In 1968 Judd purchased (for $68,000) 101 Spring Street, a five-story nineteenth-century cast-iron building at the corner of Spring and Mercer Streets in the then deteriorating neighborhood of SoHo. The cavernous space, a former manufacturing loft with floor-to-ceiling windows and wood floors, served not only as the artist's New York residence and studio, but as the genesis of his concept of "permanent installation," in which an art piece's placement was as critical as the work itself. "Everything from the first was intended to be thoroughly considered and to be permanent," Judd wrote. The artist, who lived here with his wife, Julie Finch, and their children, filled its floors with nearly two thousand pieces, ranging from household objects —including Judd-designed metal sinks and wood beds, desks, and chairs— to artworks by himself, Marcel Duchamp, Frank Stella, and Dan Flavin, and furniture by Gerrit Rietveld and Thonet. His approach in SoHo helped inspire another site of permanent installations: his living and working spaces in Marfa, Texas, along with the Chinati Foundation, an arts center inside former military barracks and artillery sheds, also in Marfa, that's now a major showcase for Judd's sculptures and the work of several contemporary artists.

FINN JUHL

Finn Juhls Hus
Charlottenlund, Denmark

Furniture designer, architect,
interior designer
👁

One of Denmark's national treasures, designer and architect Finn Juhl (1912–1989) was a pioneer of the Danish Modern movement, combining cool functionality with daring organic sensuality. His house in Ordrup, just north of Copenhagen, is a perfect example of how Juhl weighed interior design and architecture equally; all elements play ingeniously off one another. The elegant, light-filled rooms in the open-plan residence flow effortlessly into each other and, seemingly, into the rugged garden, designed by landscape architect Troels Erstad. One wing contains the living room and study, the other the kitchen, dining room, and bedrooms. Juhl's drool-worthy furniture graces every room, including sinuous FJ 44 dining chairs and FJ 45 armchairs; his Chieftain lounge chair, inspired by indigenous tools, its armrest and back "liberated," as he put it, from its supporting frame; and a pared-down Japan chair, one of Juhl's first industrially produced pieces. Juhl's art collection includes alternately quiet and disorderly works by Vilhelm Lundstrøm, Asger Jorn, Georges Braque, and Juhl himself. Almost everything else, from crafts to cutlery, is by Juhl or one of his colleagues, creating an all-encompassing experience infused by assured creativity. "Art has always been my main source of inspiration," Juhl said. "I am fascinated by shapes which defy gravity and create visual lightness."

DUŠAN SAMO JURKOVIČ

Jurkovič House
Brno-Žabovřesky, Czech Republic

Architect, furniture designer
👁

While born in Slovakia, early Modern architect Dušan Samo Jurkovič (1868–1947), nicknamed the "poet of timber" for his singular finesse with wood, is best known for his buildings in what is now the Czech Republic. His distinctive style was influenced by local folk tradition, but the home he designed for his wife and three children, just outside Brno, represented a huge leap forward, progressing from familiar vernacular to an eclectic fusion of Modern and traditional that was all his own. It's just as essential to Brno as the city's famed Modern homes, including Mies van der Rohe's Villa Tugendhat. Located atop a steep slope in a forest above the Svratka River, the home's facade is articulated by varied shapes and materials, like gabled roofs, a quarry-stone base, colorful tiles, a glass

mosaic (its motif derived from local fairy-tales), and intricately painted decoration. Unified by its double-height central hall, the home's rooms, with their dazzling hand-painted wallpaper and colorful articulation of structure, become energetic pieces in a three-dimensional work of art. Living spaces show off Jurkovič's well-earned reputation with timber: balconies become dark gridded sculpture; beams are etched with abstract moldings, and they contain shelves for the family's splendid porcelain collection; and bentwood furniture brings traditional Czech designs into a more streamlined era.

FRIDA KAHLO

La Casa Azul
Mexico City, Mexico

Painter
👁

Few house museums are as intimately linked to their inhabitants as Frida Kahlo's (1907–1954) La Casa Azul, or Blue House, in Mexico City's Coyoacán neighborhood. Kahlo, a painter revered for her vivid colors and compositions, and fusion of indigenous Mexican and modern European techniques, was born and died in the 1904 house, which wraps around a lush central courtyard. Kahlo and her husband, legendary painter, muralist, and activist Diego Rivera, added new spaces, colors, and textures over the years. Kahlo, often incapacitated due to a horrific bus accident, employed hundreds of creative objects—folk sculptures, ceramics, masks, photographs, modern art, vivid indigenous-inspired clothing, painting implements, and many of her best-known paintings—as both expression and escape;

a connection to Mexico and the world. Every piece of the 12-room house reveals something about her: crutches and wheelchairs reveal Kahlo's physical maladies; gifts from famed artists like Isamu Noguchi demonstrate her lofty place in the cultural world; portraits of Vladimir Lenin, Joseph Stalin, and Mao Zedong give evidence of her political leanings. (Leon Trotsky and his wife even lived in the Blue House for two years before moving a couple of blocks away.) Rivera decorated spaces with mosaics and seashells, and installed a colorful stepped pyramid in the courtyard.

FRIDA KAHLO AND DIEGO RIVERA

Museo Casa Estudio Diego Rivera y Frida Kahlo
Mexico City, Mexico

Painter (Kahlo); painter, muralist (Rivera)
👁

While the Colonial-style La Casa Azul of painter Frida Kahlo (1907–1954) in Coyoacán, Mexico City, is one of the most famous artist homes in the world, the nearby studio home of Kahlo and her husband—painter, muralist, and activist Diego Rivera (1886–1957)—is still a surprise. In 1932 Rivera commissioned Mexican architect Juan O'Gorman to design one of the first Modernist residences in Latin America. Hidden behind a fence of cacti, Rivera's studio incorporates many elements from Le Corbusier's architecture manifesto *Five Points of Architecture*—such as its concrete frame, slender pilotis, external spiral staircase, open floor plan, and roof terrace. Inside, the double-height studio, along with Rivera's mezzanine bedroom, is topped with sawtooth skylights and filled with his canvases, paints, papier-mâché sculptures, and a collection of native crafts and pre-Hispanic objects. A rooftop bridge connects to his wife's adjacent living quarters, the blue-colored Casa Frida, which contains small, relatively bare spaces and Kahlo's top-floor studio. The couple moved to the complex in 1934 but only lived together there for six years, until Kahlo left Rivera and moved to La Casa Azul. Even after they reconciled, the couple maintained the separate homes. Rivera died here in 1957, his vigil held in the studio. In 2012 the 1929 Cecil O'Gorman House—an equally modern neighboring home that O'Gorman designed for his father—was annexed to become part of the museum.

RAY KAPPE

Kappe Residence
Los Angeles, California, USA

Architect
🔒

Ray Kappe (1927–2019) was one of Southern California's greatest treasures. He not only created one of the richest bodies of architectural work in the area's history, but also helped upend the region's existing pedagogy, establishing the architecture programs at SCI-Arc (Southern California Institute of Architecture) and Cal Poly Pomona. His own home was similarly inventive in approach. For a beautifully forested but steeply inclined hillside site in Rustic Canyon, Kappe created a glass-and-wood elevated house supported by six concrete towers. The resulting interior is a "floating," multi-layered open space, with private areas, such as the architect's studio, cannily hidden under or behind more public ones. Kappe designed all the cabinetry in the house and also much of the furniture, including an electric blue sofa-and-chair arrangement. This striking color motif is carried through into the surfaces and objects of other areas, such as the kitchen, all visible from the living room. Expansive windows and redwood decking complete the seamless embedding of the room—and the entire house—in the surrounding landscape. You feel like you're in a tree house in the woods. Surrounding the residence are several other Kappe homes. Ranging from post-and-beam cedar cabins to multistory timber-and-glass compounds, they all tap into a primal sensation of uplift, excitement, and raw architectural power, and provide a sensual merging of building and nature.

KANJIRŌ KAWAI

Kawai Kanjirō's Memorial House
Kyoto, Japan

Ceramicist
👁

In the 1920s and 1930s, Japanese potter Kawai Kanjirō (1890–1966) helped found Mingei, a Japanese folk art movement inspired by nature and the handcrafted art of ordinary people. His ceramics evoked the unknown craftsman, from porcelain flower vases to temple-shaped *tsubos* (jars), glazed in his signature orangey copper, deep brown, and cobalt blue colors. (He prided himself on merging modern processes and traditional designs.) Kanjirō also created sculpture, furniture, wood carvings, poetry, and calligraphy. He designed his own two-story home and studio, as well as most of its objects; his brother was the builder. Tucked on a single-lane side street in eastern Kyoto, it evokes a glorified rural Japanese past, with its timber floorboards and beams, weighty dark wood furniture,

courtyard rock garden, shoji panels, and open fireplaces. A good description can be found in Yoshiko Uchida's book *We Do Not Work Alone: The Thoughts of Kanjirō Kawai*: "The moment one enters . . . it is easy to see that it is the home of an extraordinary person. One is immediately impressed with its massiveness and sturdiness." Kanjirō's studio is a shrine to his craft. This is, after all, a man who said "life is work, work is life," as well as "When you become so absorbed in your work that beauty flows naturally, then your work truly becomes a work of art."

JOHN KEATS

Keats House
London, England, UK

Poet
👁

A master of heartfelt emotion and the sensual description of nature, John Keats (1795–1821) was one of the most affecting poets of the English Romantic movement. He died of tuberculosis at just twenty-five, having published for only four years. Yet his work has inspired countless scribes, from Oscar Wilde to Jorge Luis Borges, who called his first encounter with Keats's work the most significant literary experience of his life. Keats House, originally known as Wentworth Place, and now owned by the City of London Corporation, is where Keats lived for just twenty-one months prior to traveling to Italy, where he died. While here he composed canonical pieces like "Ode to a Nightingale" and "The Eve of St. Agnes," and met and became engaged to his neighbor Fanny Brawne. (The garnet engagement ring Keats gave Brawn is on display in the house.) The gracious, rather unornamented home is perched behind thick foliage on the edge of Hampstead Heath in London. Inside its parlor, expansive windows admit light and provide views of greenery, while furnishings and sculpture speak to an age reveling in the splendor and order of ancient Greece and Rome. Upstairs is the modest bedroom where Keats first coughed blood, a traumatic indicator of his dire illness. A copy of a portrait by Joseph Severn depicts a pensive Keats writing here—one of several period paintings enlivening the spaces.

ELLSWORTH KELLY

Ellsworth Kelly Studio
Spencertown, New York, USA

Painter, sculptor, printmaker
🔒

A pioneering artist who tirelessly shaped and sculpted mesmerizing, hard-edge abstraction and color, Ellsworth Kelly (1923–2015) lived with his partner, photographer Jack Shear, for thirty-two years in an unassuming wood-clad colonial house in Spencertown, New York, along the Massachusetts border. Kelly worked inside an adjacent studio, a barnlike, 15,000-square-foot (1,394-square-meter) space that he enlarged and reconfigured in 2002 with the help of architect Richard Gluckman. There are no windows, only bands of skylights beaming angled light down onto the walls. The quiet, contemplative space was the perfect escape from reality, a minimalist white void on which to affix his vibrant primary tones and curves. Kelly died in 2015, but the box-shaped studio,

now home to the Ellsworth Kelly Foundation, remains largely the same. It contains not just places for painting, but also storage, archives, a viewing gallery, and an office. The cavernous painting space is still the center of attention. An empty horizontal canvas hangs on the wall, as if ready for treatment. Around it is a splattered mess of history. Most things are still speckled with color: Kelly's shoes, glasses, mask, stool, brushes, and solvents. His foundation continues to fund arts education programs in the area, making Kelly a sort of folk hero in this quiet wooded place, where for years he was able to live a civilized country life and evolve his work.

RUDYARD KIPLING

Bateman's
Burwash, East Sussex, England, UK

Novelist, short-story writer, journalist
👁

Rudyard Kipling (1865–1936), most famously the author of *The Jungle Book*, has been both praised and reviled as a genius of prose and narrative and a promulgator of imperialism and Empire. Born in Bombay (now Mumbai), India, he eventually settled with his family in an East Sussex home, Bateman's, in 1902. "That's She! The Only She! Make an honest woman of her—quick!" Kipling famously said (like only he could) when he saw the property. It's a stunning place whose grounds would inspire several poems and children's classics, including *Puck of Pook's Hill*, "The Glory of the Garden," and "The Land." The seventeenth-century home is a perfect example of stern Jacobean architecture, with its layered sandstone facade, closely aligned chimneys, and leaded windows. Rooms,

described by Kipling as "untouched and unfaked," remain well intact. Dark paneled walls, monolithic stone fireplaces, hefty oak beams, and exquisite Renaissance furniture exude old English tradition, while voluminous exotic artifacts—Oriental rugs, large globes, terra-cotta Hindu statues, and books from afar—reflect Kipling's strong affinities with the East. Each room tells a story. Kipling tracked down the dining room's exquisite gold leather wall hangings, whose specific origin is still disputed. The colonial-era author especially comes alive in the study, with its cloth-covered maps; animal rug; book-lined walls; messy, ink-spotted desk; and daybed with seemingly fresh cigarette burns.

STEVEN KLEIN

West Kill Farm
Bridgehampton, New York, USA

Photographer
🔒

Photographer Steven Klein (b. 1965) is a master of brash provocation and sallow darkness. His disquieting, cinematic vision has inspired a generation of fashion photographers, artists, and filmmakers and reframed our relationships with countless celebrities. Not surprisingly, his house, West Kill Farm, in Bridgehampton, New York, is the antithesis of its area's light-toned, preppy persona. "White and green is not a great color combination," he told *Architectural Digest*. Almost every surface of his residence—a merger of three barn spaces—is jet black, like a sci-fi or S&M movie set. This is a function not just of the artist's sinister aesthetic, but also of a desire to alter the seaside area's predictable bright light. Klein's extralarge bedroom, its ring of windows edged in creamy black and delineated with shadowy slats, is all various shades of black, except for a white pitched ceiling. Working with longtime collaborator Chris Rucker, Klein creates tension between soft and hard, crude and refined. Glossy leather sofas, a glass-topped coffee table, and stained wood floors reflect; matte walls, a leather duvet, and a modern hanging fireplace suck light away. Klein's brooding *Girl in a Lace Dress* overlooks the seating area, which is dominated by a sepia-toned horsehead statue. Leather and metal surfaces are not all about naughtiness: they're also references to Klein's other passion: horses. He has several in his stables and rides them frequently.

YVES KLEIN

Klein Residence
Paris, France

Performance artist
🔒

Yves Klein (1928–1962), a flamboyant and sometimes shamanic figure in postwar European art who became renowned for the use of his brilliant International Klein Blue, shared this modest Parisian apartment with German artist Rotraut Uecker, known as Rotraut. Before moving in, Klein, who strove to "liberate" intangible elements like color from their typical constraints, painted the walls, doors, and brick fireplace white. As Rotraut noted, it was like *The Void*, referring to Klein's exhibition in which he famously displayed an empty gallery as an artwork. Several of Klein's blue works appear, disembodied from the context. The rectangular glass coffee table houses powdery International Klein Blue pigment. Often filled with critics and artists, such as Pierre Restany, Niki de Saint Phalle, Jean Tinguely, and Christo, the apartment is where Klein cofounded Nouveau Réalisme and conceived notable works, such as performances, sculptures, and blue, pink, and gold-leaf monochromes. By departing from representation, Klein saw his work as, in his words, the attainment of immateriality. He died in 1962, at only age thirty-four. When in Paris, Rotraut still uses another area of the apartment but keeps the central space as it was during Klein's life. As Rotraut has said, "I thought it should always stay. You feel the richness of creation, of all the events and all the tremendous art he made here."

LEE KRASNER AND JACKSON POLLOCK

Pollock-Krasner House
East Hampton, New York, USA

Painters
👁

The leader of the Abstract Expressionist movement, Jackson Pollock (1912–1956) flung, dripped, scrawled, and poured paint onto his floor-placed canvases to create works that he described as "energy and motion made visible." In 1945 the brooding artist moved with his wife, equally talented artist Lee Krasner (1908–1984), to a humble clapboard house in Springs, a hamlet of East Hampton that somehow still maintains its air of seclusion and simplicity. The nineteenth-century fisherman's home, with its views across a salt marsh to Accabonac Creek, is as quiet and unassuming as the couples' work is not. It remains as it did at the time of Krasner's death, containing the couple's furniture; their phonograph, jazz record collection, and library (framing the threshold between living and dining rooms); and paintings and prints by both artists, including Pollock's *Composition with Red Arc and Horses*. Their nearby wood-shingled studio, a former storage barn, is an artwork in itself. Paint on the wood floor from Pollock's improvisational works creates an amalgam of his efforts; it's often clear where certain pieces—such as *Autumn Rhythm, Convergence,* and *Blue Poles*—were created. After Pollock died, Krasner, who previously worked in one of the home's bedrooms, used the studio to create her uniquely innovative, gestural works; ample evidence of her efforts grace the walls.

KARL LAGERFELD

Lagerfeld Residence
Rome, Italy

Fashion designer
🔒

According to writer Cathy Horyn, Karl Lagerfeld (1933–2019), who arrived in Paris in the 1950s from his native Hamburg, Germany, lived in about twenty residences in Paris, Rome, Brittany, Monaco, Berlin, Biarritz, and even Vermont (where he occupied a nineteenth-century house). "The well-furnished mind of Karl Lagerfeld needs an ever-changing stage. . . . He seems to reinvent himself through his homes," Horyn wrote in the *New York Times*. Lagerfeld designed the interiors, sometimes with the aid of designer friends, such as the late Andrée Putman or Christian Liaigre. "It's like an alarm clock of taste and change," he told Horyn. "Suddenly I want something else." Seen here is a wood-paneled bathroom with a spiral staircase that leads to a bedroom above; it is from one of Lagerfeld's apartments in Rome, where he and Putman once mixed her objects with Fortuny fabric and furniture from the Wiener Werkstätte. A seemingly absurd combination (particularly for a lavatory) of glass block, landscape art, classical bas-relief, and carved timber furniture seems somehow inevitable. Always ahead of his time, and thanks to published photographs of his residences (many of which he took himself), he showed new ways of living that are meaningful and personal. As photographer Helmut Newton once said, Lagerfeld was a "clairvoyant, who brings the future to us."

KENNETH JAY LANE

Lane Residence
New York, New York, USA

Jewelry designer
🔒

Bursting onto the American fashion scene in the 1960s, costume jewelry designer and style arbiter Kenneth Jay Lane (1932–2017) created spectacular faux-gem pieces that were worn by the likes of Jacqueline Onassis, Princess Diana, Sarah Jessica Parker, and Elle Macpherson. He made costume jewelry respectable, even to royalty. His fabled Park Avenue apartment, in a five-floor Gilded Age mansion dating back to 1892, was designed by Stanford White, architect to the New York elite. Lane acquired the first and second floors, with their ornate moldings, veined-marble fireplaces, and French Empire ceilings, when the building was converted into apartments in the 1970s. Of the drawing room, Lane said, "Because it's so Edwardian, I wanted the room to have a kind of clubby feeling."

Fringed lampshades from Vincent Fourcade create just that kind of vibe; the walls are covered in a dark brown olefin, a man-made fiber more commonly used for car upholstery. On this, Lane installed his eclectic collection of Orientalist paintings. Thrown into the mix are dishcloth-covered cushions from India, leopard-print chairs from a flea market in Palermo, Italy, antique books angled this way and that, and Continental silver and ceramics. The look is a supreme example of "nondecorating"—objects seemingly flung together in a hap-hazard fashion—but of course, it is all meticulously thought through and executed.

JEANNE LANVIN

Lanvin Residence
Paris, France

Fashion designer
🔒

The grand mansion at 16, rue Barbet-de-Jouy in Paris's seventh arrondissement formerly belonged to the Marquise Arconati-Visconti before becoming the home of haute couture legend Jeanne Lanvin (1867–1946) in 1920. Lanvin, a talented milliner who transformed her small 1880s hat shop into an international fashion house (Lanvin Modes, now simply Lanvin), wasn't one to waste time. She swiftly set about modifying the residence to suit her needs, adding a reception wing containing a hall, library, gallery, and dining room. For the interior, she commissioned French designer Armand-Albert Rateau, described as "the most eminent of *ensembliers*," who had also crafted exquisite Lanvin perfume bottles and a famed Lanvin store on the rue du Faubourg Saint-Honoré. In Lanvin's private apartment, his innovative, theatrical style played out in a highly polished scheme that combined classical art and sinuous plaster with luxurious materials, such as patinated bronze, carved wood, and colored marble. Her bedroom was clad entirely in silk, the color of which has since been immortalized as "Lanvin blue." The silk was decorated with white and gold rosettes, daisies, and palm leaves, beautifully embroidered in Lanvin's workshops. The space also featured carved wooden archways and a recessed canopy bed with an ornate base, as well as seats made of varnished oak with needlepoint tapestry—which, apparently, was one of Lanvin's favorite pastimes.

CARL AND KARIN LARSSON

Carl Larsson-gården
Sundborn, Sweden

Painter, illustrator (Carl); textile designer, tapestry weaver, interior designer, painter (Karin)
👁

Tucked into an extraordinary blooming garden in Sundborn, Sweden, Lilla Hyttnäs is the product of two gifted artists focused on egalitarian and creative living. Carl Larsson (1853–1919) and Karin Larsson (1859–1928) transformed the 1837 timber cottage into the perfect canvas for their vision, and the backdrop for their idyllic depictions of family life. They received the home from Karin's father in 1888, filling it with Karin's modern textiles and tapestries, furniture inspired by peasant design, hand-carved doors, and Carl's wistful, earnest pictorial murals and paintings. (You could call him the Norman Rockwell of Sweden.) The result was an experimental, personal, and playful domestic space that accommodated their large family (the couple had eight children). Ignoring the conventional, heavy,

and ornate decor of the time, as well as the muted colors of a bourgeois palette, the couple took inspiration from the Swedish countryside and the English Arts and Crafts movement, which promoted simple folk styles and craftsmanship over industrial manufacturing. The rooms of Lilla Hyttnäs are spontaneous, colorful, and relaxed, with a lifetime of accumulated modifications, paintings, and projects. Bold bursts of orange paint, bright pink landings, brimming bookshelves, and striped and checked patterns are just a few of the home's startlingly fresh touches. It is easy to imagine the Larssons living and working here, especially Karin, who considered the home an expression of her artistic practice.

RALPH LAUREN

Oatlands
Bedford, New York, USA

Fashion designer
🔒

Despite having launched his Ralph Lauren Home collection in 1983 with no fewer than 2,500 pieces, Ralph Lauren (b. 1939) makes no claims to be an interior designer. Instead, he compares his process to that of a film director creating a point of view. "It's always a world," Lauren explained. Published photographs of his homes in places like Colorado, New York, and Jamaica have always induced an emotional response. A prime example of Lauren's dream weaving is Oatlands, his estate in the monied enclave of Bedford, New York. Designed in the 1920s by architectural firm Delano & Aldrich, Oatlands was named by its original owner, banker and landscape architect Robert Ludlow Fowler Jr. Lauren has described his ivy-drenched Norman-style estate as "a combination 'hunting lodge' and stately home." Surrounded by 250 acres (101 hectares) of rolling lawn and forest, the mansion is the embodiment of the patrician gentleman's ideal, with its layered arrangements of oil paintings, mahogany paneling, Georgian furniture, Persian carpets, and tartan accents. "What is important here is that only this designer, with his particular style radar, the man who gave us the oxford-cloth button-down pillowcase and the wingtip brogue wing chair, could take the symbols of a civilized life and arrange them into so potent an interior," interiors arbiter Stephen Drucker once wrote. "The atmosphere in this house is intense, like breathing pure oxygen. It goes to your head."

LE CORBUSIER

Le Cabanon
Roquebrune-Cap-Martin, France

Architect, furniture designer,
urban planner, painter, writer
👁

Illustrious machine-age architect Le Corbusier (1887–1965) envisioned some of the largest, most futuristic developments the world had ever seen. Yet his summer house was built of timber and had just one room. Le Cabanon, his "castle" built on a hillside overlooking the Mediterranean in Cap Martin, measured 151 square feet (14 square meters), contrasting dramatically with the area's extravagant villas. Inspired by nearby trappers' cabins, Le Corbusier designed the residence as a birthday gift for his wife, Yvonne Gallis, and for eighteen years they spent every August there. (Their primary apartment and studio was located on the west edge of Paris.) One focus of Le Corbusier's work, functionality, stands out. Minimal prefabricated elements, from built-in furniture to plywood walls,

serve multiple purposes, allowing the tiny space to perform several functions, including entertaining, cooking, dining, sleeping, and producing art. It was here that Le Corbusier designed what was arguably his most famous building, the Chapelle Notre Dame du Haut in Ronchamp, France. And the cabin contains a superb collection of Le Corbusier murals, including *Taureau* and *La Mer*, whose varied colors and forms offset the space's ascetic simplicity. Thick surrounding gardens are filled with Mediterranean plants, including a carob tree, prickly pears, yuccas, and agaves. Le Corbusier drowned in the ocean nearby in 1965, spending his last night at his beloved getaway.

149

FREDERIC, LORD LEIGHTON

Leighton House Museum
London, England, UK

Painter, draftsman, sculptor
👁

Frederic, Lord Leighton (1830–1896), a celebrated British artist of the Victorian age, crafted colorful, hazily lit paintings full of history, exoticism, and romance. His style nodded to the subtle, personal abstractions of his contemporaries, the Impressionists, but with a traditional, realist streak. His London home, designed by architect George Aitchison, was anything but realist—an eclectic "palace of art," contrasting English tradition with Orientalist splendor. Leighton acquired the plot in London's Holland Park neighborhood in 1864, and over thirty years exuberantly expanded and embellished it. The first phase, an austere brick structure centered around his double-height studio, also contains a generous entry hall, dining room, drawing room, and relatively meager spaces for sleeping. Its additions—

inspired by Leighton's faraway travels—grew more elaborate. The first was the Arab Hall, modeled after the twelfth-century Palace of Zisa in Palermo, Sicily, showing off blue Moorish tile mosaics, gilt friezes, classical columns, and an ornate, partially recessed dome ceiling decorated with mashrabiya fretwork. More new spaces followed, including the Silk Room, an art gallery lined with embroidered green silk, and the Winter Studio, in brown brick with cast-iron columns. Leighton crowded the home with his own paintings, sculptures, and more than seven hundred sketches and studies; bronzes, marbles, carved furniture and ceramics; and artworks by his friends and contemporaries, including George Frederic Watts and Frederick Sandys.

LEONARDO DA VINCI

Le Château du Clos Lucé – Parc
Leonardo da Vinci
Amboise, France

Painter, sculptor, architect, inventor,
engineer, scientist, mathematician,
cartographer, musician, writer
👁

The true definition of a Renaissance man, Leonardo da Vinci (1452–1519) was one of the world's great geniuses, excelling in a breathtaking array of fields, from painting to mechanical engineering. But few are aware that the Tuscan master spent the final years of his life in Amboise, France, at the Château du Clos Lucé, next to the Château royal d'Amboise. Invited by King Francis I, who named him "Premier Painter, Engineer and Architect of the King," Leonardo, aged sixty-four, traveled through the Alps in 1516, hauling with him notes, sketches, manuscripts, and paintings, including the *Mona Lisa*, *Saint John the Baptist*, and the unfinished *Virgin and Child with Saint Anne*. The château, built of pink bricks and intricate freestone, is filled with splendid rooms furnished with tapestries, frescoes,

portraits, royal crests, stone fireplaces, leaded windows, and period furniture. Leonardo's first-floor bedchamber, where he died, has clear views of the Château royal d'Amboise, while, according to legend, a nearby tunnel linked him directly to the king's chambers. Even more extraordinary are his recently renovated working quarters, including a library, study, and workshop that showcases reconstructions of blueprints, pigments, and paintings. In the basement more than forty models have been created from Leonardo's designs, including water wheels, and weapons of war. Outside in Parc Leonardo da Vinci are giant machines based on the master's sketches, including a revolving bridge, a flying machine known as an "aerial screw," and giant crossbow.

NORMAN LINDSAY

Norman Lindsay Gallery and Museum
Faulconbridge, New South Wales,
Australia

Painter, cartoonist, novelist, sculptor
👁

Prolific Australian artist Norman Lindsay (1879–1969), recognized for his biting political cartoons and sensual book illustrations, was also a gifted painter, sculptor, art critic, and novelist. Longtime cartoonist for the Sydney *Bulletin* and creator of the famed children's book *The Magic Pudding*, Lindsay's evocative, imaginative style melded with a bold willingness to raise controversy. Lindsay and his wife Rose lived for fifty-seven years at their 42-acre (17-hectare) estate in Faulconbridge, in the Blue Mountains of New South Wales. The artist, working with a local carpenter, substantially remodeled the sandstone, bungalow-style residence, adding several new rooms and wide verandas, among other things. He also built a separate painting studio and redesigned the

garden, installing his own statuary (including suggestive female nudes drawn from mythology) as well as a wisteria colonnade, rose arbor, cypress grove, and several urns and fountains. Many of Lindsay's works are displayed inside the home, which is now the Norman Lindsay Gallery and Museum. Boisterous, orgiastic watercolors and meticulous model ships mingle with oil paintings and sculptures combining classical techniques with knowing gazes and a wholly modern tone. The artist's studio is a gabled pavilion with high casement windows that admit natural light, bouncing off pinkish roughcast walls. The spare space contains just bookshelves, a folding table, and a few paintings and sculptures.

FRANZ LISZT

Liszt-Haus
Weimar, Germany

Composer, pianist
👁

A prodigiously talented pianist and composer, Franz Liszt (1811–1886) became one of the emblematic figures of the Romantic era. Born in the village of Doborján, Hungary, he began composing at age eight, performing publicly the next year, and by his twenties was traveling Europe as an adored virtuoso. In 1847 he moved to Weimar, Germany—a capital of avant-garde music—to focus on composition. He would later depart for Rome but returned in 1869, at the invitation of Grand Duke Carl Alexander, the city's most powerful arts patron. He spent the rest of his life in the top-floor apartment of the grand duke's eighteenth-century garden house on the edge of Park an der Ilm. The classicist building, surrounded by the park's trees and greenery, was sumptuously furnished by Grand Duchess Sophie herself, its airy rooms decked with wrought Saxon furniture, pearl-drop chandeliers, porcelain urns, oil paintings, and red-and-green drapery, invoking the national colors of Liszt's home country. "Nothing was overlooked to make my apartment comfortable and elegant," Liszt noted. Piano maker Carl Bechstein sent him one of his grand pianos—an excellent advertisement—which graced the salon, as did a smaller Ibach piano. Liszt, by then in his late sixties, spent his time here teaching piano virtuosos from around the world. After he died the grand duke almost immediately opened his apartment as a memorial.

CHRISTIAN LOUBOUTIN

Château de Champgillon
Vendée, France

Fashion designer
⌂

Paris-born Christian Louboutin (b. 1963) always wanted to design shoes, and at age sixteen he dropped out of school to pursue his dream. By 1992, in his late twenties, Louboutin opened a boutique full of luxury stilettos in the Galerie Véro-Dodat—one of his first customers was Princess Caroline of Monaco. He added his iconic red soles in 1993, expanded into handbags in 2003, and in 2011 added a men's shoes line to his empire, which now includes stores across the globe. One of Louboutin's homes is the thirteenth-century Château de Champgillon in the Vendée region of western France. He shares it with his business partner, Bruno Chambelland, whose great-great-grandfather owned the property centuries ago. Previously an auctioneer, Chambelland was in charge

of decorating, and he opted for an eighteenth-century style, returning a number of pieces that had remained in his family, including an antique grandfather clock. Each fanciful room is unique: the bright white entrance hall, glowing from its floor-to-ceiling windows, leads to a twisting wrought-iron staircase; the pinkish grand salon is crowded with Italian Baroque armchairs, Louis XV mirrors, and sketches by Jean-Auguste-Dominique Ingres; Louboutin's peaceful room is lined with wallpaper made of pressed flowers from his romantic, mist-filled garden. There's also an oak barn on the property, which is now an archive of more than eight thousand pairs of Louboutins.

AUGUSTE AND LOUIS LUMIÈRE

Musée Lumière
Lyon, France

Filmmakers, inventors
👁

Brothers Auguste (1862–1954) and Louis Lumière (1864–1948) changed film history by inventing the cinematograph, an early motion picture camera and projector that, unlike Thomas Edison's peephole-employing kinetoscope, allowed movies to be shown to large audiences, not just individuals. They also created the world's first motion picture, *La sortie des ouvriers de l'usine Lumière*. Most of their creations were born at their family's "Hangar," a factory producing photographic plates and, later, the world's first film set. But their majestic home was a villa in Lyon's Monplaisir neighborhood, an outgrowth of their family's success in industry. (Their father, Antoine, built other lavish properties, and his profligate spending eventually prompted the brothers to remove him from the business.)

The Art Nouveau villa, known locally as the Château, was designed by Antoine himself, following the plans of architects Paul Boucher and Charles-Joseph Alex. Its ever-changing volumes feature a rich variety of colors and textures, including glazed-tortoiseshell roof tiles, yellow limestone walls, and white limestone balconies. Inside, Antoine employed artist and artisan friends to embellish the home—now a museum, as is the Hangar—with endless intricate details: painted floral motifs, plantlike glass chandeliers, ceramic friezes, marble plinths, colorful stained-glass windows, pediment doors, pressed cement tile, marquetry wooden floors, and marble plinths. Beyond the foyer, living spaces, and grand staircase, there's a conservatory with beautiful bay windows.

EVERT LUNDQUIST

Evert Lundquists Ateljémuseum
Drottningholm, Sweden

Painter
👁

With a career spanning more than fifty years, Swedish painter Evert Lundquist (1904–1994) created quiet but unruly work that seemed unsure whether it wanted to be abstract or figurative, contemporary or traditional. In this way, it still defies categorization. His whitewashed studio, with its Art Nouveau architecture and large arched windows, was in the early 1900s a power station for Drottningholm Palace, the private residence of the Swedish royal family. When the palace was connected to the public power supply in the 1950s, the station was converted into Lundquist's studio by the palace architect, Ivar Tengbom. Lundquist worked there from 1953 to 1993, first living alone, then with his family (his wife, painter Ebba Reutercrona, and their twin sons, Manne and Hymme, also

artists) in the house next door. The studio, which looks exactly as Lundquist left it, was both his artistic center and a boisterous meeting place for friends. Its orderly chaos still features scattered art utensils, collectibles, empty bottles, and Lundquist's tobacco pipes. Strange, incongruous pieces add a sense of creative mystery and intimacy: taxidermized birds, an antique sewing wheel, a print of the *Mona Lisa*, feathery curtains, and various types of light bulbs, presumably to create varied lighting effects. Other surfaces are filled with art—reproductions, oil paintings, charcoal drawings, and etchings, including paintings by Lundquist and Reutercrona and watercolors by Manne and Hymme.

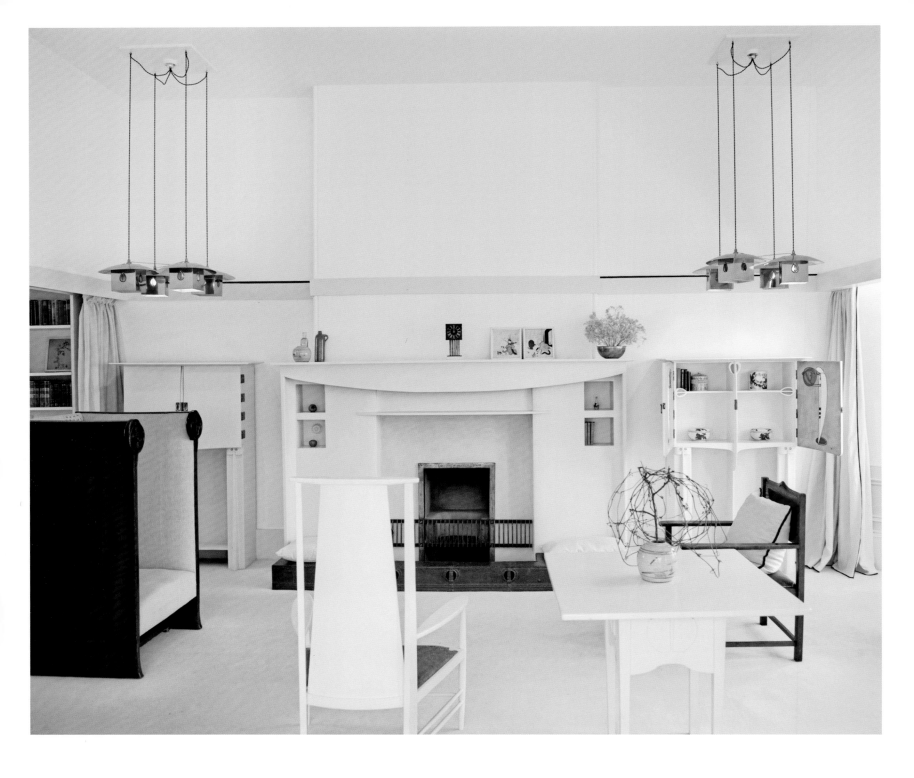

CHARLES RENNIE AND MARGARET MACDONALD MACKINTOSH

The Mackintosh House
Glasgow, Scotland, UK

Architect (Charles); painter (Margaret)
👁

Scotland's most beloved architect, Charles Rennie Mackintosh (1868–1928) was a visionary who channeled Arts and Crafts, Art Nouveau, and Art Deco styles to create something very much his own. You can visit his home on Glasgow's West End, which he designed with his talented wife, Margaret Macdonald Mackintosh (1864–1933). Their original three-story townhouse at 6 Florentine Terrace was torn down in the 1960s. But its original furniture, art, windows, doors, fireplaces, and even staircase were preserved, and the home was meticulously reassembled inside the University of Glasgow's Hunterian Art Gallery, about 328 feet (100 meters) away. It's a sublime Gesamtkunstwerk, or total work of art, incorporating the Mackintoshes' many gifts along every square inch.

You progress from the ground-floor entry and dining room to the light-filled second-floor studio/drawing room to the top-floor bedroom. You're surrounded by art upon art: black-and-silver friezes and textiles; ornate high-back chairs; metallic chandeliers etched with purple glass seed motifs; a mahogany "kimono" writing cabinet decorated with abstract square patterns; white-painted furniture embossed with dark wood plant motifs; a beautiful gesso painting by Margaret (could it be a self-portrait?); white-painted furniture with sculptural detailing of plant and bird details. Visitors can also explore the Hunterian's separate Mackintosh House Gallery, entered from the second-floor landing.

ALEXANDER MCQUEEN

McQueen Residence
London, England, UK

Fashion designer
🔒

Alexander McQueen (1969–2010) made an extraordinary rise from a humble upbringing in London's East End to the summit of the fashion world. His career rose sharply after he left school at sixteen to work as an apprentice on Savile Row. He won the British Fashion Awards' British Designer of the Year four times and was even honored by the Queen. He bought this two-bedroom property on the top two floors of a building in London's exclusive Mayfair area in 2009. A blue plaque outside the property shows it had been home to author P. G. Wodehouse from 1927 to 1934. McQueen was in the process of converting it from several apartments to one residence when he took his own life in February 2010. Design house Paul Davies London spent sixteen months transforming the

1,790-square-foot (166-square-meter) penthouse into a homage to the late designer, filling the walls with pictures of McQueen and friends, including Isabella Blow and Annabelle Neilson, and his signature skull motifs are evident in the wall mirrors. A dramatic spiral staircase leads to two bedroom suites and bathrooms that have rare Calacatta marble. A black, cream, and silver color scheme, typical of McQueen's designs, with an Art Deco flavor is the inspiration for much of the property, and there is a spectacular roof garden with 2,400 square feet (223 square meters) of black, timber-decked entertaining space.

RENÉ MAGRITTE

René Magritte Museum
Brussels, Belgium

Painter
👁

One of the exemplars of Surrealism, and arguably Belgium's most famous artist, René Magritte (1898–1967) worked by the mantra "we always want to see what is hidden by what we see." Magritte spent the majority of his life in Brussels, where he and his wife, Georgette, bounced around seven different addresses. Their longest stretch, from 1930 to 1954, was spent inside a one-bedroom apartment at 135, rue Esseghem in Jette, on the northwest outskirts of the city. The modest, sparsely furnished dwelling was where Magritte created about half of his oeuvre, usually laboring in his dining room. The home's cramped spaces provided endless inspiration: cloudy skies in paintings like *The Telescope* and *The Human Condition* were borrowed from the view from the family's powder blue living room. More fodder came from that room's simple white fireplace (*Time Transfixed*) and birds in the garden (*The Sky Bird and The Return*). The dining room served as the setting for regular Sunday meetings of the Brussels Surrealist Group. In 2019 the adjoining building was transformed into Belgium's first abstract art museum. The Magritte Museum, which opened in 2009 in the center of Brussels, contains much of Magritte's work, but 135, rue Esseghem is the artist's only house museum in the city.

SAM MALOOF

The Sam and Alfreda Maloof
Foundation for Arts and Crafts
Alta Loma, California, USA

Furniture designer
👁

Furniture maker and woodworker Sam Maloof (1916–2009) was born in Chino, California. Self-taught and diligent, he crafted pieces that were both simple and sculptural, austere and radical. A leader in the California Modern arts movement, Maloof's work is held by museums across the United States, and Presidents Carter and Reagan each owned one of his chairs. Central to Maloof's identity was his sprawling, hand-built redwood residence and adjoining woodshop, nestled in a lemon grove near Alta Loma, in the Pomona Valley. Over a half a century, it evolved into an incomparable showpiece, accruing piece by piece, room by room, employing astounding hand-made detail—sinuous or jagged joints, doors, windows, rafters—and whimsical humor. In 2004 it was saved from destruction,

moved in pieces to accommodate the extension of the I-210 freeway. The twenty-six-room home is filled with more than one hundred pieces of Maloof's furniture—from rocking chairs and dressers to music stands and cradles—clarifying the evolution and diversity of his work. It also contains one of the country's most outstanding Arts and Crafts collections: hundreds of bowls, vases, dolls, furniture, and utensils crowding shelves and tables. The woodshop, where Maloof collaborated with the same craftsmen for decades, is packed with tools, template pieces, and more. The thick native gardens and forest around the house are filled with craft and sculpture from Maloof and dozens of others.

CÉSAR MANRIQUE

Casa-Museo César Manrique Haría
Haría, Lanzarote, Spain

Painter, sculptor, landscape artist
👁

Spanish painter and sculptor César Manrique (1919–1992) was a stunningly original, ambitious figure who literally transformed his birthplace, the volcanic island of Lanzarote, in the Canary Islands. His wildly expressionist architecture—often combining volcanic stone, whitewashed walls, and colorful murals and statues—surrounds the island, where he designed monuments, parks, grottos, gardens, restaurants, and museums. You could spend days exploring it all, but to get a sense of Manrique's life and work, visit the Fundación César Manrique, where he lived from 1968 to 1988, and the Casa-Museo César Manrique Haría, his residence for the last years of his life. The Tahíche-based foundation is sited in the middle of a massive lava coulee. Its light-filled upper story,

framing views of the nearby lava fields, draws from Lanzarote's traditional whitewashed architecture, and adjoins a mural and statue-filled garden. The lower level of the house, built around volcanic bubbles connected by tunnels, contains lively rooms enhanced by Manrique's built-in furniture, murals, and statues, and by copious plant life and basalt walls. Manrique's house museum, located in a converted farmhouse in the tranquil village of Haría, sets a distinct contrast, as a peaceful, traditional escape. Textured with basalt stones and heavy timber beams, it offers a more personal look at Manrique's life, with access to his personal belongings, including ceramics, sculptures, plants, clothes, and books and, in the adjacent studio, his oils, tools, easels, and unfinished paintings.

PAUL MARMOTTAN

Musée Marmottan Monet
Paris, France

Art critic, art collector, historian
👁

Born into a substantial fortune, Paul Marmottan (1856–1932) began his career as a provincial barrister. But when his father, Jules, a successful industrialist and avid art collector, died, he renounced his career, moved to his inherited Empire-era mansion on the western edge of Paris, and began studying history and art. Marmottan became a prolific author and a recognized expert in French art of the Consulate and Empire periods. His knowledge and wealth helped him assemble an astounding art collection of his own, with which he filled the mansion, decorated in the austere Empire style, including abstract parquet floors, heavy dentil molding, mythical gilt friezes, and furniture from the Tuileries Palace and one of Napoleon's residences. Marmottan bequeathed his home to the Académie des Beaux-Arts, which opened it as a museum in 1934, expanding the collection to include countless Impressionist paintings, including the largest collection of Claude Monet's work in the world. While the museum has become renowned for its Impressionist collection, walking through Marmottan's two-story home is a journey through seven hundred years of art. Highlights include paintings, furniture, bronzes, clocks, ceramics, and art objects of the Napoleonic era; sixteenth-century Renaissance tapestries; fifteenth-century wooden sculptures, and colorful thirteenth-century texts. A modern underground addition showcases Monet's work, from urban landscapes to dozens of waterlilies, in every conceivable arrangement and color.

RAFAEL MASÓ

Casa Masó
Girona, Spain

Architect, poet, urban planner
👁

While splendid Catalan architect Antoni Gaudí is revered worldwide, Rafael Masó (1880–1935), one of his equally talented contemporaries, has been left off all but the most obscure reference guides. Masó, who grew up admiring Gaudí, was part of a group of artists and architects who formed the Noucentisme movement, an early twentieth-century effort injecting Catalan spirit and tradition into forward-looking design. His boisterous buildings, prevalent in his hometown of Girona and elsewhere in Catalonia, share Gaudí's boisterous, organically expressive character, but with additional local and historical references. Casa Masó, facing both the Onyar River and Carrer de les Ballesteries, was Masó's childhood home. Between 1911 and 1920 Masó, now an architect, undertook a radical intervention, connecting it with three neighboring buildings and filling it with Noucentista painting and decoration. The building's street facade is austere, composed of heavy stones in a varied configuration. The river side is quite the opposite: a white facade ornamented with blue windows, yellow tiles, wooden shutters, and hanging plants. Inside, this mix of austerity and verve continues, with warm tones and traditional massing infused with the bright colors and vivid forms of the many objects Masó designed himself: ceramics, furniture, stained glass, screens, planters, textiles, and lamps. If you're intrigued by this recently renovated masterpiece, follow the "Rafael Masó Route" in Girona, which includes his even-more-expressive Farinera Teixidor and Casa de la Punxa.

BRUNO MATHSSON

Södra Kull
Tånnö, Sweden

Furniture designer, architect
🔒

Swedish furniture designer Bruno Mathsson (1907–1988) became an international star thanks to seating designs with monikers like Grasshopper, Eva, Swivel, Pernilla, and Jetson. Mathsson, the son of a carpenter and furniture maker, designed each piece with an intense attention to function, studying the mechanics of sitting by reclining in a snowdrift, for example. Virtually all of the iconic pieces named above grace Mathsson's own home, called Södra Kull, which translates to "Southern Hills." The low-slung 1965 residence is tucked into the woods by the shores of Lake Vidöstern, just south of Mathsson's hometown, Värnamo. The luminous, contemplative space incorporates the artist's other major innovation: his design of glass-clad houses, inspired by a 1948 trip to the United States.

Open-plan living and dining rooms command views of the water through glazed walls, as daylight softly illuminates the interior, reflecting off matte tiled floors and metallic ceilings. A furry brown Pernilla recliner stares out to the lake, which seems to drift back into the home. Family photographs, records, and rustic modern art, ceramics, and fixtures are sparely distributed, while books and magazines are stacked on light wood shelves. In the kitchen, beautifully designed cupboards pop open with a gentle push. Mathsson's bedroom has access to a courtyard, where the designer, who loved the outdoors, often slept outside.

ANDREW MAYNARD

My-House
Melbourne, Victoria, Australia

Architect
🔒

A native of Tasmania, Andrew Maynard established his own architectural practice, Austin Maynard Architects, in 2002 in Fitzroy, Melbourne. He likes his work to reflect his left-of-center political views, and he is a firm advocate of a sensible work/life balance that promotes good mental health. These priorities strongly influenced his design of the practice's office, which doubles as his family home. The 1880s terrace has been revamped to admit as much sunlight as possible (and so provide large doses of vitamin D, on the advice of Maynard's doctor), to the point that it is sometimes necessary to wear sunglasses inside. The architect designed a glazed extension to the rear of the house, with a roof made of a translucent polycarbonate called Thermoclick. To minimize heat loss,

the roof is built with an insulating air gap, and a hydronic heating system generates heat. The dining room occupies the extension, filled with potted plants to enhance the feel of a greenhouse. Bright yellow floors, stairs—leading up to a lounge area—and chairs were chosen after Maynard consulted his Instagram followers. The original terrace, with high ceilings and small windows, was retained, accentuating the contrast with the new addition. Maynard and his family live on the top floor, which includes two bedrooms, and regain the rest of the property when the office is closed—staff are mandated to leave at 5:30 p.m. every night.

JÓZEF MEHOFFER

Józef Mehoffer House
Kraków, Poland

Painter, printmaker, textile designer,
stained-glass window designer,
set designer, furniture designer,
interior designer

👁

Józef Mehoffer (1869–1946) was a crucial figure in the Young Poland movement, formed by a turn-of-the-century cadre of Polish artists determined to break from the past. He created a remarkable body of work, with paintings influenced by Symbolism and Post-Impressionism exhibited at the Musée d'Orsay in Paris; sketches at the Polish National Museum in Kraków; and frescoes, murals, and stained-glass windows installed in several national monuments and cathedrals. In 1932 he bought his home on Krupnicza Street in Kraków's Old Town and immediately began renovating the classically proportioned, two-story 1874 villa. Nicknaming it the "Cone Palace," he delineated new interior spaces to accommodate his family and carefully restored elements like the central

wooden stair. Even during the Nazi occupation, he and his family hosted artistic, musical, and literary gatherings here. Having lost access to his atelier in the Academy of Fine Arts in Matejko Square, Mehoffer began to work here as well. The home, covered in ivy on its rear facade, is a welcome escape from the city, with its modest proportions and deep green garden, filled with benches, chairs, and tables, not to mention lovely flowers and hedges. Meho Café, also in the garden, serves brunch. The residence itself mingles antique and early-modern furnishings, as well as Mehoffer's paintings, sketches, designs, and even stained-glass windows. Especially personal pieces include lively, elegant portraits of Mehoffer's wife, Jadwiga.

STEVEN MEISEL

Meisel Residence
Los Angeles, California, USA

Photographer
🔒

Fashion photographer Steven Meisel (b. 1954) injects his work with attitude, camp, and story, teasing out supermodels' personalities and transporting them into strange worlds. It seems perfect that he chose to live in Trousdale Estates, the once cool, then kitsch Beverly Hills stomping grounds of midcentury celebrities like Barbara Stanwyck and Frank Sinatra. Meisel's home was designed in 1963 by popular architect George MacLean. Working with architecture firm Marmol Radziner and designer Brad Dunning, the photographer has rejuvenated it, with a unique fusion of retro and contemporary, just in time for midcentury design to come back into fashion. (Renovated Trousdale homes now belong to stars like Jennifer Aniston, Ellen DeGeneres and Portia de Rossi, and

Eugenio López Alonso.) Massive windows and large overhangs bring the outside in, while rough stone walls and columns set a quirky, Palm Springs/Hawaii Modern tone. Polished stone floors and dark-veneered-wood surfaces layer on a faux-vintage glam. Then come the eclectic furnishings, bridging hard and soft, flashy old and cool new. In the living spaces are a silk-covered ottoman; an octagonal rug by Edward Fields; a sunburst mirror from JF Chen, accenting a wall of mica tile, and a driftwood-and-glass table. Meisel has sheathed his office/master bathroom (you read that combination right) with green onyx walls, silk curtains, and hardwood cabinetry and screens, while a Dorothy Draper resin sculpture sits on a vintage black Jansen desk.

GARI MELCHERS

Gari Melchers Home and Studio
Fredericksburg, Virginia, USA

Painter
👁

Now eclipsed by more illustrious and inventive turn-of-the-century American painters like John Singer Sargent, Winslow Homer, and Mary Cassatt, Gari Melchers (1860–1932) was one of the most popular artists of his time, working extensively in the United States and Europe and gaining particular renown for his vibrant, picturesque scenes of rural life. Born in Detroit, he was entranced with European art and studied painting at the Royal Academy of Art in Düsseldorf and the École des Beaux-Arts in Paris. He and his wife, Corinne, also an artist (and occasionally his model), settled in Falmouth, Virginia, purchasing Belmont, a two-story, c. 1800 white frame house where they would stay from 1916 until their deaths. Thanks to their frequent travels and residencies, the couple acquired

a spectacular and eclectic collection of treasures. The highlights of their traditional, albeit colorful home are a French Savonnerie carpet, a Dutch Rococo secretary, shelves stacked with Chinese porcelain, Delft and Wedgwood dishes, and works by Corinne, including *The Model*, a clever "picture within a picture" portrait of her husband at work. Melchers's own gilt-framed art is displayed in his adjacent studio, a tall, large-windowed space designed by his friend John Donaldson in 1924. Intended from the beginning to serve as a work space as well as a private gallery, the well-appointed quarters contains Melchers's art supplies, worktables, and easels.

KONSTANTIN MELNIKOV

Melnikov House
Moscow, Russia

Architect
👁

Probably the world's most celebrated surviving example of Soviet avant-garde architecture, the defiantly radical home of Konstantin Melnikov (1890–1974) transports you into late 1920s Russia, a brief, dizzying time, when anything seemed possible. Tucked between apartment buildings in what is now an affluent section of Moscow, the white, three-story structure, built of brick faced with plaster, consists of two interlocking cylinders, famously perforated with over sixty hexagonal windows. The cylindrical shape, argued Melnikov, enhanced structural stability, opened the interior, and minimized usage of materials, which were very scarce at the time. The windows evenly disperse light, not to mention creating one of the most memorable building facades ever conceived. Inside,

the residence progresses in a spiraling fashion, from congested first-floor spaces, full of family artifacts, to airy upper rooms that include just one family bedroom (divided by partial yellow walls); a stylish, violet-colored salon, dominated by a massive window; and Melnikov's dazzling, cavernous studio, filled with a cloud of glowing hexagonal windows. Drawings, paintings, and sculptures throughout were created by Melnikov and his son and protégé, Viktor. Melnikov was eventually banned by the Soviet government from producing his architecture, and he subsisted in relative obscurity in the home until his death. Despite interfamily squabbles, the dwelling opened (albeit in limited fashion) to visitors in 2014 as a branch of the Schusev State Museum of Architecture.

HERMAN MELVILLE

Herman Melville's Arrowhead
Pittsfield, Massachusetts, USA

Novelist, short-story writer, poet

👁

Drawing on his private affliction, frustration, and inspiration, not to mention his unique experience as a seaman, Herman Melville (1819–1891) wrote what was to become one of the most revered novels in American history: *Moby-Dick; or, The Whale*. He penned several other novels, short stories, and poems, but had a relatively unappreciated career, ending up as a full-time Customs House inspector in New York. From 1850 to 1863, Melville and his family lived at Arrowhead—their home and farm in Pittsfield, Massachusetts, in the Berkshires—which he named after Mohican relics he found while plowing its fields. The yellow clapboard farmhouse was home to Melville, his wife, Elizabeth, their four children, and other family members. Melville's escape from the tumult was his second-floor study,

with its dark wood desk and views of the Berkshires. Here he wrote *Moby-Dick*, its whale inspired by the snow-covered curves of Mount Greylock, as well as *The Confidence-Man: His Masquerade*, *Israel Potter: His Fifty Years in Exile*, and several short stories. He used the spare, simple house, with its wood-paneled walls and sense of New England asceticism interrupted only by lovely dressers, clocks, beds, and china, as a subject of many of his works. He described its "grand central chimney" in the story *I and My Chimney*, and its beautiful surroundings in *Israel Potter*: "In fine clear June days, the bloom of these mountains is beyond expression delightful," he wrote.

HENRY CHAPMAN MERCER

Fonthill Castle
Doylestown, Pennsylvania, USA

Tile designer, ceramicist, archaeologist,
anthropologist, antiquarian
👁

Turn-of-the-century archaeologist, historian, collector, and tile maker Henry Chapman Mercer (1856–1930) believed that the Industrial Revolution would wipe away the handmade remnants of American culture. He gathered a collection of almost thirty thousand items, including hand tools, horse-drawn vehicles, and ceramic tiles, and built the Mercer Museum, a concrete, castle-like structure, to store most of them. His own home, Fonthill Castle, became a showplace as well, specifically for his collection of tiles and prints. An early example of reinforced-concrete construction, the towering castle is an eclectic hybrid of Gothic, Byzantine, Picturesque, and other styles. It includes forty-four rooms, over two hundred windows, and eighteen fireplaces, among other elements. The interiors

emulate a classical European estate, with vaulted ceilings, hooded fireplaces, tall columns, and hundreds of paintings and prints. But they're also adorned with a mind-bending collection of tiles of varying shapes, textures, and colors, inset into walls, floors, ceilings, and columns. Mercer built the nearby Moravian Pottery and Tile Works as well, another cast-in-place concrete structure that produces appropriately eclectic handmade tiles to this day. After his death in 1930, he left his "Castle for the New World," as he called it, in trust as a museum of decorative tiles and prints. In 1990 the trustees of the Bucks County Historical Society became its permanent overseers.

ALESSANDRO MICHELE

Michele Residence
Civita di Bagnoregio, Italy

Fashion designer

Alessandro Michele (b. 1972), Gucci's long-haired, mustachioed creative director, has a "fake vintage" aesthetic, inspired by the past and the present (never the future), that has reshaped one of Italy's premier fashion houses. "It's not easy to live now. I think we need to dream. So I wanted to present an idea of something romantic, in dream time—like in a movie," he once remarked to *Vogue*. Born in Rome, Michele and his partner, Giovanni Attili, spend much of their time there in an eighteenth-century apartment, which they converted from a formerly bleak office. But their favorite escape is a restored country house perched directly on top of a pointed mountain in Civita di Bagnoregio, a cinematically lovely and virtually empty town two hours north of Rome. "It's a very eccentric place for very eccentric people," Michele said. The home was built from the rubble of a former monastery, the kind of place you might dream exists. It looks like a painting, inside and out. Dark wood framing, whitewashed walls, and red stone tile floors mingle poetically with Michele's mix of antique and antique looking. The downside is that the mountain's crumbling volcanic rock necessitates constant rebuilding. But that seems to suit him fine. "I love the house because it's like it's falling down every year," he told the *New York Times*. "You don't know how long it will be there. And you don't care. It's a reflection of our life, you know?"

LEE MILLER AND ROLAND PENROSE

Farleys House and Gallery
Muddles Green, East Sussex, England, UK

Photographer (Miller); painter, photographer, poet (Penrose)
👁

From outside, Farleys House, the Sussex home of American photographer Lee Miller (1907–1977) and British Surrealist painter Roland Penrose (1900–1984), appears to be a typical English brick farmhouse, as its name suggests. But inside, it tells a different story, its bright-colored walls, rambling corridors, and asymmetrical rooms providing an overwhelming glimpse into the lives of its remarkable occupants. The couple and their son Antony moved here in 1949 and immediately transformed it into a hotbed of modern art's icons. Guests included Pablo Picasso, Max Ernst, Joan Miró, Eileen Agar, and Man Ray (Miller's mentor and former lover), to name just a few. The riotous work of the couple and their visitors saturates the residence in the form of paintings, sketches, sculptures, murals,

and tiles. Above the kitchen stove is a crude face, painted onto ceramic by Picasso. A pink-walled room is a monument to Miller's prominent wartime work—she documented the Normandy landings and the liberation of concentration camps, among other moments. A grid of her photographs illustrates Britain during the Blitz, and nearby there is a drink tray that she stole from Hitler's apartment. Penrose's work includes a raw, abstracted painting of Miller pregnant, her face and heaving belly painted lilac blue. A vivid, collage-style fireplace mural in the dining room depicts a birdlike man staring out, seemingly fascinated by all the fuss.

CARL AND OLGA MILLES

Millesgården
Lidingö, Sweden

Sculptor (Carl); painter (Olga)
👁

Sculpting traditional motifs from mythology, religion, and history in a fresh, vigorous way, Carl Milles (1875–1955), a protégé of Auguste Rodin, dominated the Swedish art world for the first half of the twentieth century with his larger-than-life pieces. Carl and his wife, Olga (1874–1967), a painter, created their dream estate, Millesgården, in an appropriately mythic location: a ridged cliff overlooking Lilla Värtan strait, on the island of Lidingö, just outside Stockholm. In 1906 they hired architect Carl M. Bengtsson to create a home for living, working, and exhibiting art. In the following decades, they expanded the property with Carl's half-brother, architect Evert Milles. The Milles's home itself, mixing Swedish romanticism with Mediterranean classicism, is brimming with beautiful art and tasteful modern Swedish furniture. But its art galleries and studios are the stars: classicist rooms filled with marble mosaic floors, colorful walls, Carl's sculptures, and the family's collection of art and antiquities. The cavernous Large Studio, with its rounded clerestory windows, is filled to the limit with plaster models. Even more heroic are the dreamlike, Mediterranean-inspired grounds, with their sculpture parks, gardens, planted terraces, loggia, stairs, architectural fragments, columns, and fountains. They're rich with Carl's dynamic works, such as the bronze-and-granite *Little Triton* fountain, a half man/half fish vigorously blowing water through a shell, and the graceful *Ice-skating Princess*, gracefully swirling on a frozen lake.

JOAN MIRÓ

Fundació Pilar i Joan Miró a Mallorca
Palma, Majorca, Spain

Painter, sculptor, ceramicist
👁

Spanish painter, sculptor, and ceramicist Joan Miró (1893–1983) compared the colors of his whimsical, soulful Surrealist art to words in poetry and notes in music. "The works must be conceived with fire in the soul but executed with clinical coolness," he said. In 1956, after years of nonstop travel, the artist finally settled down in Palma on the Spanish island of Majorca, a place that had inspired him since childhood. His friend, architect Josep Lluís Sert, then dean of Harvard's Graduate School of Design, designed his studio. The building's gridded concrete structure (Sert's specialty) contrasted with typical Mediterranean architecture, but its clay tile infill softened its impact, as did its undulating roof, which mirrors both Miró's vibrant creations and the local topography. The two-level studio's vaulted ceiling and clerestory windows flood it with natural light. Its work and storage areas are separate, opening space for large paintings and letting the prolific artist work on numerous pieces at once. Canvases, oils, watercolors, crayons, paintbrushes, and sponges intermingle with Miro's collection of objects, including postcards, newspaper clippings, butterflies, and shells. In 1959 Miró purchased Son Boter, an adjacent eighteenth-century Majorcan house that would become his second studio. And in 1992 the Spanish architect Rafael Moneo completed the final piece of the complex: two stunning stone-and-concrete structures containing the headquarters of the Fundació Pilar i Joan Miró a Mallorca.

JONI MITCHELL

Mitchell Residence
Los Angeles, California, USA

Singer, songwriter, painter
🔒

When folk-rock goddess Joni Mitchell (b. 1943) acquired a 1920s Spanish Revival house in Bel Air, Los Angeles, she looked to Sally Sirkin Lewis to tailor its decor to her personality. The famously soulful Mitchell admitted to *Architectural Review* that she had had her doubts about hiring an interior designer. "Decorated rooms sometimes sacrifice feelings and emotions for the sake of chic," she said. "The look is sometimes too polished. I couldn't live in a house like that." Lewis's understated style has become known as "California Design," blending glamour with clean, elegant lines and sumptuous craftsmanship. Lewis's description of her strategy for this house reflects Mitchell herself: "colorful, charming, free." The designer balanced the singer's desire for "pure and simple" with sharp statements that make sure it doesn't all blend too seamlessly: green walls and bronze-framed mirrors in the bedroom, a velvet sofa and snakeskin-covered table in the living room. She styled the singer's dining room as an eclectic mix of baronial grandness and Californian laissez-faire, with soft echoes of Mission-style nostalgia. Warm burnt-sienna tones permeate the upholstered chairs and the terra-cotta flooring. The supple coffered ceiling is flecked with turquoise, orange, and yellow paint. Surfaces are soft and luxurious, with Indian artifacts lining the eighteenth-century Welsh sideboard, flanked by suede dining chairs. The result is neither too smooth nor too polished, resonating with Mitchell's spirit.

MOBY

Moby Residence
Los Angeles, California, USA

Songwriter, singer, music producer
⌂

The musician Moby (b. 1965) specializes in driving, emotional songs that bridge the gulf between electronic dance music and pop. After moving from New York to Los Angeles in 2010, the one-named star (his parents nicknamed him Moby for the great whale) developed a reputation as a local architecture aficionado. He started his own architecture blog and bought a legendary 1920s Norman-style château called Wolf's Lair in the Hollywood Hills. The peripatetic artist loves a new design challenge, and in 2015 he sold the cavernous property, which was a bit much for a single guy. His downsizing came in stages. He bought two homes in a hilly section of Los Feliz, an older neighborhood next to Griffith Park, where he hikes almost daily. He sold one—a five-bedroom 1926 Tudor-style mansion—

in 2018 to none other than Leonardo DiCaprio, another serial homeowner. The remaining property, just down the street, overlooking Griffith Park, is smaller, but better suited to his goals of simplicity, wellness, and absorption in nature. "An ex-girlfriend who saw my house said, 'I don't know how you managed to move Westport, Connecticut, to L.A,'" he told the *Wall Street Journal*. His main living space is decorated sparsely, with just a few midcentury furnishings, including a beige sofa and a rounded teak table and chair. Representing his core interests are a centerpiece black laminate Baldwin piano and a small white meditation mat by the window.

CARLO MOLLINO

Casa Mollino
Turin, Italy

Architect, furniture designer,
interior designer, photographer,
engineer, car designer
👁

Radical Turinese architect, engineer, photographer, car designer, stunt pilot, downhill skier, and (yes) occultist, Carlo Mollino (1905–1973) was a fascinating, restless figure whose legacy is only starting to be uncovered. His apartment in a nineteenth-century villa, located near the Piazza Vittorio Veneto in Turin's center, shares many of its owner's attributes. Restored as a museum in 1999, the shadowy space, filled with pops of color and light, is packed with the gorgeous and the bizarre, often both at the same time. It's like visiting a timeless shrine composed of symbolic objects, while instigating a design treasure hunt. Mollino's taste, both classic and modern, is unassailable. His own furniture employs ingenious engineering to create unprecedented, sinuous pieces, and his sprawling oeuvre of sensuous photographs is exceptional. Around this he installed an artful mix of sumptuous Japanese lanterns and sliding doors, classical busts, gilded mirrors, richly colored tiles, and Eero Saarinen Tulip chairs. He paired this with eccentricities like arboresque photographic enlargements, clam-shells as sculptures, and found objects like 1930s-era brass fixtures. According to the home's curator (and decoder), designer Fulvio Ferrari, Mollino was inspired by the Egyptian vision of a pyramid-house for the next life, realized in a timeless aesthetic. Mollino spent more than a decade renovating and furnishing the apartment, but he never lived there and kept it a secret without ever photographing it.

CLAUDE MONET

Giverny
Giverny, France

Painter
👁

If you've ever dreamed of walking into an Impressionist painting, your best opportunity can be found about an hour west of Paris, in the village of Giverny, France. It's here that one of the world's greatest painters, Claude Monet (1840–1926), created his magical home and gardens of the same name. According to legend, Monet discovered the town in 1883 while looking out a train window, and he soon rented a large farmhouse with a vegetable garden and orchard. In 1890 he bought the property, transforming it into an inspiring oasis brimming with flowers and plants. The home is quite long—more than 130 feet (40 meters)—thanks to Monet's addition of two sizable wings. Furniture and other objects are just as they were when he lived here. The artist, who obviously loved color, chose every tone in the house, from the exterior's pink walls and green shutters, to the blue sitting room and yellow dining room. The barn next door became Monet's first studio. The gardens, created for leisure and painting, are divided into two parts. The Clos Normand, with its stunning flowerbeds, ornamental trees, and climbing roses, slopes gently from the front of the house. The fabled water garden, across the street, contains Monet's oft-painted Japanese bridge, covered with wisteria, as well as weeping willows, a thick bamboo wood, and glinting waterlilies, whose shifting, multichromatic reflections drove a revolution in the artist's work.

CHARLES MOORE

Moore/Andersson Compound
Austin, Texas, USA

Architect
☖

One of the godfathers of postmodernism, architect Charles Moore (1925–1993) came to prominence with subtle nods to vernacular design and finished his career with a colorful pastiche of historical, modern, and pop motifs. He made his final home in Austin, Texas, where he taught at the University of Texas at Austin School of Architecture. Collaborating with colleague Arthur Andersson, Moore created what would become one of the icons of the postmodern movement. Located in a neighborhood west of Downtown Austin, the residence grew and evolved from an existing bungalow to a complex of two homes and studios (including live-work space for Andersson) channeling its neighborhood's (now quickly disappearing) mix of Hispanic and German influences—an

internal courtyard, board-and-batten paneling, stucco facing, and a galvanized roof—along with exceedingly eclectic references, from John Soane and Karl Friedrich Schinkel to Irish country estates, Pompeii, and pueblo. Inside, lofty spaces reflect Moore's madcap reflexes, like decorated pilasters, turrets, naves, alcoves, a barn door, a cowhide chaise, and Rococo colors and patterns. But they're also cozy, human scale, with built-ins, books, and soft tactility. Moore filled his rooms with a sensational collection of toys, folk art, and irreverent nods to Texas and contemporary culture. Wild, brightly painted ceramics include conquistadors loading slaves into the galley of a ship with a dragon's head for a prow, statuettes of Texas heroes, deer heads, and kachina dolls.

HENRY MOORE

Henry Moore Studios and Gardens
Perry Green, Hertfordshire, England, UK

Sculptor
👁

With his fluid, semiabstract sculptures gracing museums, universities, and gardens in thirty-eight countries, Henry Moore (1898–1986) was one of the most renowned sculptors of the twentieth century. After his home in London's arts colony of Hampstead was damaged by bomb shrapnel in World War II, Moore and his wife, Irina, moved to a red-shingled farmhouse called Hoglands in bucolic Hertfordshire. "I think we may stay here for some time," Moore wrote to his friend Jane Clark in 1940. Indeed, they remained for the rest of their lives, gradually acquiring more land and outbuildings, with Irina designing a lovely garden now filled with Moore's sculptures. The outbuildings would become Moore's stunning array of unadorned studios, added as demand, and Moore's repertoire, grew.

It started with Top Studio, a skylit shed where Moore created significant works like *Three Standing Figures* and *Harlow Family Group*. Others include the Yellow Brick Studio (a carving studio where Moore made pieces in wood and stone), Plastic Studio (a lofty glazed structure allowing him to enlarge working models to monumental scale), Bourne Maquette Studio (used to create study models), Summer House (which Moore used for drawing), and Aisled Barn (a sixteenth-century building that Moore moved from a nearby farm and now houses a set of tapestries based on Moore's drawings that the artist commissioned from West Dean College of Arts and Conservation in Sussex).

GUSTAVE MOREAU

Musée National Gustave Moreau
Paris, France

Painter
👁

Nineteenth-century French Symbolist painter Gustave Moreau (1826–1898) specialized in exotic, vividly kinetic scenes focusing on the mythological and the religious. But beneath his varied work was a drive to capture something deeper. Not just human feeling, but our brief flashes of genius and magic, revealing a fleeting connection to the divine. He lived in his imposing home, edging a narrow, inclined street in Paris's ninth arrondissement, from 1852 until his death. Just two years before the painter passed away, he commissioned young architect Albert Lafon to convert the property's first floor, including its dining room, reception room, and study, into a museum showcasing Moreau's impressive collection of precious objects, and the second and third floors into vast studios that would eventually become

a museum to his own work. Reflecting Moreau's deep, eclectic fascinations, the first floor, saturated with intricately ornamented, gold-accented wallpapers and furnishings, brims with pieces that span the globe and the centuries. A glass case is filled with statuettes depicting Greek mythical figures. On top rest fifth- and sixth-century ceramic and plaster, and below lie fifteenth- and sixteenth-century treatises on architecture by Vitruvius and Sebastiano Serlio. Linked by a breathtaking spiral stair, the massive, pinkish-orange walled studios, lit by north-facing windows, are dominated by Moreau's larger-than-life paintings, stretching from floor to ceiling.

MAX MOREAU

Carmen de Max Moreau
Granada, Spain

Painter
👁

Born just after the debut of the twentieth century, Belgian painter Max Moreau (1902–1992) began his career rendering lively, semiabstracted street scenes in Paris and Brussels that blurred the line between the mundane and the exotic. But his true muse was the East, a mysterious world where he dove into the intense scenes and sensations of souks, narrow streets, and, more than anything, local men and women, their sharp features accentuated by desert light and traditional dress. After long moving between Paris and places like Morocco and Tunisia, Moreau settled with his family in Granada, Spain, a city that mingles Spanish and Middle Eastern cultures. Their modest home, in the city's hilly Moorish neighborhood of Albaicín, is one of the city's Carmen residences, noted for their high walls

and interior gardens. Moreau's contains a courtyard with a star-shaped fountain and a terraced green space filled with grape vines and fruit trees. Inside the home's spare white walls, rustic Spanish furniture and pensive Moreau portraits mix with labyrinthine Moorish textiles, lights, and furnishings, as well as art and craft collections from the painter's travels. Charming windows open to the garden, the city, and the majestic Alhambra, perched atop the al-Sabika hill. The family's second Carmen building houses Moreau's studio, just as he left it: the easel next to the window, a piano, and a collection of oriental objects.

WILLIAM MORRIS

Red House
Bexleyheath, Kent, England, UK

Textile designer, wallpaper designer, furniture designer, poet, novelist, publisher

👁

"Have nothing in your house that you do not know to be useful, or believe to be beautiful." So said artist, designer, craftsman, writer, and activist William Morris (1834–1896), who went on to become the most significant figure of the Arts and Crafts movement, a rejection of industrialization in favor of quality handmade materials and a simpler way of life. Morris commissioned architect Philip Webb to design Red House, his residence in Bexleyheath, on the outskirts of London, in 1859. The bucolic address would become what he called a "Palace of Art," his talented friends decorating the walls and ceilings on long visits. It was here that Morris cofounded the firm that would later be known as Morris & Co., producing intricately conceived wallpaper, stained glass, furniture, and textiles.

Red House recalls the neo-Gothic, with its pointed arches, picturesque masses, and steep rooflines. But its tile roof and red-brick construction, largely devoid of ornament, speak to Morris's insistence on simplicity. It is filled with the work of Morris, Webb, Morris's wife, Jane, and others: handcrafted textiles, furniture, Gothic wall murals, timber beams, brick fireplaces, and Morris & Co.'s colorful tiles and stained glass. The garden still contains fruit trees, berry bushes, and vegetable patches. Burdened by his commute into the city, he only stayed till 1865, when he moved his family into a space above his firm's workshop.

ALFRED MUNNINGS

The Munnings Art Museum
at Castle House
Dedham, Essex, England, UK

Painter
👁

One of Britain's finest Impressionist painters, Alfred Munnings (1878–1959) spent his career capturing aspects of English rural and sporting life. He is best known for his images of horses, animals which he both admired and drew from early childhood. He referred to horses as "my supporters, friends—my destiny." The subjects of his captivating depictions ranged from gypsy ponies and racehorses to the gallant steeds of war and royalty. In 1919, at age forty, he purchased Castle House, which he called "the house of my dreams." He and his second wife, Violet McBride, with their horses and dogs, lived here together until his death. The Tudor and Georgian, daffodil yellow home, situated on the edge of the idyllic Essex village of Dedham, contains the world's largest collection of the artist's work—

hundreds of paintings, drawings, and sculptures—presented in changing displays within its eight rooms. The couple's genteel furniture and personal items remain in situ. Munnings transported his first purpose-built studio from Norfolk to the home's garden. Its rustic appearance contrasts with the main house's tranquility and reveals an artist who was thoroughly absorbed in his work. Topped by a thatched roof, the white room, with its scuffed black wood floor, contains his original paint-spattered easels, smocks, paintbrushes, and paint boxes.

GEORGE NAKASHIMA

George Nakashima Woodworkers
New Hope, Pennsylvania, USA

Furniture maker, woodworker, architect
👁

Japanese American craftsman George Nakashima (1905–1990), whose lithe organic naturalism fused Japanese, Arts and Crafts, and Modernist approaches, was one of the most eminent furniture makers in US history. Born to Japanese immigrants in Spokane, Washington, Nakashima trained and worked in locations around the world. During World War II, he and his family were sent to a relocation camp until his former employer (and Frank Lloyd Wright protégé) Antonin Raymond petitioned for his release, lending Nakashima the former milk house on his farm in New Hope, Pennsylvania. The best way to understand Nakashima's work, and to be wowed by his architecture, is to head to his former studio in the hills of New Hope. The facility is still used by his daughter, Mira, who

leads a team of furniture makers on-site. The 8¾-acre (3.5-hectare) complex contains twenty-one sculptural, Rustic Modern buildings, all designed by Nakashima, scattered across slopes, lawns, and forests. Eight of the buildings are open to tours, including the luminous Conoid Studio, topped with an arched reinforced-concrete roof and fronted with expansive glazed walls, and the Arts Building, a 2.5-story structure topped by a parabolic roof formed out of plywood. Showcasing Nakashima's furniture and art, the tranquil building's angled walls are fronted with alternating timber and glazed squares, and a horizontal mosaic.

PABLO NERUDA

Casa Museo Isla Negra
Isla Negra, Chile

Poet
👁

Nobel Prize-winning Chilean writer and political figure Pablo Neruda (1904–1973) was one of the most important Latin American poets of the twentieth century. His passionate style and controversial, movie-worthy life informed a diverse body of work that included surrealist poems, love odes, historical epics, and political manifestos. One clue to Neruda's profound influence and restless lifestyle: there are three house museums dedicated to him, La Sebastiana, La Chascona, and Isla Negra. He lived at Isla Negra, his seaside home about 60 miles (97 kilometers) west of Santiago, from 1937 until his death, with extended periods away. Naming the property for a dark outcrop of rocks just offshore, he expanded it with the help of Catalan architect Germán Rodríguez Arias, inserting a stone tower atop the original structure and attaching an ocean blue wing. Blessed with clear views of the craggy coastline, and the sound of constant pounding surf, the home is a testament to Neruda's imagination and the "wild and blue" sea that he loved. Inside, varnished wood surfaces, narrow spaces, and the occasional porthole evoke the interior of a ship. Unusual possessions (Neruda called himself a *cosista*, or "thingist") cover every surface: masks, antique shoes, and smoking pipes, as well as seagoing objects like a ship's buxom figurehead, compasses, maps, ships in bottles, seashells, and whale's teeth. There's even a large rusty anchor in the garden.

RICHARD NEUTRA

Neutra VDL Research House
Los Angeles, California, USA

Architect
👁

The Neutra VDL Research House, named for Dutch philanthropist C. H. Van Der Leeuw, who provided pioneering Modernist architect Richard Neutra (1892–1970) the loan to build it, is arguably Neutra's most famous work, although there is stiff competition. Edging Los Angeles's Silver Lake Reservoir, the glass house and studio is filled with what were radical elements like interlocking and projecting planes, large glazed walls, modular dividers, and clerestories. Strikingly ahead of its time, it also showcases the engineering innovations that allowed it to open to the elements, including glass-aluminum sandwich panels, foil insulation, and other variations on the standard balloon-frame. While the street facade opens to the reservoir, the rear unfolds onto a luxuriant patio, where there is a small

garden house. A 1963 fire destroyed most of the main residence (though the garden house remained unscathed), and Neutra and his son Dion redesigned it, better accounting for the sun, including large vertical solar louvers, shimmering water roofs, and adjusted orientation. They created more complex shifts in space and form, while turning the home further inward, toward the courtyard. Visiting is a must, particularly a climb up to the top-floor porch, where you can take in the reservoir and, even better, the kaleidoscopic collection of midcentury homes perched precariously in the hills above it. These include a colony of Neutra-designed homes immediately adjacent.

MARC NEWSON
AND CHARLOTTE
STOCKDALE

Newson-Stockdale Residence
London, England, UK

Product designer, furniture designer,
interior designer, fashion designer
(Newson); fashion stylist (Stockdale)
🔒

Marc Newson (b. 1963), considered one of the most influential industrial designers of his generation, applies his amorphous, space-age aesthetic to everything from aircraft interiors and cars to furniture, kitchen appliances, cameras, watches, footwear, and luggage. The London home Newson shares with his wife, fashion stylist Charlotte Stockdale (b. 1971), and their two daughters is a former mail-sorting office in Howick Place, Westminster, London. Although it was an empty shell when they bought it, Newson and Stockdale wanted to preserve the building's volume but avoid a cold, loftlike space. So they turned to mountain chalets and Newson's subtle futurism for inspiration. The open-plan first floor now features a wall of blond river rocks from Nova Scotia, a fireplace, two Svenskt

Tenn sofas upholstered in a plant-filled Josef Frank fabric, two of Newson's Micarta chairs (machined from linen phenolic composite, a natural material sensitive to ultraviolet light), and almost no art or ornament. Other rooms take the pastoral/futuristic aesthetic in different, often strange directions—mergers of the couple's conflicting aesthetics. Curving kitchen cabinets lacquered in the same mint green as the Newsons' much-loved 1960 Aston Martin DB4; a wood-paneled, mock Victorian library; a bathroom wallpapered with thin trees and lit by a large square skylight; coral-shaped shelving; and of course Newson's formless, riveted aluminum chaise longue. "I can't disassociate work from pleasure," Newson said. "In a way, my job is my hobby."

OSCAR NIEMEYER

Casa das Canoas
Rio de Janeiro, Brazil

Architect
🔒

Oscar Niemeyer's (1907–2012) Casa das Canoas, which was designed as his family home, is widely regarded as his finest domestic work, combining the architect's free, organic style with modern materials and a masterful response to context. Located on a plateau in a forested hillside outside Rio de Janeiro, the amoeba-shaped residence intermittently wraps around and even incorporates the site's rocky outcrops. Many other Modernists created structures from glass, steel, and concrete to blur the boundary between interior and exterior space, but few so willingly abandoned straight lines to allow structure to follow its environment. The ground-floor living space incorporates a boulder that seems to slide inside the home. Limited wood-paneled walls add natural warmth and

shield the kitchen, while expansive glazed walls are framed in narrow sashes and shaded by thin slab overhangs and exterior vegetation. As a result, the living space is naturally shaded, without curtains blocking the view. On this level, one is totally exposed, while bedrooms downstairs are refuges, dug into the earth, with small windows revealing only a tiny part of the luxuriant growth outside. The elegant interior design at Casa das Canoas was a collaboration between Niemeyer and his daughter, Ana Maria, who went on to have a distinguished career in the field, designing a range of furniture items with her father as well as spaces for the presidential palace in Brasília.

ISAMU NOGUCHI

The Isamu Noguchi Garden
Museum Japan
Takamatsu City, Japan

Sculptor, furniture designer,
landscape architect, ceramicist,
architect, set designer
👁

Isamu Noguchi (1904–1988), the child of a Japanese father and American mother, lived and studied around the world, creating sculptures and landscapes that amalgamated lively modern abstraction with a sinuous, organic forms. In 1985 he helped found the Isamu Noguchi Museum, a collection of exhibition spaces and sculpture gardens in and around a former printing plant in Queens, New York, across the street from his studio. Noguchi's lesser-known studio, now the Isamu Noguchi Garden Museum, was located across the world on the mountainous Japanese island of Shikoku, in Mure, a small town that produced the crystal-textured Aji stone Noguchi often worked with. He approached the site holistically, as an "environmental sculpture." Hugging the hillside, surrounded by rough stone walls

and laced with outdoor sculpture, its traditional Japanese buildings—an Edo period workshop, former merchant's residence, and Meiji period warehouse, commune with their surroundings. Noguchi's barnlike storehouse studio feels peaceful, like time is standing still, with granite-and-timber walls, tree-trunk columns, pebbly stone floors, and high fretted windows. Large-scale works here include the black-granite *Energy Void*. Designer Issey Miyake described it perfectly: "The space embodies and responds to the . . . rules of nature and of the universe. After a while, you begin to have the sensation that you too are drifting, weightless through space."

RUDOLF NUREYEV

Nureyev Residence
Paris, France

Dancer, choreographer
🔒

With its views of the Seine and the Louvre, the opulent, densely decorated Paris apartment at 23, quai Voltaire became the main residence of Soviet-born ballet dancer and choreographer Rudolf Nureyev (1938–1993) after he defected to the West in 1961. Using a mix of neoclassical elements from Russian, French, and Italian decorative arts, interior decorator and theater designer Emilio Carcano pursued a consistently lavish color scheme throughout: deep golds, browns, and reds, permeating the heavy Genoese velvet sofas, leather-paneled walls, French Academic paintings, and other items from Nureyev's ever-growing assemblage of antiques, carpets, and art. Such opulence reflects a flamboyant performer whose appetite for everything—dance, sex, collecting—was insatiable. "Everything he had was like a set," observed artist Jamie Wyeth, who sketched hundreds of Nureyev portraits. "He never thought he had enough of anything." Carcano, who studied under Italian costume designer Lila De Nobili, extended the decadent marble floors from the library into the bathroom, where a French copper bath is filled from an elaborate brass faucet, and the walls covered with trompe l'oeil garden screens. When the apartment was completed, midway through his directorship at the Paris Opera Ballet, Nureyev was diagnosed with HIV. He died, at the age of fifty-four, from complications related to AIDS.

JUAN O'GORMAN

Juan O'Gorman House-Studio
Mexico City, Mexico

Architect, painter, muralist
👁

Best known internationally for designing Diego Rivera's functionalist Mexico City home and studio, architect and muralist Juan O'Gorman (1905–1982) is a lofty figure in Mexico, particularly thanks to his colorful, untamed mosaic murals, which have adorned important local structures like Mexico City's first airport and the library of the National Autonomous University of Mexico. Perhaps his most extra-ordinary work was his own house in Pedregal, just outside Mexico City, a meandering brick and lava stone structure filled with his pre-Hispanic-inspired murals and mosaics. That building was unfortunately demolished in 1969, but O'Gorman's other Mexico City home, near Rivera's home-studio and Frida Kahlo's La Casa Azul, still survives. Built in 1933, it is

a fascinating amalgam of tradition and modernity, incorporating the layout of the surrounding area's colonial residences, including a luxuriant interior courtyard, but filled with extra-large windows, gleaming white surfaces, Art Moderne curves, and tall, flowing spaces. O'Gorman, who sadly took his life here, incorporated his artwork, primordial stone wall mosaics, and deep red, blue, and green walls and tilework. The new owner, artist Paulina Parlange, is the perfect steward for the home. Co-owner of Colorindio, a local textile company, she works with traditional Mexican weaving communities to create vivid patterned fabrics that feel both timeless and new. Parlange has added eclectic furniture, art, and craft, blending thrillingly with O'Gorman's original palette.

GEORGIA O'KEEFFE

Georgia O'Keeffe's Home and Studio
Abiquiú, New Mexico, USA

Painter
👁

When iconic American painter Georgia O'Keeffe (1887–1986) first came upon the 5,000-square-foot (465-square-meter) Spanish colonial-era adobe compound that would become her second New Mexico home and studio, it was in a state of ruin. O'Keeffe purchased the property in Abiquiú, about an hour north of Santa Fe, in 1945 (one year before her husband, photographer Alfred Stieglitz, would die), taking three years to painstakingly restore it with her friend Maria Chabot. The sensuous adobe walls seem to grow out of the earth, and the fissured timber beams, cozy built-ins, and luminous cinematic window scenes envelop you. The sound of the wind and the stillness and enormity of the landscape all contribute to a sense of peace and simple sublime. The house inspired more

than two dozen O'Keeffe paintings, including her *Cottonwood* series. She often painted her sweeping shapes and sentient swaths of color from inside her bedroom window overlooking the Chama River Valley, but inspiration could come from anywhere, such as the patio door she painted more than a dozen times. O'Keeffe's home is furnished with midcentury design pieces like a Womb Chair, Noguchi lamps, and a Le Corbusier-style lounge. Her crowded pantry still contains bottled spices, Kerr mason jars, Le Creuset pots, and Chemex coffee carafes.

JIM OLSON

Cabin at Longbranch
Longbranch, Washington, USA

Architect
🔒

Founding partner of Seattle architecture firm Olson Kundig, Jim Olson (b. 1940) has created a serene body of work that shuttles fluidly between his love of architecture, art, and nature. When he was just eighteen, at the urging of his father, who gave him $500, he built a 14-by-14-foot (4-by-4-meter) retreat for himself slotted into the hilly woods of Longbranch, Washington. "It was probably the best opportunity I ever had," he said. Elevated on stilts, the minimal, timber-clad home is shaped by its wooded surroundings, but also by Olson's commitment to a simple, modern approach. An exposed-wood framework reveals his deep affinity for the ancient building methods of Japan. But the star of the show is the gorgeous site: the fir and cedar trees, rutted brush, and glistening lake.

The building is designed to look out, not in. Unadorned furnishings and built-in shelving create a unified palette that doesn't draw attention to itself. Olson has added several additions over the years, including new rooms, larger glass walls, a cupola-shaped skylight, and small pavilions linked by wood platforms. The extra tall windows are a crucial update. Sometimes it seems like they aren't there at all. "We're all part of the natural world. That's where it begins and ends," Olson remarked.

NATHANIEL OWINGS

Wild Bird
Big Sur, California, USA

Architect
🔒

As a founding partner of Skidmore, Owings & Merrill, Nathaniel Owings (1903–1984) is chiefly associated with the portfolio of architecturally significant skyscrapers the firm produced during the mid-twentieth century. Owings and his wife Margaret's Big Sur, California, home could not be more different in terms of scale or setting. The couple, impressed with a local A-frame house by architect Mark Mills, hired Mills to collaborate on what would become the Wild Bird house, which appears to take off from its lofty perch. Its A-frame structure suited the otherwise difficult plot on the rocky cliffs and maximized its views across the Pacific Ocean. A line of glass skylights topped its split frame, and there were walls of glass at either end of the main living space, allowing an abundance of natural light.

The concrete support beams were ornamented, becoming sculptural elements, while the use of wood echoed the region's redwood forests. The stone flooring and rugged rock hearth blended the property further into the landscape. This was a key concern for the Owingses; as a committed conservationist, Margaret in particular did much work to prevent property developers from altering the Big Sur landscape in the decades following Wild Bird's completion. The Owings' home still stands, but it has been reconfigured since passing into new ownership in 2000 and suffering a fire in 2012.

CARLOS PÁEZ VILARÓ

Museo Taller de Casapueblo
Punta Ballena, Uruguay

Muralist, painter, ceramicist, sculptor, composer, screenwriter

👁

In 1958 Uruguayan artist Carlos Páez Vilaró (1923–2014), best recognized for his boisterous, dazzlingly colorful paintings, murals, and sculptures, started work on one of the greatest mergers of architecture and sculpture in the world: his home and studio, Casapueblo. Overlooking the ocean on the southeastern Uruguayan peninsula of Punta Ballena, the cement-and-stucco "livable sculpture," as he called it, evolved (without plans) until his death, eventually resembling a gigantic whitewashed drip castle from a fairy-tale. Now a museum and hotel, Casapueblo rambles down the hillside, its warped, stylized surfaces covered in Páez Vilaró's murals (his own symbols demarcate each room, not numbers), and its dozens of corridors and terraces meandering in all directions,

as if a castle had been melted in a microwave. In the building's center is Páez Vilaró's home and studio, consisting of five rooms and three terraces, their white, cavelike walls filled with the artist's paintings, pottery, and sculpture, including works inspired by, among other things, tango lyrics, working-class struggle, folk culture, 1960s abstract painting, female forms, and the sun. The design of the museum's rooms are informed by what Páez Vilaró described as his "briefcase full of colors," as well as his "struggle against the straight line." Every day, timed to the sunset, the hotel plays a track of Páez Vilaró reciting his "Ode to the Sun."

JIMMY PAGE

The Tower House
London, England, UK

Guitarist, songwriter, record producer
🔒

Rock star Jimmy Page (b. 1944) owns an extraordinary Grade I-listed building in London's Holland Park that was designed by architect William Burges between 1875 and 1881. Built in the French Gothic style, the house is recognizable due to its cylindrical tower and conical roof. The main rooms have the themes of time, love, and literature, with embellishments and adornments wherever one looks: carvings, frescoes, stained-glass windows. The chimney figures are dominant in each room; the library's represents the Principles of Speech in Caen stone. Much of the house's contents were sold off in 1933, but English Heritage inspectors described its interiors as having "high heritage value" in 2014. Burges entertained in the drawing room, where the theme is love. A medieval cupid is painted on the ceiling above an astrological-themed table. Other remarkable spaces include the Butterfly Room, where a ceiling of butterflies and frieze of wildflowers contrast with embellished gold-and-red decor. Page bought the house from actor Richard Harris in 1972; at the tender age of twenty-eight, the Led Zeppelin guitarist was comfortable taking on the burden—and privilege—of its listed status, which provides strict regulations aimed at preserving a building's historic structure and character. He is so sensitive to protecting the interiors that he only ever plays acoustic guitar at home, has no television, and does not hold parties here.

VERNER PANTON

Binningen House
Binningen, Switzerland

Product designer, furniture designer,
lighting designer
⌂

Born in Gamtofte, Denmark, Verner Panton (1926–1998) studied architecture at the Royal Danish Academy of Fine Arts, then worked for fellow design icon Arne Jacobsen before setting up his own practice in 1955. Like many postwar designers, Panton was preoccupied with new materials and their potential for mass production, a quest that ultimately led him to create the piece of furniture for which he is most famous: the gravity-defying Panton chair—the first successfully molded out of a single piece of plastic. But it was as an experimental architect that Panton came into his own. He broke with convention, designing rooms as landscapes that were an assault on the senses, thanks to his use of intense colors, op art patterns, organic shapes, and unusual textures. The look was given free rein in his home in Binningen, on the outskirts of Basel, where he and his family lived from 1972 to 1987. During that time, he transformed the common areas into a showroom for his work. Hedonistic highlights include the entrance hall, its walls webbed with glowing, concentric-ringed lamps; a rainbow-colored upholstered living sculpture for climbing and lounging; and a light installation made of thousands of individually cut, translucent shell pieces that created a stalactite-like lunar landscape on the dining-room ceiling. The ceiling distracts from additional noteworthy elements, like multihued three-dimensional tile walls and an ivory shag carpet embedded with colorful circles.

ALEXANDROS PAPADIAMANTIS

Papadiamantis House
Skiathos, Greece

Novelist, short-story writer,
poet, translator
👁

Born to a Greek Orthodox priest on the idyllic Aegean island of Skiathos, Alexandros Papadiamantis (1851–1911) was known as the "Saint of Greek Letters," his work delving into universal moral and philosophical quandaries, and the intractable challenges of Greek society. Even as a successful and prolific author of short stories and novels, he lived a pious, ascetic, solitary life, always staying in rooming houses when in Athens. He returned for good to Skiathos (the setting for his most famous novel, *The Murderess*) in 1908, less than three years before he was to die of pneumonia. The humble, whitewashed two-story home where he spent his last years had been built by his father in 1860. Close to the island's port, on a small side road stemming from what is now called Papadiamantis Street,

the residence reflects a family, and an island culture, rooted in simplicity and tradition. Its three rooms are spare but beautiful, with tactile dark wood floors, furnishings, and ceilings, dominated by the color most prevalent in Greek architecture: white. In Papadiamantis's "study," a cupboard and mantel reveal some of the author's supposed possessions—clocks, teacups, lamps, and books—while a single bed hugs the wall, as if this were a monk's cell. Other spaces, like the living room, exhibit more color, texture, art, and collectibles, but all maintain a spirit of gracious austerity and poverty.

CORNELIA PARKER

Parker Residence
London, England, UK

Sculptor, installation artist

Artist Cornelia Parker (b. 1956) is renowned for her sculptures and installations, including her performance piece *The Maybe* (1995), in which actress Tilda Swinton slept inside a glass box, eight hours a day, for seven days. Parker moved to London's Shoreditch in 1994, where she stayed for twenty years, long enough to see the area mutate from a deprived inner-city neighborhood to a bubbling center of creativity, to a magnet for cash-rich property developers. The last fifteen of those years were spent in this residence, a Victorian print warehouse that became her studio and family home. The front of the property was built in the late nineteenth century and retains the appearance of a warhouse. Inside, the ceilings are enormously high. The main room is the family's hub—its open-plan setting means conversation continues while her artist husband Jeff McMillan cooks. Parker's work is often unsettling, which manifests itself in corners of the home. She owns an original William Burroughs drawing, with the words "No Morphine MD," as well as a Jimmy Lee Sudduth portrait, drawn with mud with his fingers. A statue Parker made of Perdita from *101 Dalmatians*, her head removed by the same guillotine used to execute Marie Antoinette, sits on the next shelf. The family left the residence in the early 2010s to move to northwest London.

LUCIANO
PAVAROTTI

Casa Museo Luciano Pavarotti
Modena, Italy

Singer
👁

Barrel-chested Italian tenor Luciano Pavarotti (1935–2007) was one of the few opera stars to become a household name far outside the musical establishment. He starred in the first *Live From the Met* telecast in 1977, starred in his own feature film, *Yes, Giorgio*, in 1982, and performed with Bono, Queen, Sting, the Spice Girls, and of course Jose Carreras and Plácido Domingo, the other two "Three Tenors." More than ten million records of their original concert were sold. For the last three years of his life, the maestro lived with his family in a newly built rustic pink stone house outside his hometown, Modena. Its spaces merge bright yellow and ivory surfaces with traditional decor, like soft-hued Italian tiles and untreated wood floors and beams. Surprisingly intimate elements include

Pavarotti's early-model cell phone, still sitting on his desk; small, framed photos of family and friends by the bed; a collection of Panama hats; and plenty of examples of his own paintings, filled with bright primary colors. Fitting for a star of this magnitude, the home's skylight-topped great room showcases Pavarotti's Grammys, Emmys, gold records, and honorary degrees. Other rooms reveal flamboyant robes, capes, opera costumes, and tuxedos; photos with legends like James Brown and Pope John Paul II, and letters from fans and celebs like Princess Di and Frank Sinatra.

JOHN PAWSON

Pawson House
London, England, UK

Architect, product designer,
set designer
⌂

John Pawson (b. 1949) is synonymous with contemporary minimalism, and inside his unassuming Victorian house in the Notting Hill neighborhood of London, where the architect lives with his wife, interior designer Catherine, the couple has masterfully reduced architecture to its pure essence. Having completely stripped out the original floor plan, they replaced it with an unornamented white interior emphasizing long, straight lines, supplemented with hidden storage. This approach is reminiscent of one of Pawson's earliest commissions, an interior for the writer Bruce Chatwin, who requested a space "as simple and spare as a ship's cabin." But, as Pawson has often explained, minimal living doesn't have to equal monastic living. While regulations prohibited altering the home's facade, the rear

elevation is sliced open with glazed apertures. At the top of the house, a glass slot allows daylight to spill down a narrow, triple-height concrete stairwell. Seating comes in the form of simple wooden furniture by Danish designer Hans Wegner and freely arrangeable white cushions placed on stone benches. The upstairs living room's simple, recessed fireplace is embedded into the plain white wall. A bench runs the entire length of one wall, an element that mirrors the kitchen counter downstairs, which seamlessly extends into the walled garden. Tables, desks, and seats are blond and brown, contrasting with the white palette around them. "I didn't want white anywhere you'd touch," Pawson said.

JOZEF PEETERS

Jozef Peeters Studio and Apartment
Antwerp, Belgium

Painter, designer, engraver,
graphic artist
🔒

In early twentieth-century Belgium, Jozef Peeters (1895–1960) pioneered his own experimental form of fractured abstraction called "Pure Plasticism," which shared affinities with the Netherlands' Neo-Plasticism—a.k.a. De Stijl. Peeters designed posters, made linotypes, and established himself as an energetic arts organizer, interacting with many of the twentieth-century's creative innovators, such as Piet Mondrian, Theo van Doesburg, Wassily Kandinsky, and László Moholy-Nagy. In 1927 he turned his attention to his Antwerp apartment, creating a space that embodied many of the principles he once applied to painting, such as "the animation of the surface." Living in his four-room apartment with his wife and two children, he designed art, furniture, and ceiling lamps, and gave each room its own geometric color scheme. Colored planes move across walls and ceilings in a completely individual manner, yet they establish a dynamic whole. To achieve that, "Symmetry has to be avoided and asymmetry applied in a way that does not appear chaotic," Peeters explained. When his wife became terminally ill in 1937, Peeters assumed her primary care, using his design skills to create a wheelchair for her. In order to make money, he painted traditional landscapes under the pseudonym H. Angtze. In 2009 Peeters's daughter bequeathed his apartment, along with its artworks, furniture, and objects, to the Antwerp City Council.

PABLO PICASSO

La Californie
Cannes, France

Painter, sculptor, ceramicist,
printmaker, set designer, costume
designer, poet, playwright
🔒

In 1955 Pablo Picasso (1881–1973) and his second wife, Jacqueline Roque, moved to the villa La Californie, an eclectic 1920 home in Le Suquet, in the hills above Cannes, France. They stayed until 1961, when construction of a nearby house obstructed their ocean views. The ground-floor salon and dining room became a sprawling studio filled with the artist's sculptures, ceramics, and paintings, some completed and some half-finished, sitting among his vast collection of ornaments. It was here that Picasso worked, usually from early afternoon until late evening, in what would be one of his most fruitful creative periods. His painting *Portrait de femme à la robe verte* was propped up on a bust and framed by lamps, papers, and instruments. A Thonet rocking chair, which

appeared in several of his works, seemed to scrutinize busts, brushes, boxes, and more oil works set on easels and tables, and affixed to walls. The messy scene gives the impression of a life lived for work, in which any object could potentially be transformed by the artist's prolific hand. One of his many visitors, the artist Brassaï, noted, "Only Picasso's immense dislike for anything in 'good taste,' his fondness for the comical, the misshapen, the baroque—the villa is staggering under the weight of stucco and round motifs—his indifferent attitude towards the places he lives, and his penchant for trusting in Providence can explain his choice."

JOŽE PLEČNIK

Plečnik House
Ljubljana, Slovenia

Architect
👁

One of Eastern Europe's most influential Modern architects, Slovenian designer Jože Plečnik (1872–1957) created work that can be discovered all over Europe. Plečnik, who began as an apprentice in his father's cabinetmaking workshop, went on to study and work with famed Viennese architect Otto Wagner. Affiliated with the Viennese Secession, Plečnik created functional, organically decorated structures in Vienna, Prague, and his home city, Ljubljana. His residence in Ljubljana's Trnovo neighborhood, where he worked from 1921 until his death, is a complex that includes a traditional house that he purchased in 1915, a cylindrical tower addition that he created in 1925, a neighboring home that he bought in 1928, and a vegetable garden. He often used his home, which he called his "trial greenhouse," to perform architectural experiments, especially with natural materials like wood, brick, and stone. His circular ground-floor studio and second-floor bedroom, both located in the tower, feel simple and rustic, filled with original artifacts, like Plečnik's original knotty-timber furniture, drawing tools, clothing, and personal mementos, as well as a stellar collection of crafts and artworks. The home also contains a large archive of sketches, plans, photographs, and models. The property is managed by the Museum and Galleries of Ljubljana, which has put together a permanent exhibition sharing Plečnik's story and examples of his work, both built and unbuilt.

LODOVICO POGLIAGHI

Casa Museo Lodovico Pogliaghi
Varese, Italy

Painter, sculptor, decorator,
set designer

👁

Nineteenth- and twentieth-century sculptor, painter, decorator, and set designer Lodovico Pogliaghi (1857–1950) was an eclectic and expressive artist and a ravenous collector. This rare combination was a recipe for what would become one of the most fascinating and underappreciated homes in Italy. Pogliaghi purchased its plot in Varese while working nearby on the restoration of the Sacro Monte, a spectacular seventeenth-century religious complex on Mount Velate. He planned a place of relaxation, creation, and display, and he kept at it until his death. The residence combines several regional and historical architectural styles and contains more than 1,500 artworks and close to six hundred archaeological objects. During his career Pogliaghi famously designed the intricate central door of the Milan Cathedral, as well as tombs, tabernacles, and altars. His facility with such work is showcased throughout the home, from colorful mosaics to themed rooms brightened by murals and frescoes. The most lavish is the Golden Gallery, its golden stucco and mirror ceiling a 1:4 replica of a ceiling he created for the shah of Persia. The cavernous space of Pogliaghi's atelier contains a plaster cast of the Milan Cathedral doors and candelabrum-grasping angels, evoking his altar in Pisa's cathedral. The Exedra, a replica of the Pantheon in Rome, displays countless antiquities, radiating from its center, including a second-century marble statue of Dionysus-Apollo, part of an Egyptian sphinx, and Etruscan tiles.

BEATRIX POTTER

Hill Top
Hawkshead, Cumbria, England, UK

Children's book writer, illustrator
👁

The creator of beloved children's characters like Peter Rabbit, Jemima Puddle-Duck, and Mrs. Tiggy-Winkle, Beatrix Potter (1866–1943) developed her love of animals and playful art-making as a child, on long family vacations in the rippling meadows of Scotland and the English Lake District. "It is all the same, drawing, painting, modeling, the irresistible urge to copy any beautiful object which strikes the eye," she wrote. Aside from her family's lovely retreats, Potter grew up in a strict Victorian household in London, which she called her "unloved birthplace." In 1905, with royalties from early books, Potter bought Hill Top, a two-story stucco farmhouse in Cumbria, in her adored Lake District. She saw the cottage as a life-size dollhouse, a place all to herself to write and escape from her life at Castle Cottage, the home across the road that she and husband, William Heelis, later purchased in 1913. Like Potter, Hill Top is practical and unpretentious, yet imaginative and sophisticated. It remains, in accordance with her will, "as if she had just gone out to the post." English and Chinese porcelains perch on a wall cupboard. The teapot was Ribby's in *The Tale of the Pie and the Patty-Pan*. Mr. Jeremy Fisher, cast in iron, stands on a table, near the dresser from *The Tale of Samuel Whiskers* and the grandfather clock from *The Tailor of Gloucester*.

ELVIS PRESLEY

Graceland
Memphis, Tennessee, USA

Singer, actor
👁

The King of Rock 'n' Roll, Elvis Presley (1935–1977) was without a doubt one of the most significant cultural figures of the twentieth century. With eighteen number one hits, and exhilarating appearances in concerts, movies, and television, he became one of the first true modern stars. His Memphis home, Graceland, is the most popular house museum in the United States after the White House. Presley bought the two-story Colonial Revival mansion and its grounds in 1957, when he was twenty-two and just becoming a superstar. The home contains twenty-three rooms, and a visit includes the lavish living and dining rooms; the music room, with its baby grand piano and stained-glass peacock doorway; and the Jungle Room, with its Polynesian decoration, indoor waterfall, and green shag carpet. Other spaces include the Trophy Building, with its endless gold records and shimmering jumpsuits; the basement Billiards Room, lined with pleated fabric in an elaborate, colorful print; and the brilliant yellow TV Room, with its mirrored ceiling. Elvis and his family are laid to rest in the meditation garden. Visitors can more or less continue forever, with the Elvis: The Entertainer Career Museum, the Presley Motors Automobile Museum, the Elvis Discovery Exhibits, Elvis's Airplanes, and of course innumerable shopping and dining opportunities.

JEAN PROUVÉ

Maison Jean Prouvé
Nancy, France

Industrial designer, furniture designer,
architect, engineer
👁

French designer, architect, and engineer Jean Prouvé (1901–1984) was a revolutionary in the notoriously backward construction world. His atelier-focused approach explicitly incorporated building, engineering, and fabrication, and he became a pioneer of prefabrication, transferring technologies from industry and mass production to the realm of architecture. His sleek, industrial-inspired design objects, including chairs, tables, and lamps, still feel groundbreaking today. Situated in thick foliage on a steep hilltop overlooking Nancy, his 1954 home is a triumph of Prouvé's approach, completed shortly after one of his greatest failures: the closing of his own factory, in nearby Maxéville, for mass-produced housing. Over the course of a single summer, Prouvé and his family created the home with the help of friends, using lightweight, prefabricated materials (some inset with portholes for increased lightness and visibility) like metal facade panels, a single exposed steel roof beam (serving as a key design element), and cross-laminated timber panels. The long, narrow home—consisting of a lofty, open-plan living room with smaller rooms on both sides, including service spaces (kitchen, bathroom) and private areas (bedrooms)—was placed on a thin reinforced-concrete platform to fit on a site that had been considered unbuildable. The base was filled with ducts to provide radiant heating. Prouvé's office, a lightweight 8 x 8-foot (2 x 2-meter) pavilion saved from the Maxéville plant, was reassembled below the house in 1957.

GIACOMO PUCCINI

Villa Museo Puccini
Torre del Lago, Italy

Composer
👁

Generally considered the greatest Italian composer after Giuseppe Verdi, Giacomo Puccini (1858–1924) crafted soaring verismo operas like *La Bohème*, *Tosca*, and *Madama Butterfly*. Most of his masterpieces were composed in the same place: his Mediterranean villa on the shores of Lake Massaciuccoli, in the tiny Tuscan town of Torre del Lago. Puccini, who grew up in nearby Lucca, moved here in 1891, and began constructing the villa—a transformation of the guard tower for which the town is named—in 1899. The austere two-story structure, now painted in its original shades of orange and yellow, truly was his retreat: a castle on the lake. You can feel the maestro's aura inside, thanks particularly to the informally arranged artifacts. In his study, bedecked with classical motifs, are Puccini's richly

ornamented Förster piano, a thicket of portraits from the course of his life, and even his death mask. In the bedroom he shared with his wife, Elvira, are furnishings inspired by the surrounding countryside, including a curving brass bed, bird-adorned dressers, flower-shaped lamps, and yellow-speckled wallpaper. Other spaces contain portraits of friends, letters, awards, and even, in his hunting room, rifles, hunting trophies, and boots. The former living room has been trans-formed into a chapel, graced with family shields. Perhaps most striking of all are the home's lush grounds, edging the lake and evoking the peace that drew Puccini here in the first place.

ALEXANDER PUSHKIN

Pushkin Memorial Apartment
St. Petersburg, Russia

Poet, playwright, novelist,
short-story writer
👁

Generally considered the greatest of all Russian poets and the founder of modern Russian literature, Alexander Pushkin (1799–1837), in hindsight, made a poor choice when it came to marriage. His exceptionally beautiful spouse, Natalya, who he married in 1831, loved attention, eventually setting the stage for a duel between Pushkin and one of her would-be suitors. Needless to say, the great poet lost, dying on February 10, 1837, aged thirty-seven. Pushkin and his family inhabited the apartment where he died in St. Petersburg, now the Pushkin Memorial Apartment, for the last four months of his life. Located on the Moika River, near Palace Square, the yellow neoclassical building—former home of the Volkonsky princes—is typical of the severe yet ornate structures that dominate this elaborate eighteenth-century city. Showcasing Pushkin's wealth, which stemmed from his noble upbringing and profound success, his ground-floor apartment contains eleven lavish, pale-hued rooms, enhanced by elegant classical-style wood moldings and furniture. Pushkin's study is dominated by his embossed leather desk, topped by letters and manuscripts, and his red leather armchair. Dark wood shelves are densely filled with the poet's exceptional collection of books. The apartment also contains a lock of the poet's hair, a death mask, Natalya's jewelry, portraits of their children, and the sofa on which Pushkin died.

SERGEI RACHMANINOV

Ivanovka
Ivanovka Village, Russia

Composer, pianist, conductor
👁

The dreamlike, passionate music of composer, conductor, and virtuoso pianist Sergei Rachmaninov (1873–1943) echoes the longing, magic, and turbulence of the late Romantic age. But it particularly resonates at his beloved country estate, Ivanovka, the former family home of his aristocratic relatives, the Satins. Edged by a tiny village, birch forests, wheat fields, and softly undulating land, it's about 300 miles (483 kilometers) from Moscow, a world away from the tumult of prerevolutionary Russia. Rachmaninov, who called Ivanovka his favorite place, composed his best work here, where he could be at one with nature, stillness, and the pastoral spirit of his country. He and his family first came to Ivanovka in 1890 and continued to return until they escaped Russia during the revolution in 1917,

then living in France, Switzerland, and the United States (Rachmaninov died in Beverly Hills, of all places). The estate, which was rebuilt in the 1970s after being destroyed (like most aristocratic residences) in the revolution, is dominated by its beautiful, wood-clad manor house, which contains many of the Satins' and Rachmaninovs' possessions, which were hauled away to safety before the revolution. This includes ornate furniture, candelabras, vases, clocks, and pianos. But the musician did most of his work in an adjacent humbler cottage, where his family lived before inheriting the entire property. It is once again draped in patterned wallpaper and filled with their simple, locally built mid-nineteenth-century furniture like tables, dressers, beds, and wardrobes.

DIETER RAMS

Rams Residence
Kronberg, Germany

Industrial designer, furniture designer,
product designer
🔒

"The composition of these rooms represents the basic intention behind my design: simplicity, essentiality, and openness." So Dieter Rams (b. 1932), chief designer at Braun between 1961 and 1995, once described the arrangement of the *Doppelbungalow* he has shared with his wife since 1971 in Kronberg, near Frankfurt. In many ways, the L-shaped home—which brackets a pool and multilevel Japanese garden, with Rams's studio facing the lower level—is a time capsule, its elements largely installed before he retired from Braun in the mid-1990s. The open-plan living room, with its white walls and white ceramic-tile floor, shares the same "less, but better" credo that made his industrial design so distinctive. Rams had a hand in designing almost all of its furniture,

electrical goods, shelving, and even doorknobs, proof of his intention to not only create products he himself would use, but also improve their designs based upon experiencing them. Comfort comes from the recliners of his 620 Chair Program, designed for Vitsœ in 1962. These are arranged around a Braun TV3 dating from 1986. Hanging on a wall is Rams's white Vitsœ 606 Universal Shelving System, a flexible and sustainable modular line launched in 1960 and still in production today. Color comes from the personal effects and books the shelves hold, and from a collection of indoor plants that bridge the interior with the garden, visible outside.

RAPHAEL

Casa Raffaello Urbino
Urbino, Italy

Painter, architect
👁

Considered with Michelangelo and Leonardo da Vinci to be among the greatest masters of the Italian Renaissance, Raphael (1483–1520), a.k.a. Raffaello Sanzio di Urbino, in his short life created a body of work that exemplified that period's ideals of beauty, harmony, and human grandeur, with a serene, rich clarity that became his hallmark. As his full name suggests, the artist—who excelled in not just painting but also sculpture, printmaking, and architecture—was born and raised in Urbino, a walled city about 30 miles (50 kilometers) south of San Marino. Raphael's grandfather, merchant Sante di Peruzzolo, bought the pale, sunbaked brick townhouse in 1463, opening a workshop where Raphael's father, Giovanni Santi, and eventually the young Raphael himself, would train and work.

Renovated in 1635, the three-story home was in 1873 converted into a museum. Its rooms, considered lavish at the time, are airy and simple, with whitewashed walls, stone tile floors, and ceilings of timber beams or arched brick vaults. Its luminous "Sala Grande" boasts a timber-coffered ceiling carved with geometric motifs, and is graced with heavy wood furniture, an imposing hearth, and tall Raphael masterpieces. His narrow bedroom is sparsely decorated, save for a small fresco of Madonna and Child created by the artist. The family's wealth and Raphael's esteem are made clearer on the top floor, where rooms showcase lavish family porcelains, portraits, and intricate gifts for the master.

KARIM RASHID

Rashid Residence
New York, New York, USA

Industrial designer, furniture designer,
lighting designer, product designer,
graphic designer, fashion designer,
interior designer

Born in Cairo, raised in Canada, and based in New York, prolific industrial designer Karim Rashid (b. 1960) is noted for his sensual but minimal style. His luminous work spans luxury and democratic goods, furniture, lighting, surface design, brand identity, and packaging for companies like Samsung, Christofle, Veuve Clicquot, Umbra, Alessi, and Issey Miyake. Rashid has also entered the realm of interiors and architecture, with designs for the Università metro station in Naples, Philadelphia's Morimoto restaurant, the Semiramis hotel in Athens, Greece, and the Hotel nhow Berlin. In his four-bedroom townhouse in Hell's Kitchen in Manhattan, Rashid created an all-white, gallery-like backdrop, to which he added a shimmering lime kitchen backsplash and a fuchsia accent wall to give the open space more dimension. At the center of the sitting area, which is 20 feet (6 meters) wide and 13 feet (4 meters) tall, is a colorful, swirling carpet that pulls all of Rashid's joyful product and furniture designs together. These include a chromatic vortex Sit Kit sofa from Luca Boffi, an orange Bounce chair from Gufram, a snowy Ottawa sideboard from BoConcept, and a streamlined pink Tide cabinet from Horm. "Color is life and for me, color is a way of dealing with and touching our emotions, our psyche, and our spiritual being," Rashid once said. The designer, who recently listed the duplex for sale, regularly swaps products, colors, and configurations, so this ensemble didn't last long.

OSCAR DE LA RENTA

Oscar de la Renta Country House
Kent, Connecticut, USA

Fashion designer
🔒

A tidal wave of wonderment hit the international interior design world when Annette and Oscar de la Renta (1932–2014) married in 1989, a second marriage for both. Annette, who is one of New York's most respected philanthropists, and her internationally known fashion designer husband were already celebrated tastemakers—the possibilities for extraordinary residential collaborations seemed endless. There was the apartment in the city, the place in the Dominican Republic, and then the matter of what to do about their separate country houses. Although Annette told *Vogue* she first wanted to tear it down, they decided that their country seat would be the Connecticut house the fashion designer had acquired in 1971 and decorated with deep-hued Orientalist touches. These were quickly exchanged (with a few notable exceptions) for a lighter, more British look with William Kent tables, Elizabethan portraits, a Georgian-style bed, and country-house chintzes. "Out went the boulle cabinets and the seraglio scenes," commented fashion journalist Hamish Bowles. Traditional architect Ernesto Buch designed a sumptuous, layered new space that functions as a living room, library, and bedroom, with a view of de la Renta's beloved garden. Vivien Greenock helped with the decoration. "I thought if I wasn't giving Annette a new house," de la Renta told *Vogue* in 2008, "I should give her a new bedroom."

ILYA REPIN

Penaty
St. Petersburg, Russia

Painter
👁

A giant of nineteenth-century painting, Ilya Repin (1844–1930) was instrumental in bringing Russian art—and Russian culture in general—into the mainstream of European culture. His starkly realist works, noted for their psychological depth and dramatic narrative, revealed the deepening tensions within his country's stagnant social order. Repin lived in his estate, Penaty (named for the Roman gods of the household, Penates), for the last thirty years of his life. Located in Repino, a seaside suburb of St. Petersburg that was posthumously named for the artist, the wondrous, unusual home reflects an inspired man who was constantly searching for techniques and content. Repin inhabited the sprawling wooden building with his wife, Natalia Nordman, and welcomed artists and thinkers like Maxim Gorky

and Isaak Brodsky. Reflecting the folk traditions of both Russia and neighboring Finland, the residence is a hodgepodge of forms, spaces, and materials—a rich palette to which the artist kept adding. It's overwhelming to take in the incongruent mix of knotty woods, silk curtains, and furnishings encompassing Scandinavian tables, Asian urns, and Classicist European chairs. Surfaces are littered with hundreds of artworks, including paintings by Repin himself, and paintings, drawings, and sketches by other illustrious Russian artists, including Repin's son Yuri. Penaty's staggered roofs, originally timber, have been converted into metal and glass, allowing natural light to flood the central spaces.

ZANDRA RHODES

Zandra Rhodes Residence
London, England, UK

Fashion designer
🔒

Color has always played a central role in the career of Zandra Rhodes (b. 1940), throughout her more than fifty years as a self-described "notorious figurehead of the UK fashion industry." The designer's trademark pink hair and outrageous clothes are as colorful as her home, the so-called Rainbow Penthouse, which she bought in 1995 on Bermondsey Street, then a down-at-the-heels corner of southeast London. The area has changed dramatically since, with bars, restaurants, markets, and art galleries combining to create a vibrant neighborhood. Rhodes played an important part in this resurgence, as her apartment sits on top of the Fashion and Textile Museum, which she founded in 2003 to celebrate great British garment design. Mexican architect Ricardo Legorreta was given the task of

rejuvenating the warehouse building, incorporating a split-level, two-bedroom home for Rhodes. The penthouse apartment houses her eye-catching art collection, including canvases by Duggie Fields and Andrew Stahl, a crystal chandelier and Gandhi mirror made by Andrew Logan, and four Roman columns from the film set of *The Rocky Horror Picture Show*. Pieces of rock are strewn around the apartment, with pebbles from Sardinia, crystals from the Atlas Mountains, and even a piece of the Berlin Wall. Light fills the apartment via the outside terrace upstairs, accentuating the vivid citrus-colored walls and bright pink Amtico vinyl flooring. The lower level houses the bedrooms, galley kitchen, and textile print room.

JOHN RICHARDSON

Richardson Residence
New York, New York, USA

Art historian, curator, biographer,
journalist, industrial designer
⚓

Through the span of an illustrious life, British art historian John Richardson (1924–2019) worked as an industrial designer, critic, curator, biographer (including a four-volume biography of Pablo Picasso), auctioneer, gallery director, and journalist. He was awarded both British knighthood and membership to the French Ordre des Arts et des Lettres. Born into nobility and accustomed to schmoozing with the likes of Picasso, Georges Braque, Fernand Léger, Andy Warhol, and the directors of major museums, he was famed for curating his own "Bohemian Aristocratic" residences in France, England, and the United States. His last was inside a loft on lower Fifth Avenue, near New York's Union Square, which provided an almost empty palette with which he could fill his epic collections, showcasing his

wealth and sophistication. Around the edges is a layer of fluted Greek columns, rusticated wainscot, neoclassical bookshelves (not surprisingly filled with thousands of books), and paintings from the likes of Warhol, Picasso, and Lucian Freud. Within this exceptional shell are endless treasures: marble busts, gilded mirrors, Chinese porcelains, antique furnishings (including his eighteenth-century desk), and pictures of Richardson with his many famous friends. The great room, its edges revealing the exposed piping of a typical Flatiron loft, is anchored by a pinkish, mystical mountain landscape by Lucien Lévy-Dhurmer. That work is surrounded by a colorful mélange of ancient and modern art, both noble and unrestrained.

GERRIT RIETVELD

Rietveld Schröderhuis
Utrecht, The Netherlands

Architect, furniture designer
👁

The Rietveld Schröderhuis in Utrecht, the Netherlands, is the architectural embodiment of De Stijl, an early twentieth-century Dutch art movement centered on simple, abstract visual elements, like geometric forms and primary colors. The undertaking was led by artists like Piet Mondrian, Theo van Doesburg, and Gerrit Rietveld (1888–1964), a designer who had previously been known for pared-down furniture, such as his Red and Blue Chair. In 1924 Rietveld was asked by a widowed mother of three, Truus Schröder-Schräder, to design a residence that complemented her unconventionality. They were a perfect match and would eventually become lovers; Rietveld lived with the family after his wife died in 1957. Together they created a cube-shaped, gray-and-white home focusing on clean horizontal and vertical planes, and the targeted use of primary colors. Walking inside is like entering a De Stijl painting. Shifting lines and squares of red, yellow, and blue accentuate every surface, along every axis, including floors, walls, windows, cabinets, and furniture. Rietveld devised ingenious solutions to augment the small home's functionality: sliding and pivoting walls can open spaces or create entirely new rooms. A table in his study folds away and disappears. A top-floor corner window swings open, with no frame at its corner, making it feel like you're outdoors. Lighting and furniture—including a tubular chandelier and Rietveld's slat-constructed Red and Blue and Berlin Chairs—serve as both utilities and art.

NIKOLAI RIMSKY-KORSAKOV

N. Rimsky-Korsakov Museum-Apartment
St. Petersburg, Russia,

Composer
👁

The youngest and most beloved of "the Five" (a.k.a. the "Mighty Handful") composers who strove to establish a Russian national music style in the late nineteenth century, Nikolai Rimsky-Korsakov (1844–1908) is best known for lyrical, unyielding pieces like *The Flight of the Bumblebee* and *Scheherazade*. The prolific composer was born in the small town of Tikhvin but went to naval college in St. Petersburg, far to the west, remaining there for the rest of his life. Working also as a teacher and inspector of military orchestras, he composed more than half of his major works in his apartment on Zagorodny Prospekt. Remaining for his last fifteen years, he hosted legendary musical soirées, attracting famed painters, singers, and musicians like Sergei Rachmaninov and Igor

Stravinsky, who often played Rimsky-Korsakov's black Becker grand piano, still located in the living room. The renovated apartment, its belongings preserved by Rimsky-Korsakov's heirs, also includes his study, dining room, and entry hall, as well as adjacent concert and exhibition spaces. Rooms capture the spirit of this lover of both folk and cosmopolitan culture, who was a creative force in a time of extravagance. His tiered wood desk is where he would write music without the aid of a piano. Simultaneously simple and excessive, it is accompanied by diminutive portraits, rich-grained cabinetry, a deep burgundy armchair, and the intricately patterned textiles that typified late nineteenth-century Russia.

NORMAN ROCKWELL

Norman Rockwell Studio
Stockbridge, Massachusetts, USA

Painter, illustrator
👁

During his stellar career, American illustrator and painter Norman Rockwell (1894–1978) worked in about twenty studios, each arranged in his typically clean, fastidious manner. But he called his studio in Stockbridge, a tiny village in the Berkshire Hills of Massachusetts, where he spent the last twenty-one years of his life, his "best studio yet." The airy, understated space features ample evidence of Rockwell's diligent, relatively conventional approach. It was split in two and moved to the grounds of Stockbridge's Norman Rockwell Museum (which contains the most significant collection of the artist's work in the world) in 1986. Rockwell refurbished the space, a ramshackle former nineteenth-century carriage barn behind his house, with the help of a local cabinetmaker. Containing a loft for extra supplies, the ivory-walled work space admits daylight through exceptionally big windows. You can peruse Rockwell's original materials, including paints, brushes, easels, and a large printing press; and his personal items, like a radio (he listened to opera while working), books (from his extensive library), fan mail, the chair he used when painting, and the couch where he took catnaps. Not surprisingly, the space is full of art, by painters who inspired him, members of his family, and, of course, himself, including a re-creation of his iconic *Golden Rule*, as if it were in progress.

OTTO
ROTHMAYER

Villa Rothmayer
Prague, Czech Republic

Architect
👁

A Czech architect of the twentieth century, Otto Rothmayer (1892–1966) created dozens of exhibitions and monuments and helped oversee the reconstruction of Prague Castle (collaborating with his mentor, noted Slovenian architect Jože Plečnik). His own villa, built in 1929, is an early monument of classicist Modernism, an understated design that ushers the traditional Mediterranean villa into a new age. The austere ivory rectangle is adjoined by a veranda and cylindrical stair. Interiors are simple and lovely: Rothmayer, born into a family of carpenters, designed most of the woodshoplike home's joinery, timber windows, built-in cabinets, shelves, benches, tables, and chairs. The veranda is connected visually with the yard, a verdant space filled with quirky objects, like stone and ceramic urns, making it feel like a secret garden. Villa Rothmayer hosts a permanent exhibition called *The Story of a House and a Family*, designed to evoke a place full of life, work, and art. Rothmayer often collaborated with his wife, Božena Rothmayerová, an acclaimed textile artist and promoter of the modern lifestyle. Its neighborhood, Střešovice, is a treasure trove of early Modernist architecture, including Villa Müller by Adolf Loos, which, like the Villa Rothmayer, is owned and run by the City of Prague Museum. More early Modern homes nearby include the Traub Villa, Hübschmann Villa, Špála Villa, and Jaroslav Vondrák Villa.

JEAN-JACQUES ROUSSEAU

Les Charmettes
Chambéry, France

Philosopher, writer, composer
◉

Helping reconceive the social contract in favor of the "collective will," writer, philosopher, and composer Jean-Jacques Rousseau (1712–1778) was one of the figures who heaved us into the modern world, inspiring political cataclysms like the French Revolution, transforming taste in the arts, and encouraging the pure expression of emotion that led to the Romantic movement. Rousseau's primary residence, now the Jean-Jacques Rousseau Museum, was in Montmorency, just outside Paris. But before he settled there, the young Rousseau lived with his benefactress and lover, Madame de Warens, from 1736 to 1742 in Les Charmettes, a seventeenth-century country house in Chambéry, near the border of his native Switzerland. Calling it "our asylum . . . where in the space of

four or five years I enjoyed a century of life and pure and full happiness," Rousseau here formed the "store of ideas" for his later publications. It's easy to see why Rousseau was filled with peace here, embraced by a green, wooded valley, with clear views of the Chartreuse Mountains. Inside, the rustic stone farmhouse reveals the splendors of its age—faux-stone trompe-l'oeil murals, ornamented baroque furniture—within a faded, country palette accentuated by exposed plank floors and ribbed timber ceilings. Upstairs bedrooms gaze onto the countryside. Rousseau's is austere, architectural, with diamond-patterned walls and a draped alcove bed. Madame de Warens's is feminine, softened with rose wall patterns; a pinkish embroidered canopy hangs like a tent over her bed.

PETER PAUL RUBENS

Rubenshuis
Antwerp, Belgium

Painter, draftsman, art collector
👁

Flemish Baroque master Peter Paul Rubens (1577–1640) is renowned for his stirring historical portraits of sensuous, zaftig women, which gave rise to the term *Rubenesque*. But Rubens, who studied and worked in Italy for almost a decade, painted innumerable other subjects, and was also a prolific muralist, sculptor, textile artist, scholar, and even diplomat. His home in Antwerp, Belgium, where he lived for twenty-five years, reveals another talent: architecture. Rubens drew the plans to renovate and expand an old Flemish structure in the city center, giving it the feel of an Italian palazzo, filled with classical motifs and antique sculptures and paintings. He added a studio, garden pavilion, portico, and domed, semicircular "Pantheon" sculpture gallery. Many of his designs were altered or even demolished in subsequent renovations, particularly in the eighteenth century. Yet its basic elements are intact, and some, like the portico and pavilion, remain exactly as they were. Other spaces, like the lofty studio where Rubens painted most of his work, are now richly decorated galleries filled with period furniture and detailing. The museum contains a large number of masterpieces by Rubens himself, including his early *Adam and Eve* and a rare self-portrait. It also shows off work by colleagues like Anthony van Dyck, Willem van Haecht, and even Titian. Outside, a quiet courtyard garden provides a getaway from the city and from the popular museum itself.

PAUL RUDOLPH

Paul Rudolph Townhouse
New York, New York, USA

Architect
🔒

For more than three decades, a Georgian Revival townhouse on New York's swanky Beekman Place served as a lab for the three-dimensional experiments of revolutionary architect Paul Rudolph (1918–1997). Rudolph began his career in Florida as one of the forerunners of the Sarasota School and went on to become famous (and infamous) for his dexterous employment of concrete and highly complex floor plans. In 1961, while chairing the Yale School of Architecture, he rented a one-bedroom apartment in the townhouse as a weekend escape. He went on to become the owner of the whole building, and by 1977 gained permits to erect a new four-story glass-and-steel penthouse. The addition is organized into four linked levels, circling a central void and dominated by cantilevered floors, staggered terraces, narrow bridges, open stairs, and windows of varying dimensions. Structures and surfaces alternate between steel beams, metal grating, stainless-steel shells, concrete panels, acrylic, Formica, Lucite, marble, leather, even plastic wrap. From the library, one progresses up through the living room, dining room, and master bedroom suite (later converted into an office), all lit via a skylight above. Outdoor balconies and terraces, covered in greenery, are outlined by a thin steel frame. Similarly complex spatial strategies are on display in the nearby Modulightor Building, the architect's final residential project, which now houses the Paul Rudolph Heritage Foundation and a ground-floor shop for Modulightor, a lighting company Rudolph helped found.

JOHN RUSKIN

Brantwood
Coniston, Cumbria, England, UK

Art critic, painter, draftsman,
art collector
👁

Known as the leading English art-and-architecture critic of the Victorian era (and a gifted artist himself), John Ruskin (1819–1900) helped elevate naturalist artists like J. M. W. Turner and set the stage for a resurgence of Gothic architecture and, later, the Arts and Crafts movement. But he had a much wider impact, calling into question, among many other things, the moral foundations of British society and what he called the barbaric impacts of capitalism and industrialism. Seminal works like *Modern Painters*, *The Seven Lamps of Architecture*, and *The Stones of Venice* still reverberate today. Brantwood, Ruskin's home in the village of Coniston, in northwest England's Lake District, overlooks the east edge of the serene Coniston Water. Ruskin bought the stone home in 1871, when he was

fifty-two, immediately renovating and expanding it with new spaces and Gothic details, such as a large turret, lancet windows, and timber carvings. Inside, the meandering residence is full of original furniture, like Ruskin's secretaire and the little bed in which he died; paintings by Turner, Thomas Gainsborough, and the Pre-Raphaelites; several drawings by Ruskin himself; and treasures compiled during his many travels. Just as significant are Brantwood's 250-acre (101-hectare) grounds, which feature a lodge, coach house, stable, pastures, and eight unique gardens, where Ruskin experimented with cultivation and irrigation. Tiny Coniston also has a small Ruskin museum, which showcases local history as well as Ruskin's.

ELIEL SAARINEN

Saarinen House
Bloomfield Hills, Michigan, USA

Architect, painter
👁

The house of Finnish-American architect and painter Eliel Saarinen (1873–1950) typifies his groundbreaking merger of Arts and Crafts, Art Deco, and Finnish vernacular. The building was his family home and studio while he served as Cranbrook Academy of Art's first resident architect, and later as the Academy's first president and head of the Architecture Department. Saarinen shared it with his wife, Loja, a revolutionary textile designer, and his soon-to-be-legendary son, Eero. Located at the heart of Eliel's famed Cranbrook campus, the two-story building is, appropriately, a complete work of art: no detail is too big or too small for attention. Outside, triangular forms, decorative bricks, leaded-glass windows, and soft ivy create a textured assemblage that is neither cluttered nor austere. The same layered, holistic approach continues inside, through geometric motifs, colorful accents, and Saarinen-designed tapestries, rugs, furniture, upholstery, and lighting. The book room, a nook just off the living room, is unified by textiles whose complex forms call to mind both Finnish traditional weaving and Art Deco abstraction. A handcrafted wooden table and cabinets recall the carpentry of the Arts and Crafts movement, but their exotic woods are indicative of Art Deco, as is the boldly geometric chandelier above. Eliel and Loja asked Eero (then twenty) to design most of their upstairs bedroom's furnishings, including the beds, nightstand, table, lamp, and mirror. He created sleek, vividly modern designs that served as a harbinger of what was to come.

VITA SACKVILLE-WEST

Sissinghurst Castle
Kent, England, UK

Poet, novelist, garden designer
👁

Victoria "Vita" Sackville-West (1892–1962) was the only daughter of Lionel Edward Sackville-West, later the third Baron Sackville. She was a prizewinning fiction writer and poet, composing vividly about her beautiful Kentish countryside (and its farms, country houses, and aristocracy). As a woman, Sackville-West was unable to inherit her childhood estate of Knole; devastatingly for her, the property went to her cousin Eddy. Perhaps this explains why she craved a historic country seat of her own. After marrying diplomat Harold Nicolson (their open marriage allowed for her famous relationship with Virginia Woolf), they bought Sissinghurst Castle, a dilapidated Elizabethan mansion of fairy-tale demeanor, with rose-colored bricks and a romantic medieval tower. The couple immediately

set about renovating the estate and its gardens. Not surprisingly, Sackville-West had an obsession with lineage, and she decorated the castle in a grand historical style. The more faded and threadbare, the better. If she bought an object that was new, it was made to look old. In her magical writing room in the castle's tower, faux-Tudor decor meets Edwardian bohemanism. Books, of course, feature heavily, as do tattered textiles and worn timber furniture. Beyond a stone archway is a tiny nook stuffed with more books, while heavy velvet curtains drape the windows. A typewriter rests on the animal-footed table. It is a place to think, write, and withdraw from the world.

YVES SAINT LAURENT

Villa Oasis
Marrakech, Morocco

Fashion designer
👁

French designer Yves Saint Laurent (1936–2008) revolution-ized fashion, shaking the stodgy haute couture world to its foundations, validating ready-to-wear style, and flashing his impeccable and ever-changing talent season after season. He founded his eponymous fashion house in 1961, moving it to a Second Empire hôtel particulier at 5, avenue Marceau (now the Fondation Pierre Bergé - Yves Saint Laurent) in 1974. All the while, he lived in a richly decorated duplex on the city's Left Bank and escaped to Villa Oasis, his marvelous residence inside Marrakech's equally stunning Majorelle Garden. The cobalt blue home, originally created by French Orientalist painter and plant collector Jacques Majorelle, is hidden within the public garden behind tall bamboo thickets. Inside, each room has its own exotic palette, inspired by Morocco's blazing colors and unified by North African themes and forms: flower tile mosaics, carved wood openings, and lushly patterned textiles and furniture. The grand salon, colored in shades of green and yellow, evokes the country's scruffy sage and juniper, and its bright desert flowers. Majorelle designed its tile work and wall decorations, and painted the exquisite Moderne console. Saint Laurent, who lived here with his partner and patron, industrialist Pierre Bergé, enlivened the home through creative restoration, not to mention lavish entertaining. He designed and painted the villa's top floor, sketching his collec-tions here on a square bamboo table that remains at the center of the space.

NIKI DE SAINT PHALLE

Giardino dei Tarocchi
Capalbio, Italy

Sculptor, painter, mosaicist, filmmaker
👁

Atop Etruscan ruins in the Tuscan village of Capalbio sit twenty-two monumental figures. It is said sculptor, mosaicist, and performance artist Niki de Saint Phalle (1930–2002) first envisioned this garden, inspired by the mystical figures in a tarot deck, when she was in an asylum. She wrote in a letter, "I'm following a course that was chosen for me, following a pressing need to show that a woman can work on a monumental scale." Known for its jubilant, shockingly colorful "monsters," the Giardino dei Tarocchi ("Tarot Garden") became her life's work. With help from husband and collaborator Jean Tinguely, she lived and worked here from 1973 until 1998, when the park opened to the public. During these decades she chose the sphinx-inspired "Empress" as her residence, with her

bedroom in one gravity-defying breast and her kitchen in the other; she made each nipple into a circular window. In the dining room Tinguely's scrap-metal chandelier hangs like a spider web amidst an explosion of shattered glass above a mirrored table; the floor is composed of earth-colored circular tiles. The combination gives the interior a hallucinatory quality, as though a fairy-tale had been blown to bits and reassembled: a manifestation of Saint Phalle's imagination. "The Empress is the great Goddess," she once said. "She is the Queen of the sky. Mother. Whore. Emotion. Sacred magic and civilization."

AUGUSTUS SAINT-GAUDENS

Aspet
Cornish, New Hampshire, USA

Sculptor
👁

Beaux-Arts sculptor Augustus Saint-Gaudens (1848–1907), revered for his tirelessly crafted, intensely realist work (one critic called it "a symphony in bronze"), is considered the foremost American sculptor of the nineteenth century. A core player in the American Renaissance, his most famous works include the statue of Abraham Lincoln in Chicago's Lincoln Park, the Sherman Monument in New York's Grand Army Plaza, and the Shaw Memorial in Boston, with its deeply emotional depiction of Union soldiers heading to war. At the encourage-ment of his wife, Augusta, Saint-Gaudens rented and eventually bought an 1817 Federal-style home (formerly a tavern) in peaceful Cornish, New Hampshire. They called the house and its rolling property Aspet, after his father's birthplace in France.

Several creative friends and colleagues followed, forming what would become known as the Cornish Colony. The Saint-Gaudenses remodeled the home's interior, which contains art from the likes of John Singer Sargent, as well as Classicist and Colonial furnishings and splendid decorative objects. They converted two smaller rooms on the first floor into a living room, whose grass-mat wall coverings, molded wood trim, decorative wood mantel, and animated textiles balance rural informality with urban refinement. Saint-Gaudens converted the property's wooden barn into his sun-drenched "Little Studio," while several structures display his sculptures, including the New Gallery, Picture Gallery, atrium, atrium pool, and Farragut forecourt.

ARY SCHEFFER

Museé de la Vie Romantique
Paris, France

Painter
👁

A stunning surprise in Pigalle, a Paris neighborhood now known for its unseemly side, the Musée de la Vie Romantique was the home of Ary Scheffer (1795–1858), a Dutch-born painter whose work typified the individualism and intense emotion of the Romantic age. At the time, the newly developed area was known as "New Athens," a center for artistic, fashionable Parisians, including neighbors like Théodore Géricault and Eugène Delacroix. Scheffer's two-story home, built in 1830 in the rigorous Restoration style, is accessed via a narrow driveway, its white facade, punctuated with curved green shutters, emerging like a vision. Scheffer added two glass-roofed studios (one for painting and one for hosting); the whole complex wraps around a lovely garden and paved courtyard.

In his tall, light-filled studio, Scheffer, good friends with King Louis-Philippe I and his family, hosted artistic and literary meetings (Franz Liszt and Frédéric Chopin would often play piano), and noted painters would collaborate with him. The home itself contains dainty spaces decorated with checked wallpaper and lined with paintings and sculptures by Scheffer and others of the Romantic age. The living room, somewhat curiously, is now a re-creation of the salon of a neighbor and frequent visitor, novelist and memoirist George Sand (the pen name of Amantine-Lucile-Aurore Dupin), including more than two hundred of her intricate objets d'art, jewelry, manuscripts, and even a lock of her hair.

FRIEDRICH SCHILLER

Schillers Wohnhaus
Weimar, Germany

Playwright, poet, philosopher, historian
👁

Although small in size, Weimar is a city of cultural giants. The metropolis of about sixty-five thousand has been home to Johann Sebastian Bach, Franz Liszt, Johann Wolfgang Goethe, Walter Gropius (and the Bauhaus), Friedrich Nietzsche, and playwright and poet Friedrich Schiller (1759–1805). Schiller is not the best known of these figures. But he was a colossus of the Enlightenment, a startlingly modern writer whose work still has tremendous relevance. In 1802 Schiller moved with his family to a spacious 1777 house near the city's Esplanade, close to his good friend and collaborator Goethe's residence. "These days I finally realized an old wish to own my own house," he wrote to his publisher. "Because I have now given up all thoughts about moving away from Weimar and think that I will live and die here." Indeed, Schiller, exhausted by his tireless work and repeated ailments, died here just three years later, at age forty-five. His yellow two-story house reveals a high standard of living for a writer at the time. Its many living spaces are spread along the first two floors; the reception room, dining room, parlor, lounge, and bedrooms are enlivened by bright wallpaper (a new invention), ornamental molding, and classical art and furnishings. Schiller had the entire attic to himself, a simple but elegant series of spaces—accented with books, furniture, and fine objects—to work in peace and receive guests.

RUDOLPH M. SCHINDLER

Schindler House
West Hollywood, California, USA

Architect
👁

When else do you get a chance to step inside one of the most famous houses in the world? The Schindler House, otherwise known as the King's Road House, is widely considered the masterpiece of prolific Frank Lloyd Wright protégé Rudolph Schindler (1887–1953). Decades ahead of its time, it personified the Austrian-born architect's progressive commitment to construction innovation, communal living, and indoor-outdoor lifestyle. Schindler designed the West Hollywood residence—which he and his wife, Pauline, shared with another couple, Clyde and Marian Chace—in just two months, from November to December 1921. There were four rooms, one for each person to "express his or her individuality," as well as upstairs sleeping porches, a shared kitchen, and a patio for each family within the verdant garden. Laid out on a pinwheel plan, which opened as much surface as possible to the garden, the home was constructed using tilt-up, precast-concrete modules. Schindler offset the concrete with a Japanese-influenced system of floor-to-ceiling redwood-framed windows and clerestories. The home became a laboratory for invention. Schindler here devised legendary homes like the Lovell Beach House, El Pueblo Ribera Court, and the Wolfe House, and hosted Wright and his son Lloyd, photographer Edward Weston, composer John Cage, and modern dancer John Bovingdon. The home now contains offices and exhibition space for the MAK Center for Art and Architecture.

AMY SEDARIS

Sedaris Apartment
New York, New York, USA

Actor, comedian, screenwriter
⌂

The one-bedroom Greenwich Village apartment of Amy
Sedaris (b. 1961) should have its own show. It's as quirky and
hilarious as Sedaris herself, if not more. In one way it does
have its own show: she regularly uses it as the inspiration for
At Home with Amy Sedaris. Called the "most cheerful home
in Manhattan" by *House Beautiful*, the unit is a brilliant combination of kitsch, camp, and charm. Nothing is done halfway;
it's all filled to the colorful limit. Patches are sewed all over fabric
furniture. Wigs and wig samples dominate the top of a
wardrobe and form a lampshade. Fake foods are a major motif.
Flowers are everywhere: floating flower wallpaper, paper
roses, fake ferns, flea market bloom paintings, and endless
bouquets. Books are color coordinated, and splashes of pink

(including pink paper towel rolls) pop up frequently. But basically nothing else matches. A fun activity is visiting Sedaris's craft
room, filled with endless random objects collected from
cheap stores around the world. (Tokyo is a major source.) It's
also where her pet rabbit sleeps. "Everywhere you look there is
a bouquet of magic," noted *New York* magazine's Wendy
Goodman. The space itself reflects New York living—small
spaces, built-in shelves and cupboards, a low couch, a marble
fireplace—but you can't tell. In fact, you can't see much of
anything behind all the stuff.

JAVIER SENOSIAIN

Casa Orgánica
Naucalpan de Juárez, Mexico

Architect, designer
🔒

While Mexico City has produced some of the world's most celebrated architects, somehow almost no one outside the city has heard of surrealist designer Javier Senosiain (b. 1948). A master of free-form, biologically inspired building, he has created curving structures that resemble snakes, mushrooms, protozoa, and seashells. "The straight line is pretty much absent from nature: everything from microorganisms to the macrocosm, from DNA strands to galaxies, shifts in spirals," he told *Pin-Up*. In 1984 Senosiain created his own house, known as Casa Orgánica, on a hillside site west of Mexico City in Naucalpan de Juárez. The home, covered in tightly cropped grass and a variety of shrubs, trees, and flowers, resembles a green dune. When you go for a walk in the garden, you're actually walking on the house. Inside the residence—divided into social spaces and private ones—is carved out in smooth, curving concrete that's coated in blond marble powder, resembling the inside of a silky cave. Plastic skylights, porthole windows, hobbit-like doors, and winding tunnels enhance an already otherworldly feeling. In the living room, which looks out onto the rolling property through amoeba-shaped glass, a curving bench is built in, its color and texture matching the surrounding surfaces. That space melts into the kitchen, which continues into another space, into another, and so on.

FRANK SINATRA

Sinatra House (Twin Palms)
Palm Springs, California, USA

Singer, actor
👁

Often credited with putting Palm Springs on the map as a stylish Southern California retreat, star crooner Frank Sinatra (1915–1998) hired local architect E. Stewart Williams to design a weekend home that would advertise his ascendant status. Sinatra, raised on the East Coast, first asked Williams to design a Georgian-style mansion, complete with a red-brick facade and white columns. Luckily, Williams, working on his first residential commission (he went on to design Palm Springs icons like the Edris House and Palm Springs Art Museum), convinced Ol' Blue Eyes to divert from his plan and opt for something more modern and desert appropriate. Sinatra asked Williams to finish the house—known as Twin Palms— on an impossibly tight schedule, hoping to have it ready for a Christmas party. The house, full of light, air, and classy modern furnishings, went on to become a symbol of West Coast glamour and casual lifestyle. It was also the setting for count- less celebrity fetes, cocktail hours, movie shoots, and dramas (like Sinatra's divorce from his first wife, Nancy, and fierce fights between Sinatra and his future wives). The 4,500-square-foot (418-square-meter), four-bedroom residence, now available as a vacation rental, still exudes Sinatra cool and Palm Springs chill, with its flowing open plan, stone and wood walls, ball chandelier, beamed ceilings, clerestory windows, sliding glass doors, sleek breezeways, Rat Pack-era furniture, original sound system, spacious patio, and, yes, piano-shaped pool.

ZADIE SMITH

Smith Residence
London, England, UK

Novelist, short-story writer, essayist
🔒

Author Zadie Smith (b. 1975) opens her readers' eyes to a London away from the glitzy tourist center, a London she knows intimately from her upbringing. Smith, who wrote her debut novel *White Teeth* in 2000, was born and raised in Willesden, until recently a relatively ordinary, though rough around the edges, area of northwest London. Now the neighborhood's demographic is changing, with gentrification making its relentless march. Smith has moved around the world in her adult life, living in Rome and the United States, but she also bought a large house in her native Willesden. The period residence is geographically close to the public housing estate where she grew up, although the class divisions created by a few streets' separation are tangible. Smith's choice of decor is tastefully restrained, with stripped wooden floorboards and predominantly white walls throughout the main living areas. On the fireplace in her study is a replica of Michael Jackson's white glove, as well as figurines of Enid from the movie *Ghost World* and Stewie from *Family Guy*. A large red statue on the floor is a souvenir from a trip to Kerala in India. A portrait of Smith and her father, who died in 2006, hangs on her study wall and is the work of her stepsister. Bookshelves abound on many walls, as you would expect in such a literary household: her husband, Nick Laird, is a novelist and poet.

JOHN SOANE

Sir John Soane's Museum
London, England, UK

Architect
👁

Located inside three townhouses on London's bucolic Lincoln's Inn Fields, Sir John Soane's Museum is one of the quirkiest, most energizing places in the city and perhaps the world. John Soane (1753–1837), one of the most important architects of Britain's Regency era, demolished and rebuilt the three buildings between 1792 and 1825, creating a labyrinth of variously sized and oriented rooms. He continuously filled the spaces with thousands of objects, ranging from the sarcophagus of the Egyptian pharaoh Seti I to architectural models of Soane's own Bank of England headquarters. Other items include furniture, sculptures, drawings, and paintings. He often placed them in dedicated chambers, like the Model Room, which includes a sort of grand tour in miniature, with destinations like

a recreation of the temples at Paestum and a cork model of Pompeii in Italy; and the Picture Room containing over one hundred paintings by artists including William Hogarth, Canaletto, and J. M. W. Turner. Other fascinating areas include the genteel drawing rooms; the Bath Room, full of wondrous porcelains; and the library, thronged with beautiful period books. Many zones are opened up via light shafts, staggered ceilings, exposed domes, atria, and large skylights. Wherever you go, nearly every inch of floors, walls, stairways, shelves, mantles, and sometimes even ceilings is filled with something extraordinary.

PAOLO SOLERI

Cosanti
Paradise Valley, Arizona, USA

Architect, urban designer,
writer, philosopher
👁

One of the modern era's most visionary designers, Italian-born Paolo Soleri (1919–2013) was an architect, urban designer, craftsman, and philosopher. He called his most noted philosophy "arcology," the fusion of architecture with ecology, and through it he formulated a radical reorganization of the urban environment into dense, three-dimensional cities that could each sustain environmental balance and human culture. In 1956 Soleri settled on a 5-acre (2-hectare) plot in Paradise Valley, Arizona, with his wife, Colly, and their two daughters, setting out to bring this philosophy to life. His dream, which was partially realized (you can visit), was to build Arcosanti, a prototype city about an hour north. But their life was at Cosanti, where Soleri and his students designed experimental structures for living and

working using an earth-casting method, in which concrete was poured over preshaped earthen forms. The concrete, and the pavilions' underground elements, act as natural insulation in the harsh desert environment. Cosanti, which served as Soleri's home and studio, is a wonder in itself. Its raw, meandering, interlocked domes and cylinders, imbedded with primal geometries, feel both ancient and futuristic. The studio space, with its elaborate web of organic vaults and alien ornament, brings you into a different world. You'll be hard-pressed not to buy one of the many bells you'll find here.

JOAQUÍN SOROLLA BASTIDA

Museo Sorolla
Madrid, Spain

Painter
👁

Spanish painter Joaquín Sorolla Bastida (1863–1923) lyrically captured his native country's people and landscapes, glowing radiantly under bright sunlight. His 1911 residence in Madrid's aristocratic Chamberí neighborhood is considered one of the best-preserved artist homes in Europe. Sorolla worked closely with architect Enrique María de Repullés y Vargas to create the rather regal Modern Historicist home. Its sumptuous domestic areas, reached via an imposing portico, encompass the salon, replete with family portraits and turn-of-the-century furniture; the dining room, with its white-marble paneling and oil paintings; the bedrooms (now temporary exhibition rooms); and a mezzanine ventilated by a timeless Andalusian courtyard, a light-suffused, tile-clad space loaded with handmade

ceramics. Sorolla's three workspaces are the heart of the home. As during Sorolla's time, they contain dark red walls and wood floors, and are covered in salon-style hangings of his work. Hall 1, a former storage space, showcases the evolution of the painter's work. Hall 2, which was his office and exhibition gallery, is dedicated to family portraits. Hall 3, Sorolla's main studio, is the most impressive, with its high ceilings and gabled roof, soaking in the Spanish light. Sorolla's original utensils are on display, as is his elaborate daybed, and his best-known works are everywhere.

GUSTAV STICKLEY

The Stickley Museum at Craftsman Farms
Morris Plains, New Jersey, USA

Furniture designer, publisher
👁

One of the pioneers of the American Craftsman movement, Gustav Stickley (1858–1942)—an early devotee of Britain's Arts and Crafts campaign—became world renowned for his wood furniture and homes that stressed simplicity, local materials, and honesty of construction. He gained early prominence via his monthly magazine, the *Craftsman*, whose first issue came out in 1901. Stickley's 30-acre (12-hectare) country estate, Craftsman Farms, is in Morris Plains, New Jersey, about an hour west of New York. Brimming with meadows, forests, trails, and streams, Stickley's "Garden of Eden," as he called it, is dotted with cottages, barns, and stables. All were sited according to the curves and slopes of the land, leaving the property in its natural state rather than flattening it. Its centerpiece is the Log House, a log cabin-inspired structure made of chestnut trunks cut from the property, and fieldstone also hailing from the site. The shingled, T-shaped home has a large gabled roof, a generous porch, and a kitchen attached to the rear. Inside, living and dining rooms, clad with exposed brown-stained logs, contain original Craftsman furniture and fixtures, and copper-hooded fireplaces. Stickley and his family lived in the four bedrooms upstairs, cozy spaces lent simple texture by stained gumwood beams, unornamented furniture, and stone walls. "When a man's home is born out of his heart and developed through his labor and perfected by his sense of beauty, it is the very cornerstone of life," wrote Stickley.

EDWARD DURELL STONE

Edward Durell Stone Townhouse
New York, New York, USA

Architect
🔒

Architect Edward Durell Stone (1902–1978), who possessed a flair for the dramatic, had geometric branding down decades before Louis Vuitton. His 15-foot-wide (5-meter-wide) 1870s New York townhouse was derelict before he decided to reclad it in a striking, three-dimensional white concrete screen of interlaced circles and squares. There is no other ornament, no tripartite separation—just this beautiful, monolithic sculpture. Inside, the architect filled the midblock home—which contrasts in every way with its Upper East Side neighbors and yet somehow fits right in—with his Modern-meets-Baroque language, creating a plate-glass window wall facing the street, installing a large skylight, tearing out partitions to create a continuous flow in the parlor floor, and utilizing lots of marble. The home,

landmarked in 1981, had fallen on hard times before Knoll CEO Andrew Cogan and his wife, Lori Finkel, hired Stone's son Hicks to restore it (Hicks's previous renovation in 1998 had attempted to remove the screen wall, a move that was rejected by New York City's Landmarks Preservation Commission). They sold the house for upward of $9 million in 2014, and it has never looked better. You have to wonder how the building stays so white. The residence is part of a superb collection of Modernist town-houses on the Upper East Side, including Philip Johnson's Rockefeller Guest House, William Lescaze's Lescaze House, and Paul Rudolph's Modulightor, Beekman Place, and Halston House.

ROBERT TATIN

Musée Robert Tatin
Cossé-le-Vivien, France

Painter, sculptor, ceramicist
👁

French polymath Robert Tatin (1902–1983), a peripatetic builder, painter, sculptor, and more, was as talented as he was eccentric. Born into modest circumstances in Mayenne, a region between the Loire Valley and Normandy, he studied drawing and painting in Paris, returned to Mayenne to start a successful career in carpentry, then went on to become a world-famous painter, sculptor, and ceramicist, working worldwide. He returned to Mayenne for good in 1962, purchasing a small stone house that he and his wife Lise would convert into La Maison des Champs, the perfectly unique outlet for, and reflection of, his talents. The house, where Tatin lived and worked for the last twenty-one years of his life, resembles the cobbled-together abode of an artistic hobbit, covered in

strange gargoyles and full of Tatin's colorful art and handmade furniture. His workshop and living spaces are open to visitors. But the true delight is what he built around them; a wonderworld of bizarre contours and structures, like stone totems, monster-shaped sculptures (including the "dragon," a fierce, mouth-shaped symbolic entrance), a water-filled meditation garden, and half-pyramidal fortresses, all imbedded with symbolic references to past civilizations, gods, planets, the animal world, and mysticism. Entrance is via the "Alley of the Giants," lined with nineteen otherworldly statues representing historical figures like Joan of Arc and artistic ones like Picasso and Jules Verne.

PYOTR ILYICH TCHAIKOVSKY

Tchaikovsky House-Museum
Klin, Russia

Composer
👁

No composer's work embodies the Romantic age's intense waves of sentiment quite like the compositions of Pyotr Ilyich Tchaikovsky (1840–1893). From *The Nutcracker* to *Swan Lake* to *Sleeping Beauty*, his languorous, catchy refrains are forever etched into the popular consciousness. Like many composers, Tchaikovsky preferred to work in the quiet of the countryside. From 1892 until his death, he rented a nineteenth-century timber villa on the outskirts of Klin, a small town about 56 miles (90 kilometers) northwest of Moscow. Enamored of the residence's beautiful views and generous garden, the composer was extremely productive here, often working from early morning until well after dinner. In the center of the home's decorous reception room and study is

Tchaikovsky's grand piano, still played on special occasions, like his birthday. Dark wood bookcases reveal a portion of his staggering collection of books on music, literature, philosophy, and science, and his thick wooden desk, where he wrote correspondence, rests at the base of a wall filled with photographs of his family, musicians (including his beloved teacher, Anton Rubinstein), artists, friends, and students. Tchaikovsky carried out most of his composing in his bedroom, on a plain birchwood table overlooking the garden. Scattered here are music scores and sketches, including some of the last pieces he ever composed.

ALFRED, LORD TENNYSON

Farringford
Freshwater Bay, Isle of Wight,
England, UK

Poet
👁

The most famous poet of the Victorian era, Alfred, Lord Tennyson (1809–1892) brought his highly wrought, melodious style to subjects mythical, philosophical, and fanciful, from Ulysses to Lancelot to the cycles of life. Wearing a flowing cape and broad-brimmed "wideawake" hat, he fashioned himself a rather heroic character, albeit a scruffy one. Farringford, his secluded estate on the Isle of Wight, served as his family home from 1853 until his death. Lying just west of the chalky cliffs of Freshwater Bay, overlooking the whale-backed ridge of Tennyson Down, the home and its bucolic grounds inspired endless poetry, including "The Flower," "The Holy Grail," and "In Memoriam A. H. H." The eclectic structure was built in the early nineteenth century as a buff-brick neo-Georgian villa,

decorated with Gothic motifs like crenellated parapets and Gothic arched windows, doorways, and cornices. Piece by piece, it grew under subsequent owners, Tennyson included. After having served as a hotel starting in 1945, the home was restored and opened to the public in 2017. Neo-Gothic details merge with a Victorian sense of splendor, color, history, and whimsy. The library, where Tennyson conducted research and stored his voluminous book collection, reveals sweeping views through its large central window. It contains his original writing desk, Windsor chair, and two large globes (evidence of his keen interest in astronomy).

DYLAN THOMAS

Dylan Thomas Boathouse
and Writing Shed
Laugharne, Camarthenshire,
Wales, UK

Poet, short-story writer, scriptwriter
👁

Welsh poet Dylan Thomas (1914–1953) became famous first for the forceful lyricism and highly charged emotion of his work, and second, tragically, for his early death from pneumonia at age thirty-nine. (His poem "Do not go gentle into that good night" begged readers to "Rage, rage against the dying of the light.") When he first visited the tiny charming township of Laugharne at age nineteen, he called it "the strangest town in Wales." He was instantly smitten and later took up residence, with his wife, Caitlin, in a small three-story fisherman's cottage hugging the rugged, peaceful shores of the Taf estuary. Every room looks out on the water, so you get the feeling of being inside a boat. The first-floor living room displays, among other artifacts, books, newspaper clippings, family photographs, and a desk that

Thomas inherited from his father. Thomas did most of his writing inside a rickety little clifftop shed nearby—he called it the "water and tree house"—which had excellent views of the town. Inside, his simple desk is scattered with books, papers, and handwritten letters. The walls are full of pinned-up photographs. Dylan and Caitlin are both buried nearby, in the grounds of St. Martin's Church in Laugharne.

FAYE TOOGOOD

Toogood/Gibberd Residence
London, England, UK

Furniture designer, fashion designer,
interior designer, sculptor, painter
🔒

Faye Toogood (b. 1977), the rare creative to master drawing, sculpture, furniture, and fashion, makes the complex look simple and shifts the familiar into the new, with a soft and informal sensuality. The home she occupies with her husband, architecture journalist Matt Gibberd, shares Toogood's breezy minimalism, although it was built before she was born. Modernist architect Walter Segal created the box-shaped structure, sandwiched between nineteenth-century town-homes in London's Highgate, as a prototype of his low-cost, do-it-yourself system, known as the Segal self-build method. The couple fell in love with it, restoring the acoustic-board ceilings, frameless windows, and exposed pale bricks. Looking for more gentle, milky tactility, they replaced faded cupboard doors with cream-felt-covered plywood, installed vertical pine cladding, and upgraded the kitchen in polished concrete. They also filled the home with quirky curiosities, another specialty of Toogood's: in addition to her playfully squat Roly Poly stools and tables and quirky Silo and Puffball pieces, there are aluminum cupboards sprayed with car paint and counters found in a junk shop. In the living room, one of Toogood's geometric tapestries hangs above a draped white sofa, behind one of her pill-shaped coffee tables, beset with objects that are beautiful cousins: both incongruous and perfectly matched. Artful, mysterious insertions are everywhere, from minimal drawings and paintings by Henry Moore and Patrick Procktor to furnishings that emerge from the walls.

BILLIE TSIEN AND TOD WILLIAMS

Williams and Tsien Residence
New York, New York, USA

Architects
🔒

Architects Billie Tsien (b. 1949) and Tod Williams (b. 1943) have brought their soft, sophisticated aesthetic to homes and cultural institutions alike, including the Barnes Foundation, the (sadly, demolished) American Folk Art Museum, and, most recently, Dartmouth's Hood Museum of Art. In a very good way, it's sometimes hard to tell which project is a residence and which is a museum. The New York couple have incorporated a lucky twist into their lifestyle. Instead of heading out of town to get away, they simply walk down the street to their Central Park South pied-à-terre. The rooftop space, measuring just 883 square feet (82 square meters), makes up for its size with well-ordered unity and an all-encompassing connection to Central Park. The focal point is a steel-framed living room, wrapped on three sides with floor-to-ceiling glass, spilling via sliders onto an expansive terrace, where nothing can get in the way of the views. That sensation continues inside. Tsien commented in Michael Webb's book *Architects' Houses*, "I feel I'm in the park even when I'm sitting in the tub." Sand-finished walls, stone paving, and smooth timber furniture and cabinetry balance a serene mix of urban and pastoral. The couple's artful aesthetic pervades the space, which features soft greenish V'Soske rugs that they themselves designed, pillows by Dutch designer Claudy Jongstra, resin-and-cast-glass tables, and gold tiles from Venice.

MARK TWAIN

The Mark Twain House and Museum
Hartford, Connecticut, USA

Novelist, journalist, publisher
👁

One of history's most acerbic, insightful observers, Mark Twain (1835–1910), born Samuel Langhorne Clemens, was a vital voice during a turbulent and transformative time in American history. Born in Missouri, he had already lived around the country before he and his new wife, Olivia (Livy), decided to move to Hartford, Connecticut, in 1871. They hired architect Edward Tuckerman Potter to build what would become a breathtaking, but money-sucking, home. By 1891 the family had left due to various financial problems. But Twain always loved the place: "It was of us, and we were in its confidence and lived in its grace and in the peace of its benediction," he said, calling the time he spent here his happiest, most productive years. (He wrote *The Adventures of Tom Sawyer* and *Adventures of*

Huckleberry Finn here, often with a Scotch in hand.) The twenty-five room Victorian mansion, which, incidentally, sits right across the lawn from writer Harriet Beecher Stowe's Victorian Gothic cottage, is, outside, a mesmerizing jumble, with steeply pitched rooflines, bricks in all colors, shapes, and positions, and elaborate wood carvings. Richly decorated rooms are like stories themselves, containing thousands of artifacts, like plush furniture, intricate wallpapers, ornamental timber paneling, manuscripts, and photographs. Twain bantered with luminaries in the dining room, and shared story after story around the living room's enormous Scottish fireplace. The adjacent museum further elucidates Twain's life and work.

CY TWOMBLY

Gaeta House
Gaeta, Italy

Painter
🔒

Artist Cy Twombly (1928–2011) created colorful, graffiti-like canvases, savage in their intensity but full of gentle wisdom. Revealing wildly varied influences, his work evoked classical mythology, sexual innuendo, and urban scrawl. He split his time between Lexington, Virginia, and Italy, where he lived both in Rome and in Gaeta, on the Tyrrhenian Sea, where he owned a home and studio. While restoring his house, he often spent time inside the white stucco residence of his assistant, Nicola Del Roscio. The property dates back about a thousand years. Del Roscio revived a structure once in tatters. "I spent all my life to restore this place and when I finish, it will collapse," Del Roscio told the *New York Times*. The centerpiece is the grand sitting room, with 14-foot (4-meter) ceilings and walls graced with eighteenth-century garland and flower frescoes in pale pink and blue. Couches and chairs are upholstered in yellow and cream silk. There's a sofa from Andy Warhol's home in Paris, and terra-cotta floor tiles, handmade in a nearby village. A table is topped with a framed poster for a Twombly exhibition in St. Petersburg, a Ross Bleckner painting, red coral, and a leaf from the Seychelles. Other rooms are spare, but their views are supremely seductive, framing the sea and the long arc of the coast below.

JØRN UTZON

Can Lis
Santanyí, Majorca, Spain

Architect
👁

A trained sculptor and talented sailor, Danish architect Jørn Utzon (1918–2008) turned out to be the perfect person to design the Sydney Opera House. With its curved, shell-like roof forms jutting over Sydney Harbor, the building would go on to become one of the most iconic structures of the twentieth century. But Utzon's acrimonious relationship with his clients, and the Australian press, led him to controversially quit the project in 1966, before its completion. He then brought his family far from the spotlight, to the Spanish island of Majorca, where in 1972 he built Can Lis, a clifftop house that ingeniously merges modern design with traditional Majorcan techniques and materials. A narrow site prompted its linear progression of separate pavilions—bedrooms, kitchen, living and dining rooms—connected by courtyards and stepping stones, and facing a partially covered patio overlooking the sea. The home's thick pink-sandstone walls, with deeply recessed windows, provide natural insulation and a sense of timelessness and shelter. Weighty permanent furniture includes a semicircular limestone-tiled couch, pinkish-gold tiled stone tables and seats, and nooks carved into the walls for beds. Graphic shapes adorn and pierce the home's hard surfaces, like a crescent moon motif, a reference to the home's former street, Avinguda Media Luna. The home was restored and transformed into a retreat for artists and architects in 2011 by the Utzon Foundation.

SUZANNE VALADON

Atelier-Apartment, Musée de
Montmartre
Paris, France

Painter
👁

Like most female artists of the nineteenth century, Suzanne Valadon (1865–1938) had to fight to achieve recognition for her work, which was highlighted by her powerful, insightful portraits of women, employing emphatic silhouettes, rich colors, and restrained crudity. Starting in Paris's bohemian Montmartre neighborhood in the 1880s as a model for artists like Pierre-Auguste Renoir and Henri de Toulouse-Lautrec, she later trained with Edgar Degas and at the age of forty-four finally began painting full time. She would eventually be feted with multiple retrospective exhibitions. Yet she does not achieve full prominence in her own house museum, the Musée de Montmartre. The institution is located inside a collection of old homes on the Butte Montmartre, housing the ateliers of

artists like Renoir, Émile Bernard, and Charles Camoin. While its spaces showcase exceptional pieces by these and other Montmartre legends, only the home and studio of Valadon and her husband and son (painters André Utter and Maurice Utrillo), known as "le trio infernal," remains as it was. Recently renovated, its cramped spaces, struggling to attain refinement, include a living room dressed with dark-but-flowery wallpaper, and the troubled Utrillo's modest bedroom, barbed wire on the windows. By contrast, the ivory-toned painting studio is luminous and inspiring, with tall windows and skylights over-looking the neighborhood and the complex's enchanting garden (often painted by Renoir), and overflowing with oil paints, canvases, stray paint marks, and notebooks.

MART VAN SCHIJNDEL

Van Schijndelhuis
Utrecht, The Netherlands

Architect, furniture designer, interior
designer, product designer, educator
👁

Dutch architect Mart van Schijndel (1943–1999) acted as
a bridge: between Modernism and postmodernism, varied
cultures, and disciplines like carpentry, furniture design,
architecture, and product design. Perhaps not surprisingly,
his "house of air and light" in Utrecht, hidden behind buildings
in the old center of the city, is a poetic, unified monument of
space, color, and illumination. All of the home's rooms, except
for the bedrooms, open onto a triangular living room, enclosed
in double-height glass and surrounded by east and west patios.
The luminous central space, an excellent example of the
arresting power of minimalism, is accentuated with abstract
details, including granite sawtooth stairs, Van Schijndel's
reductive furniture, and clear and frosted windows, which pivot

at the corners. Other glass surfaces, like kitchen cabinets, as
well as some doors and windows, have invisible hinges made
with silicone sealant. The space's walls first appear the same
color, but each has its own subtle light pastel shade. Light
and color contribute what Van Schijndel liked to call the "fourth
dimension," an important addition to the building's depth and
form. The home, which was completed in 1992, won the Rietveld
Prize (named for fellow Dutch architect Gerrit Rietveld) in
1995. In 1999, the Van Schijndelhuis was added to the Utrecht
Municipal Historic Buildings Register due to its special architectural value, making the house the youngest architectural
monument in Holland.

GIUSEPPE VERDI

Villa Verdi
Sant'Agata di Villanova sull'Arda, Italy

Composer
👁

Italian composer Giuseppe Verdi (1813–1901), still a hero in his home country, was the creator of more than two dozen forcefully passionate, often grandiose operas, including *La traviata*, *Aida*, and *Rigoletto*. Born near Busseto, an ancient commune about an hour southeast of Milan, Verdi lived around Europe, notably in Milan and Paris. But he spent much of the last fifty years of his life just outside Busseto, in a yellow two-story neoclassical villa that he shared with his wife, opera singer Giuseppina Strepponi. Verdi, who bought the property in 1848, rigorously renovated its spaces and added two terraced wings. Visitors can view Verdi and Strepponi's quarters, located on the ground floor of the south wing. Filled with pompous, red velvet Louis Philippe-style furniture and curtains and gold accents,

the sumptuous, flowing rooms are crowded with priceless relics like pianos, busts (including Vincenzo Gemito's elegant sculpture of Verdi himself), portraits, period photos, and music books and scores. Strepponi's room, with its canopy bed, is where she died in 1897; the dressing room is dominated by Verdi's Fritz piano; and Verdi's study showcases his desk, piano scores, and memorabilia. The final space, the Grand Hotel de Milan room, contains the furniture (as well as Verdi's shirt and death mask) from Room 157 of the Hotel de Milan, where the composer died. The villa's vast, romantic park is filled with over one hundred varieties of trees.

GIANNI VERSACE

The Villa Casa Casuarina at the former
Versace Mansion
Miami Beach, Florida, USA

Fashion designer
👁

Many of us still remember when iconic fashion designer
Gianni Versace (1946–1997) was tragically murdered outside
his Miami Beach mansion. But few know that his lavish
Ocean Drive property has become a five-star hotel called the
Villa Casa Casuarina. That name was the original moniker
of the residence, designed in 1930 by wealthy architect Alden
Freeman. Freeman built the home as a homage to the Alcázar
de Colón, the Santo Domingo home of Diego Columbus, son
of Christopher Columbus. After Versace bought the estate
and an adjacent hotel (he demolished the latter) in 1992, he
spent three years renovating, adding a garden, swimming pool,
and South Wing. Obsessed with antiquity and extravagance,
Versace installed a wealth of over-the-top classical details.

While many of his possessions were auctioned off in 2001 (for
$28 million), you can still enjoy auburn, peach, violet and sky
blue walls, floors, ceilings, and railings, along with pedimented
windows, Hellenic moldings, crown-shaped chandeliers, and
Roman frescoes, coupled with the hotel's equally baroque—
but sometimes modern or zebra-patterned—furnishings. There
are also marble statues of Neptune and Medusa in the garden;
the Thousand Mosaic Pool, its floor and surrounds depicting
Poseidon through thousands of 24-karat gold tiles; and
rotundas, fountains, murals, grand stairs, tiled courtyards, and
more evocations of a Roman villa. The hotel's twelve suites
range from $600 to over $2,000 per night, so start saving
up now.

267

GUSTAV VIGELAND

Vigelandmuseet
Oslo, Norway

Sculptor
👁

Without a doubt the most famous sculptor in Norwegian history is Gustav Vigeland (1869–1943), whose palpably emotional, zestfully physical sculptures dominate Vigeland Park in Oslo. (He also designed the Nobel Prize medal.) The Vigelandmuseet, located in Oslo's Frogner neighborhood, contains Vigeland's home and studio. The red-brick building, designed by architect Lorentz Ree, was built for Vigeland by the city in return for the pledge of his art collection. Marked by a central tower with two symmetrical wings, the museum collection contains 1,600 sculptures, twelve thousand drawings, and four hundred woodcuts, among other holdings. Vigeland's apartment, where he lived from 1924 until his death, is situated on the second floor of the building. While Vigeland had not pursued interior design prior to the move, here he did an about-face, creating about fifty pastels to grace these spaces and designing natural-toned, geometric patterns for carpets, pillows, tablecloths, and even candlesticks and lamps. Intimate possessions on display include Vigeland's pocket watch, stationery, keys, and even his boots and nightrobe. The astounding Vigeland sculpture park just next door showcases more than two hundred of the master's works in bronze, cast iron, and stone. If you're willing to take a long trip, Vigeland's childhood home, Vigeland Hus, is located in Mandal, on Norway's southern tip.

VOLTAIRE

Château de Voltaire
Ferney-Voltaire, France

Philosopher, playwright
👁

Playwright and philosopher François-Marie Arouet (1694–1778), known to the world by his pen name Voltaire, was one of the sparks that kindled the Enlightenment. He used his sharp, often witty pen as a weapon against the political and religious establishment. Often forced into exile for his controversial work, the Paris-born Voltaire shuffled around Europe. In 1759, after falling out of favor in Geneva, and unwelcome in the courts of Paris, he purchased and rebuilt an estate in Ferney, along the border of France and Switzerland, where he could be independent and entirely free. Here, working in his bedroom, he wrote some six thousand letters, as well as his *Treatise on Tolerance* and his *Philosophical Dictionary*. The lavish new home, which Voltaire designed with renowned Genevan architect

Jean-Michel Billon, was completed in 1766. Famed for saying, "We must tend to our garden," Voltaire laid out the formal grounds himself. The rose-colored neoclassical residence, topped with an imposing mansard roof, was restored in 2018. Inside, it shows off Voltaire's notable talent for design, not to mention his outsize personality. It's filled with over 460 original items, like crystal chandeliers, classical paintings, Louis XIV furniture, and more than seven thousand books. The bedchamber of Voltaire's niece (and lover) Madame Denis, around the corner from his, is the most ornate of all: a dizzying spectacle of chinoiserie, yellow and gold textiles, veined marble, and parquet.

DIANE VON FURSTENBERG

Von Furstenberg Residence
New York, New York, USA

Fashion designer

Diane von Furstenberg (b. 1946) founded her eponymous company in 1972, expanding it into an international luxury fashion brand renowned for its bold, creative approach to color and print. Look above her flagship store in Manhattan's Meatpacking District, and you will see the crystalline roof that marks the fashion designer's private penthouse. Von Furstenberg's home is not just close to work; she is also a neighbor of the High Line, the green artery that she helped rejuvenate with a $20 million donation. Von Furstenberg hired the architecture firm WORKac to unite a pair of Victorian red-brick buildings she bought in 2006. They filled the gap between the structures with a concrete staircase that leads diagonally up to a live-work area, above which is a 900-square-foot

(84-square-meter) master suite with a terrace. This 80-foot (24-meter) staircase acts like a chandelier, its three thousand Swarovski crystals reflecting light throughout the residence. The surfaces throughout the penthouse are filled with books and photographs, and inspiring words are painted on the walls. A large Zhang Huan portrait of Von Furstenberg, created with ash, fills much of one wall. There are sconces by André Dubreuil, and contrasts can be seen everywhere: zebra-hide chairs stand on leopard-print carpets; a Salvador Dalí lip sofa shares space with an Anh Duong self-portrait; a bed stands in a bamboo pavilion hung with panels of linen.

OTTO WAGNER

Otto Wagner Villa I
Vienna, Austria

Architect
👁

Vienna Secession architect Otto Wagner (1841–1918), first working in the neo-Renaissance style, soon broke free, helping launch the Modern architecture movement in Europe with designs in which simplified—but still resoundingly elegant—decoration followed the demands of structure, material, and function. "The only possible point of departure for our artistic creation is modern life," he insisted in 1895. In 1888 Wagner completed a remarkable villa for his family in Hütteldorf, a Vienna suburb. He crafted the building, perched atop a hillside and accessible via a grand staircase, in the new Jugendstil (a German decorative style parallel to Art Nouveau), which merged his classical training with a growing interest in abstraction and functionalism. The aqua-and-ivory structure, its open

portico fronted by large Ionic columns, is covered in simplified classical motifs and flanked by symmetrical, modular pergolas. Inside, the villa spreads out into lofty, colorful salons. The most exquisite and modern is the Adolph Böhm hall, rebuilt in 1900 and named for the designer of its brilliant-colored floral Tiffany glass windows. Wagner adorned the hall, considered Vienna's greatest Art Nouveau space, with Greek-inspired furnishings and fluid, gold-leaf decoration. In 1912 Wagner sold the estate and built Villa II, a neighboring home incorporating colorful abstractions that highlight function and assert his modern evolution more forcefully. His original villa is now the Ernst Fuchs Museum, filled with work by the fantastical realist artist, who was its final resident.

EMERY WALKER

Emery Walker's House
London, England, UK

Printer, photographer, typographer
👁

English printer and photographer Emery Walker (1851–1933) was, along with his friends William Morris and Philip Webb, a key figure in the English Arts and Crafts movement at the close of the nineteenth century. Walker ran his own company specializing in the innovative technique of photogravure, the reproduction of photographic tones, especially useful for books using photographs as illustrations. But he was also an expert in traditional typography, supporting Morris in the foundation of the celebrated Kelmscott Press and joining with Thomas James Cobden-Sanderson in creating the Doves Press. His home on the west side of London, 7 Hammersmith Terrace, is essentially a museum of Arts and Crafts: every space is alive with its influence. Abutting the north bank of the

Thames, the Georgian townhouse neighbored the residences of several of the movement's most prominent members. Morris & Co.'s floral textiles and hand-blocked wallpapers cover virtually every surface—walls, floors, furniture, and fireplaces. Darker greens and blues dominate the dining room; lighter blues, purples, and pinks the drawing room. The layered spaces are crowded with Arts and Crafts furnishings, including exquisite dark wood cabinets and chairs by Webb, and rich embroidery by May Morris, William's daughter. The eclectic property is also full of personal mementos—photos of family and friends, art and artifacts made especially for the Walkers, as well as seventeenth- and eighteenth-century English furniture and Chinese and Moroccan ceramics.

JOHN WARDLE

Shearers Quarters
Bruny Island, Tasmania, Australia

Architect
🔒

One of Australia's most celebrated contemporary architects, John Wardle threads the needle between innovation and tradition, employing new building techniques but drawing, after long observation, on a site's history and its lessons. The architect and his wife, Susan, spend most of their time in their oft-renovated home in Melbourne's Kew neighborhood. To create their weekend getaway—Shearers Quarters on rugged Bruny Island, off Tasmania—Wardle used a spectacular blend of his greatest strengths. Perched next to an existing cottage (which they also employ) on the couple's working sheep farm, the residence occupies the site of an old shearing shed that was destroyed by fire. Wardle designed a long building that unfolds along its length. Its narrow east end is covered in corrugated iron, like the hull of a ship, and its west edge opens to the ocean with a broad gable and large windows. Most rooms, fitted with timber joinery, furniture, and built-ins, are clad in a golden cypress surface, while bedrooms are lined in local recycled apple crates. Windows shift from extruded cubes to cinematic rectangles to thin vertical slits. The impact of the varied views—and the slowly moving wedges of light hitting the home's open, changing, tactile surfaces—cannot be overstated. Nor can the soft flow from space to space, leading one's psyche inevitably to the sea.

GEORGE FREDERIC AND MARY WATTS

Limnerslease
Compton, Surrey, England, UK

Painter, sculptor (George); sculptor, ceramicist, illustrator, painter (Mary)
👁

The Victorian era in England was a golden age for curious and stimulating artists' houses. Limnerslease, the home of prominent painter George Frederic Watts (1817–1904), is one of the most extraordinary. Designed by architect Ernest George, the half-timbered Arts and Crafts structure was constructed in 1891 as a winter home: a doctor-ordered escape from the pollution of Watts and his wife Mary's (1849–1938) thriving base in London's Holland Park. It is nestled in Compton in the picturesque Surrey Hills. The interior—largely designed by Mary—displays intricate gesso ceiling ornament, herringbone wood floors, intimate alcoves, and fluidly milled furniture. The east wing accommodates Watts's recently restored studio, a soaring red space showcasing the artist's work and process:

finished and unfinished canvases, strangely named pigments, and the artist's very stiff brushes, used to essentially sculpt paint. The couple thrived here. Watts, often referred to as "England's Michelangelo" because of his resplendent allegorical painting, dove into sculpture and realized long-delayed paintings. Mary, whose history-inspired work is displayed in her own studio in the house, shifted her focus from fine art to design and architecture, establishing the successful Compton Potters' Arts Guild and designing the nearby Watts Chapel, a fusion of Art Nouveau, Celtic, and Romanesque. After her husband's death, she loyally oversaw the nearby Christopher Hatton Turnor's Watts Gallery, dedicated to her husband's work.

EDITH WHARTON

The Mount
Lenox, Massachusetts, USA

Novelist, short-story writer, poet
👁

One of America's greatest writers, Edith Wharton (1862–1937) broke through the sexist, hierarchical limitations of Gilded Age society to create seminal novels like *The Age of Innocence*, *Ethan Frome*, and *The House of Mirth*. She also created authoritative works on architecture, gardens, interior design, and travel, including *The Decoration of Houses*, which she coauthored in 1897 with architect Ogden Codman Jr. In 1901 she and Codman designed her hilltop house, the Mount, on 113 acres (46 hectares) in Lenox, Massachusetts. She penned much of her best work here, while her marriage disintegrated. The Whartons sold the Mount in 1911 and divorced in 1913; Edith moved permanently to France. But the home stands as a testament to her talent and clear-eyed fortitude. Informed by

French, Italian, and English designs (particularly Belton House, a seventeenth-century English estate), Wharton, determined to break from the excess and frilly ornament of her upbringing, focused on classical moderation, order, scale, and harmony. The white stucco home, set off by dark green shutters, is punctuated by vertical clusters of gables and chimneys. Classically decorated main-floor rooms, judiciously spaced with tasteful furniture, open onto a long, vaulted gallery. Books on the shelves of Wharton's library include works from every period of her life. The author, who in 1904 wrote *Italian Villas and Their Gardens*, also partnered with Beatrix Farrand on her home's serene, layered landscape.

VIRGINIA WOOLF

Monk's House
Rodmell, East Sussex, England, UK

Novelist, literary critic, essayist
👁

Dancing between literary triumph and personal desolation (which led, tragically, to suicide), Virginia Woolf (1882–1941) helped push literature into the modern age, experimenting with devices like varied narrative perspective, dream states, and free association. She keenly explored challenging subjects like human relationships, mental illness, and feminism in novels such as *Mrs. Dalloway*, *To the Lighthouse*, and *Orlando*. In 1919 Woolf and her editor, publisher, and activist husband, Leonard, purchased Monk's House, a rustic sixteenth-century cottage in the tiny village of Rodmell, East Sussex, far from the distractions of London. Their charming rural escape, which they expanded and renovated over decades, became a full-time residence after their London home was damaged in

an air raid. Still filled with the couple's possessions, Monk's House is elegant and tasteful, but simple, never haughty. Cozy rooms take on differing hues, most notably mint green in the sitting room. That space's walls are covered in artwork by fellow Bloomsbury group members Vanessa Bell (Virginia's sister) and Duncan Grant, who also painted its matching table and chairs. Stephen Tomlin's incomplete bust of Virginia rests on the windowsill, next to Leonard's narrow desk, still covered with letters. The couple's colorful country garden contains Woolf's writing lodge, which afforded her views of their flowers, vegetables, and orchard (which inspired her short story "In the Orchard"), not to mention the rolling Sussex Downs.

FRANK LLOYD WRIGHT

Taliesin West
Scottsdale, Arizona, USA

Architect
👁

Nestled in the desert foothills of Scottsdale, Arizona, Taliesin West is a monument not only to the unmatched vision of Frank Lloyd Wright (1867–1959), but to his unparalleled ability to reinvent himself. Wright, already in his seventies, imagined a desert utopia where he could escape the harsh winters of Taliesin, his home and studio in Wisconsin—not to mention the preconceptions of the architectural world—with his wife and several apprentices. Inspired by the sweeping, abstract lines of the desert, the master designed a low-lying series of buildings hugging the landscape and formed of rutted, blond desert stone, sandy concrete, and rich redwood. "Our new desert camp belongs to the Arizona desert as though it had stood there during creation," said Wright, who had the rare ability to merge timeless and the futuristic concepts. Visiting Taliesin West takes you out of the banal world of housing developments and strip malls that have sprung up in Scottsdale, and into an ethereal realm, infused with creativity and nature. Tours take you into the original studio and living spaces, and through the drafting studio, dining facilities, theaters, and workshop. All combine elegance and rawness and are seamlessly connected to each other and to a series of terraces, gardens, and pools. Taliesin West is still an engine of creativity as the home of the Frank Lloyd Wright Foundation.

RUSSEL WRIGHT

Dragon Rock House and Studio,
Manitoga
Garrison, New York, USA

Industrial designer
👁

Industrial designer Russel Wright (1904–1976) helped usher American families into the modern age, producing biomorphic housewares and furnishings made of easy-to-maintain materials like wood, aluminum, stainless steel, clay, and plastic. His American Modern line was one of the most successful dinnerware sets in history, and Wright's book *Guide to Easier Living*, cowritten with his wife, Mary, became a perennial best seller. Visiting Manitoga, his home and 75-acre (30-hectare) woodland, is a transporting experience. Acquiring an abandoned quarry and hillside in Garrison, New York, Wright, inspired by the area's native Wappinger people, named it Manitoga, which means "place of great spirit." Wright employed an all-encompassing vision, blending and sequencing the site's built and natural elements. Visitors undertake a procession past a meadow, up a craggy hillside, around a pond, through a cathedral-like canopy of trees, and over a waterfall. They reach the house and studio, Dragon Rock, designed by architect David Leavitt with Wright, which echoes the twists, turns, and steps of the natural landscape while also contrasting them with man-made straight lines and modern materials like glass, steel, and resin. The home's main structural support is a large cedar tree trunk, while boulders, plantings, and stone terraces bring the outdoors in. Vast expanses of glass reveal views of the waterfall, the quarry pool, and the surrounding landscape. Few places achieve this level of harmony between the natural and the built.

N. C. WYETH

N. C. Wyeth House and Studio
Chadds Ford, Pennsylvania, USA

Illustrator, muralist
👁

American painter and illustrator N. C. Wyeth (1882–1945) was a master of dramatic effect and palpable realism. Explore his works, and you sense the look, feel, even smell of a scene. While best known for his illustrations for *Harper's, Scribner's,* and the *Saturday Evening Post*, he practiced painting with equal verve, creating more than three thousand canvases. With proceeds from his illustrations for Robert Louis Stevenson's *Treasure Island*, in 1911 Wyeth purchased an 18-acre (7-hectare) plot near Chadds Ford in rural Pennsylvania, not far from a Revolutionary War battlefield. Calling it "the most glorious site in the township," he built his family home and studio here, overlooking the rolling hills of the Brandywine Valley. He and his wife, Carolyn, raised five children in the two-story Colonial

Revival structure, designed by architect William Draper Brinkle. Both rustic and elegant, the home, with its timber paneling, beams, and floors, unveils rich, handcrafted detail that can't be imagined from its rather pedestrian exterior. The L-shaped studio, luminous thanks to a massive Palladian-style window, feels like a local barn, albeit a splendid one. Expertly crafted local furniture and painting supplies mingle with illustration props like firearms and a hanging canoe. Three of the Wyeths' children—Henriette, Carolyn, and particularly Andrew—became famous artists in their own right. Andrew's nearby studio, which he repurposed from an old schoolhouse, is also open to the public.

ANDREA ZITTEL

A–Z West
California, USA

Painter, sculptor
👁

The art of Andrea Zittel (b. 1965) merges about every medium imaginable, including sculpture, fashion, architecture, and performance art. More importantly, her work blurs the line between art and life. Like a modern-day Georgia O'Keeffe or Donald Judd, Zittel left a powerful career in New York (and her showroom, A–Z East) to form a 70-acre (28-hectare) "artwork" that she calls A–Z West, a community in Joshua Tree, deep in the Mojave Desert east of Los Angeles. Zittel describes A–Z West as an "evolving testing grounds for living." Her "life practice" comprises shipping-container work spaces, sculpture installations, bare-bones "experimental living cabins" for guests (including Wagon Station Encampment, twelve domed aluminum-clad units), and a giant studio for crafting the textiles and ceramics of A–Z West Works. The artwork also encompasses her lifestyle, in which she wears the same outfit (of her design) every day for a season and constantly changes her own home, a space that began as a shack and has expanded into a colorful oasis filled with succulents, vivid patterns, plywood walls, and her own usable art, such as *Aggregated Stacks*—wall shelves made from plaster-covered cardboard shipping boxes—and *Linear Sequence*, a sculpture of tabletops and floor cushions that functions as a living room. You can book a visit in one of the guest cabins, but be warned: they have no electricity or running water.

ANDERS ZORN

Zorngården
Mora, Sweden

Painter, etcher, sculptor
👁

One of Sweden's most illustrious artists, painter Anders Zorn (1860–1920) employed free-flowing brush strokes, a restricted color palette, and keen insight into human emotion to vividly capture his subjects' spirit. He painted the portraits of kings, presidents, and common people with equal gusto, to stunning effect. Zorngården, Zorn's home in Mora, Sweden, which he designed himself, remains virtually untouched after more than a century. The fairy-tale cabin—equal parts grand and cozy—is a hybrid, combining elements from local timber cottages, English manors, and Zorn's conception of Viking-era dwellings. A sharply pitched roof, timber siding, and intricate windows dialogue with the interior, with its painted wood beams, tall brick fireplace, built-in benches and cabinets, and cavernous, chalet-like great hall. For his personal collection, Zorn mixed local craftwork, like hand-woven tablecloths, pillowcases, and wooden chairs, with valuable objects acquired from abroad, such as medieval tapestries, antique sculptures, and old master paintings. The home showcases what were luxuries in its day: refrigeration, central heating, hot and cold running water, and even a vacuum cleaner. The emerald green garden, full of berry bushes and fruit trees, is accentuated by a sinuous bronze fountain sculpture by Zorn himself. The home sits next to the Zorn Museum, which contains hundreds of Zorn's watercolors, oil paintings, sculptures, drawings, and etchings.

283

ARTISTS' HOMES BY LOCATION

This book features 248 homes that belong (or belonged) to some of the world's most creative people from around the world. The directory below is organized alphabetically by location so that you can see a full list of all the properties in an individual country or city. After each artist's name we have included either an eye symbol to denote that the residence can be viewed by the public or a padlock symbol to indicate that it is a private home.

ARTISTS' HOMES OPEN TO THE PUBLIC

Many of the properties featured in this book can be visited by the public; some operate as museums, others can only be visited by appointment. Each artist entry includes either an eye symbol to denote that the residence can be viewed by the public or a padlock symbol to indicate that it is a private home.

Below are the details of the 167 properties that are open to the public, organised alphabetically by the surname of the creative person who lived there. While every care has been taken to ensure accuracy, details are subject to change and therefore it is advisable to check information prior to making travel plans.

ALVAR AALTO
The Aalto House
Riihitie 20
FI-00330 Helsinki
Finland
Website: alvaraalto.fi/en

LOUISA MAY ALCOTT
Orchard House
399 Lexington Road
Concord
MA 01742
USA
Website: louisamayalcott.org

ANNA AND MICHAEL ANCHER
Anchers Hus
Markvej 2–4
9990 Skagen
Denmark
Website: skagenskunstmuseer.dk/museer/anchers-hus

LOUIS ARMSTRONG
Louis Armstrong House Museum
34–56 107th Street
Corona
Queens
NY 11368, USA
Website: louisarmstronghouse.org

JANE AUSTEN
Jane Austen's House
Winchester Road
Chawton
Hampshire
GU34 1SD
UK
Website: jane-austens-house-museum.org.uk

FRANCIS BACON
Francis Bacon's Studio
Dublin City Gallery The Hugh Lane
Charlemont House
Parnell Square North
Dublin 1
D01 F2X9
Republic of Ireland
Website: hughlane.ie

LUIS BARRAGÁN
Casa Luis Barragán
General Francisco Ramírez 12–14
Colonia Ampliación Daniel Garza
11840 Mexico City
Mexico
Website: casaluisbarragan.org
Note: Tours by appointment only.

FREDERIC CLAY BARTLETT
Bonnet House Museum & Gardens
900 North Birch Road
Fort Lauderdale
FL 33304
USA
Website: bonnethouse.org

GEOFFREY BAWA
Number 11
33rd Lane
Colombo
Sri Lanka
Website: geoffreybawa.com/number-11
Note: Tours by appointment only.

VANESSA BELL AND DUNCAN GRANT
Charleston
Firle
Lewes
East Sussex
BN8 6LL
UK
Website: charleston.org.uk

ANTONIO BLANCO
Blanco Renaissance Museum
Campuan
Ubud
Bali 80571
Indonesia
Website: blancomuseum.com/museum

KAREN BLIXEN
Karen Blixen Museet
Rungsted Strandvej 111
2960 Rungsted Kyst
Denmark
Website: blixen.dk

LINA BO BARDI
Casa de Vidro
Rua General Almério de Moura 200
Vila Morumbi
São Paulo
São Paulo 05690-080
Brazil
Website: institutobardi.org

ROSA BONHEUR
Château de By
12, rue Rosa Bonheur
77810 Thomery
France
Website: chateau-rosa-bonheur.fr/

ÉMILE-ANTOINE BOURDELLE
Musée Bourdelle
18, rue Antoine Bourdelle
75015 Paris
France
Website: bourdelle.paris.fr/en

DAVID BOWIE
David Bowie and Iman Residence
Mandalay
Mustique
St. Vincent and the Grenadines
Website: mustique-island.com/villa/mandalay
Note: The villa is available for private rental.

ROBIN BOYD
Boyd House II
290 Walsh Street
South Yarra
Melbourne
VIC 3141
Australia
Website: robinboyd.org.au
Note: Tours by appointment only.

ROBERT BRADY
Museo Robert Brady
Netzahualcóyotl 4
Col. Centro
Cuernavaca
Morelos
CP 62000
Mexico
Website: museorobertbrady.com

REMO BRINDISI
Casa Museo Remo Brindisi
Via Nicolò Pisano 51
44029 Lido di Spina
Italy
Website: casamuseoremobrindisi.com

CHARLOTTE, EMILY, AND ANNE BRONTË
Brontë Parsonage Museum
Church Street
Haworth
Keighley
West Yorkshire
BD22 8DR
UK
Website: bronte.org.uk

OLE BULL
Ole Bull Museum Lysøen
Museet Lysøen
5215 Lysekloster
Norway
Website: lysoen.no/en

ROBERTO BURLE MARX
Sítio Roberto Burle Marx
Estrada Roberto Burle Marx 2019 -
Barra Guaratiba
Rio de Janeiro
Rio de Janeiro 23020-255
Brazil
Website: portal.iphan.gov.br/pagina/detalhes/399
Note: Tours by appointment only.

GEORGE, LORD BYRON
Newstead Abbey
Newstead Abbey Park
Ravenshead
Nottinghamshire
NG15 8NA
UK
Website: newsteadabbey.org.uk

GUSTAVE CAILLEBOTTE
Maison Caillebotte
8, rue de Concy
91330 Yerres
France
Website: proprietecaillebotte.com

PAUL CAUCHIE
Maison Cauchie
Rue des Francs 5
1040 Etterbeek
Brussels
Belgium
Website: cauchie.be

PAUL CÉZANNE
Atelier de Cézanne
9, avenue Paul Cezanne
13090 Aix-en-Provence
France
Website: cezanne-en-provence.com/en

CHARLES CHAPLIN
Manoir de Ban
Chaplin's World
Route de Fenil 2
1804 Corsier-sur-Vevey
Switzerland
Website: chaplinsworld.com/en

AGATHA CHRISTIE
Greenway
Greenway Road
Galmpton
Near Brixham
Devon
TQ5 0ES
UK
Website: nationaltrust.org.uk/greenway

FREDERIC EDWIN CHURCH
Olana State Historic Site
5720 State Route 9G
Hudson
NY 12534
USA
Website: olana.org

JEAN COCTEAU
Villa Santo Sospir
14, avenue Jean Cocteau
06230 Saint-Jean-Cap-Ferrat
France
Website: santosospir.com

THOMAS COLE
Thomas Cole National Historic Site
218 Spring Street
Catskill
NY 12414
USA
Website: thomascole.org

SAMUEL TAYLOR COLERIDGE
Coleridge Cottage
35 Lime Street
Nether Stowey
Bridgwater
Somerset
TA5 1NQ
UK
Website: nationaltrust.org.uk/coleridge-cottage

SALVADOR DALÍ
Casa Salvador Dalí
Portlligat
17488 Cadaqués
Girona
Spain
Website: salvador-dali.org/en/museums

ROBERT DASH
Madoo
618 Sagg Main Street
Sagaponack
NY 11962
USA
Website: madoo.org
Note: The garden is open to visitors. The interiors are shown only by private tour.

GIORGIO DE CHIRICO
Casa Museo di Giorgio de Chirico
Piazza di Spagna 31
00187 Rome
Italy
Website: fondazionedechirico.org/en

CHARLES DICKENS
Charles Dickens Museum
48 Doughty Street
London
WC1N 2LX
UK
Website: dickensmuseum.com

KARL DULDIG
Duldig Studio – Museum and Sculpture Garden
92 Burke Road
Malvern East
VIC 3145
Australia
Website: duldig.org.au

ALBRECHT DÜRER
Albrecht-Dürer-Haus
Albrecht-Dürer-Straße 39
90403 Nuremberg
Germany
Website: museums.nuernberg.de/albrecht-duerer-house

CHARLES AND RAY EAMES
Eames House
Eames Foundation
203 Chautauqua Boulevard
Pacific Palisades
Los Angeles
CA 90272
USA
Website: eamesfoundation.org
Note: Tours by appointment only.

JIM EDE
Kettle's Yard
University of Cambridge
Castle Street
Cambridge
CB3 0AQ
UK
Website: kettlesyard.co.uk

RALPH WALDO EMERSON
Ralph Waldo Emerson Memorial House
28 Cambridge Turnpike
Concord
MA 01742
USA
Website: ralphwaldoemersonhouse.org

WHARTON ESHERICK
Wharton Esherick Museum
1520 Horseshoe Trail
Malvern
PA 19355
USA
Website: whartonesherickmuseum.org

WILLIAM FAULKNER
Rowan Oak
916 Old Taylor Road
Oxford
MS 38655
USA
Website: rowanoak.com

DANIEL CHESTER FRENCH
Chesterwood, A Site of the National Trust for Historic Preservation
4 Williamsville Road
Stockbridge
MA 01262
USA
Website: chesterwood.org

ALBERT FREY
Frey House II
686 Palisades Drive
Palm Springs
CA 92262
USA
Website: psmuseum.org/visit/frey-house
Note: Tours by appointment only.

JAMES GALLIER, JR.
Gallier Historic House
1132 Royal Street
New Orleans
LA 70116
USA
Website: hgghh.org/gallier-house

ELIZABETH GASKELL
Elizabeth Gaskell's House
84 Plymouth Grove
Manchester
M13 9LW
UK
Website: elizabethgaskellhouse.co.uk

GESELLIUS, LINDGREN, & SAARINEN
Hvitträsk
Hvitträskintie 166
FI-02440 Luoma
Finland
Website: kansallismuseo.fi/en

JOHANN WOLFGANG GOETHE
Goethes Wohnhaus
Frauenplan 1
99423 Weimar
Germany
Website: klassik-stiftung.de/goethe-nationalmuseum/goethes-wohnhaus

ERNÖ GOLDFINGER
2 Willow Road
Hampstead
London
NW3 1TH
UK
Website: nationaltrust.org.uk/2-willow-road

EILEEN GRAY
Villa E-1027
E-1027 Sentier Massolin
06190 Roquebrune-Cap-Martin
France
Website: capmoderne.com/fr/lieu/la-villa-e-1027
Note: Tours by appointment only.

EDVARD GRIEG
Edvard Grieg Museum Troldhaugen
Troldhaugvegen 65
5232 Paradis-Bergen
Norway
Website: griegmuseum.no/en

WALTER GROPIUS
Gropius House
68 Baker Bridge Road
Lincoln
MA 01773
USA
Website: historicnewengland.org/property/gropius-house

CHAIM GROSS
The Renee & Chaim Gross Foundation
526 Laguardia Place
New York
NY 10012
USA
Website: rcgrossfoundation.org
Note: Tours by appointment only.

PATRICK GWYNNE
The Homewood
Portsmouth Road
Esher
Surrey
KT10 9JL
UK
Website: nationaltrust.org.uk/the-homewood
Note: Tours by appointment only.

GEORGE FRIDERIC HANDEL
Handel House
Handel & Hendrix in London
25 Brook Street
Mayfair
London
W1K 4HB
UK
Website: handelhendrix.org

WILLIAM S. HART
William S. Hart Museum
24151 Newhall Avenue
Newhall
CA 91321
USA
Website: hartmuseum.org

ERNEST HEMINGWAY
Ernest Hemingway Home and Museum
907 Whitehead Street
Key West
FL 33040
USA
Website: hemingwayhome.com

JIMI HENDRIX
Hendrix Flat
Handel & Hendrix in London
25 Brook Street
Mayfair
London
W1K 4HB
UK
Website: handelhendrix.org

BARBARA HEPWORTH
Barbara Hepworth Museum and
Sculpture Garden
Barnoon Hill
St. Ives
Cornwall
TR26 1AD
UK
Website: tate.org.uk/visit/tate-st-ives/
barbara-hepworth-museum-and-
sculpture-garden

WINSLOW HOMER
Winslow Homer Studio
Prouts Neck
Maine
USA
Website: portlandmuseum.org/
studiotour
Note: Tours by appointment only.

VICTOR HORTA
Horta Museum
Rue Américaine 25
1060 Saint-Gilles
Brussels
Belgium
Website: hortamuseum.be/en

ELBERT HUBBARD
Roycroft Campus
31 South Grove Street
East Aurora
NY 14052
USA
Website: roycroftcampuscorporation.
com

VICTOR HUGO
Maison Victor Hugo
6, place des Vosges
75004 Paris
France
Website: maisonsvictorhugo.paris.fr/en

CLEMENTINE HUNTER
Melrose Plantation
3533 Highway 119
Melrose
LA 71452
USA
Website: melroseplantation.org

HENRIK IBSEN
Ibsenmuseet
Henrik Ibsensgate 26
0255 Oslo
Norway
Website: ibsenmuseet.no/en

THOMAS JEFFERSON
Monticello
931 Thomas Jefferson Parkway
Charlottesville
VA 22902
USA
Website: monticello.org

PHILIP JOHNSON
The Glass House
199 Elm Street
New Canaan
CT 06840
USA
Website: theglasshouse.org
Note: Tours by appointment only.

DONALD JUDD
101 Spring Street
New York
NY 10012
USA
Website: juddfoundation.org
Note: Tours by appointment only.

FINN JUHL
Finn Juhls Hus
Kratvænget 15
2920 Charlottenlund
Denmark
Website: ordrupgaard.dk/en/finn-juhls-
house

DUŠAN SAMO JURKOVIČ
Jurkovič House
Jana Nečase 335/2
616 00 Brno-Žabovřesky
Czech Republic
Website: moravska-galerie.cz/
jurkovicova-vila?lang=en

FRIDA KAHLO
La Casa Azul
Londres 247
Colonia del Carmen
Coyoacán
04100 Mexico City
Mexico
Website: museofridakahlo.org.mx/en/
the-blue-house

FRIDA KAHLO AND DIEGO RIVERA
Museo Casa Estudio Diego Rivera y
Frida Kahlo
Calle Diego Rivera s/n
San Ángel Inn
Álvaro Obregón
01060 Mexico City
Mexico
Website: estudiodiegorivera.inba.gob.
mx

KANJIRŌ KAWAI
Kawai Kanjirō's Memorial House
569 Kaneicho
Gojozaka
Higashiyama-ku
Kyoto 605-0875
Japan
Website:kanjiro.jp

JOHN KEATS
Keats House
10 Keats Grove
Hampstead
London
NW3 2RR
UK
Website: cityoflondon.gov.uk/things-to-
do/keats-house

RUDYARD KIPLING
Bateman's
Bateman's Lane
Burwash
East Sussex
TN19 7DS
UK
Website: nationaltrust.org.uk/batemans

LEE KRASNER AND JACKSON POLLOCK
Pollock-Krasner House
830 Springs-Fireplace Road
East Hampton
NY 11937-1512
USA
Website: stonybrook.edu/commcms/
pkhouse
Note: Tours by appointment only.

CARL AND KARIN LARSSON
Carl Larsson-gården
Carl Larssons väg 12
790 15 Sundborn
Sweden
Website: carllarsson.se/en

LE CORBUSIER
Le Cabanon
Avenue Le Corbusier
06190 Roquebrune-Cap-Martin
France
Website: capmoderne.com/en/lieu/
le-cabanon
Note: Tours by appointment only.

FREDERIC, LORD LEIGHTON
Leighton House Museum
12 Holland Park Road
London
W14 8LZ
UK
Website: rbkc.gov.uk/subsites/
museums/leightonhousemuseum1.aspx

LEONARDO DA VINCI
Le Château du Clos Lucé – Parc
Leonardo da Vinci
2, rue du Clos Lucé
37400 Amboise
France
Website: vinci-closluce.com/en

NORMAN LINDSAY
Norman Lindsay Gallery and Museum
14 Norman Lindsay Crescent
Faulconbridge
NSW 2776
Australia
Website: nationaltrust.org.au/places/
norman-lindsay-gallery

FRANZ LISZT
Liszt-Haus
Marienstraße 17
99423 Weimar
Germany
Website: klassik-stiftung.de/en/
liszt-house

AUGUSTE AND LOUIS LUMIÈRE
Musée Lumière
25, rue du Premier - Film BP 8051
69352 Lyon
France
Website: institut-lumiere.org

EVERT LUNDQUIST
Evert Lundquists Ateljémuseum
Kantongatan 23
178 93 Drottningholm
Sweden
Website: evertlundquistsateljemuseum.
se

**CHARLES RENNIE AND MARGARET
MACDONALD MACKINTOSH**
The Mackintosh House
Hunterian Art Gallery
82 Hillhead Street
University of Glasgow
Glasgow
G12 8QQ
UK
Website: gla.ac.uk/hunterian/
collections/permanentdisplays/
themackintoshhouse

RENÉ MAGRITTE
René Magritte Museum
Rue Esseghem 135
1090 Jette
Brussels
Belgium
Website: magrittemuseum.be

SAM MALOOF
The Sam and Alfreda Maloof Foundation
for Arts and Crafts
5131 Carnelian Street
Alta Loma
CA 91701
USA
Website: malooffoundation.org
Note: Tours by appointment only.

CÉSAR MANRIQUE
Casa-Museo César Manrique Haría
C/ Elvira Sánchez nº30
35520 Haría
Lanzarote
Spain
Website: fcmanrique.org

PAUL MARMOTTAN
Musée Marmottan Monet
2, rue Louis-Boilly
75016 Paris
France
Website: marmottan.fr/en

RAFAEL MASÓ
Casa Masó
Ballesteries 29
17004 Girona
Spain
Website: rafaelmaso.org/cat/casa.php

JÓZEF MEHOFFER
Józef Mehoffer House
Krupnicza 26
31–123 Kraków
Poland
Website: mnk.pl/branch/the-mehoffer-house

GARI MELCHERS
Gari Melchers Home and Studio
University of Mary Washington
224 Washington Street
Fredericksburg
VA 22405
USA
Website: garimelchers.org

KONSTANTIN MELNIKOV
Melnikov House
Krivoarbatsky Pereuolok 10
Moscow 119002
Russia
Website: muar.ru/en/melnikov-house
Note: Tours by appointment only.

HERMAN MELVILLE
Herman Melville's Arrowhead
780 Holmes Road
Pittsfield
MA 01201
USA
Website: mobydick.org

HENRY CHAPMAN MERCER
Fonthill Castle
525 East Court Street
Doylestown
PA 18901
USA
Website: mercermuseum.org

LEE MILLER AND ROLAND PENROSE
Farleys House and Gallery
Farley Farm
Muddles Green
Chiddingly
East Sussex
BN8 6HW
UK
Website: farleyshouseandgallery.co.uk

CARL AND OLGA MILLES
Millesgården
Herserudsvägen 32
181 50 Lidingö
Sweden
Website: millesgarden.se/home.aspx

JOAN MIRÓ
Fundació Pilar i Joan Miró a Mallorca
Carrer de Saridakis 29
07015 Palma
Majorca
Spain
Website: miromallorca.com/en

CARLO MOLLINO
Casa Mollino
Via Giovanni Francesco Napione 2
10124 Turin
Italy
Note: Tours by appointment only.

CLAUDE MONET
Giverny
84, rue Claude Monet
27620 Giverny
France
Website: fondation-monet.com/en

HENRY MOORE
Henry Moore Studios and Gardens
Dane Tree House
Perry Green
Much Hadham
Hertfordshire
SG10 6EE
UK
Website: henry-moore.org

GUSTAVE MOREAU
Musée National Gustave Moreau
14, rue de la Rochefoucauld
75009 Paris
France
Website: en.musee-moreau.fr

MAX MOREAU
Carmen de Max Moreau
Camino Nuevo de San Nicolás 12
18010 Granada
Spain

WILLIAM MORRIS
Red House
Red House Lane
Bexleyheath
London
DA6 8JF
UK
Website: nationaltrust.org.uk/red-house

ALFRED MUNNINGS
The Munnings Art Museum at Castle House
Castle Hill
Dedham
Colchester
Essex
CO7 6AZ
UK
Website: munningsmuseum.org.uk

GEORGE NAKASHIMA
George Nakashima Woodworkers
1847 Aquetong Road
New Hope
PA 18938
USA
Website: nakashimawoodworkers.com/visit
Note: For information about guided tours, visit nakashimafoundation.org.

PABLO NERUDA
Casa Museo Isla Negra
Poeta Neruda s/n
Isla Negra
El Quisco 2660131
Chile
Website: fundacionneruda.org/en

RICHARD NEUTRA
Neutra VDL Research House
Neutra VDL Studio and Residences
2300 Silver Lake Boulevard
Los Angeles
CA 90039
USA
Website: neutra-vdl.org/visit

ISAMU NOGUCHI
The Isamu Noguchi Garden Museum
Japan
3519 Mure
Mure-cho
Takamatsu City
Kagawa 761-0121
Japan
Website: isamunoguchi.or.jp/index_e.htm
Note: Tours by appointment only.

JUAN O'GORMAN
Juan O'Gorman House-Studio
Mexico CIty
Mexico
Website: airbnb.co.uk/rooms/640803
Note: The house is available for private rental.

GEORGIA O'KEEFFE
Georgia O'Keeffe's Home and Studio
Abiquiú
New Mexico
USA
Website: okeeffemuseum.org/store/products/abiquiu/abiquiu-home-studio-tour
Note: Tours by appointment only.

CARLOS PÁEZ VILARÓ
Museo Taller de Casapueblo
Calle Mar de Liguria
Punta Ballena
Maldonado 20003
Uruguay
Website: casapueblo.com.uy/en

ALEXANDROS PAPADIAMANTIS
Papadiamantis House
Papadiamanti 12
Skiathos 370 02
Greece

LUCIANO PAVAROTTI
Casa Museo Luciano Pavarotti
Stradello Nava 6
41126 Modena
Italy
Website: casamuseolucianopavarotti.it/en

JOŽE PLEČNIK
Plečnik House
Karunova ulica 4–6
1000 Ljubljana
Slovenia
Website: mgml.si/en/plecnik-house

LODOVICO POGLIAGHI
Casa Museo Lodovico Pogliaghi
Via Beata Giuliana 5
21100 Varese
Italy
Website: casamuseopogliaghi.it

BEATRIX POTTER
Hill Top
Near Sawrey
Hawkshead
Ambleside
Cumbria
LA22 0LF
UK
Website: nationaltrust.org.uk/hill-top

ELVIS PRESLEY
Graceland
Elvis Presley Boulevard
Memphis
TN 38116
USA
Website: graceland.com

JEAN PROUVÉ
Maison Jean Prouvé
6, rue Augustin Hacquard
54100 Nancy
France
Website: musee-des-beaux-arts.nancy.fr

GIACOMO PUCCINI
Villa Museo Puccini
Viale G. Puccini 266
55049 Torre del Lago
Italy
Website: giacomopuccini.it/en/

ALEXANDER PUSHKIN
Pushkin Memorial Apartment
12 River Moika Embankment
St. Petersburg 191186
Russia
Website: museumpushkin.ru/vserossijskij_muzej_a._s._pushkina/muzej-kvartira_a.s.pushkina/the_pushkin_apartment_museum.html

SERGEI RACHMANINOV
Ivanovka
Sergei Rachmaninov 1
Ivanovka Village
Uvarovo District
Tambov Region 393481
Russia
Website: ivanovka-museum.ru

RAPHAEL
Casa Raffaello Urbino
Via Raffaello Sanzio 57
61029 Urbino
Italy
Website: casaraffaello.com

ILYA REPIN
Penaty
Primorskoe Shosse 411
Repino
St. Petersburg 197738
Russia
Website: eng.nimrah.ru/musrepin/

GERRIT RIETVELD
Rietveld Schröderhuis
Prins Hendriklaan 50
3583 EP Utrecht
The Netherlands
Website: rietveldschroderhuis.nl/en

NIKOLAI RIMSKY-KORSAKOV
N. Rimsky-Korsakov Museum-
Apartment
Zagorodny Prospekt 28
St. Petersburg 191002
Russia
Website: rkorsakov.ru/eng

NORMAN ROCKWELL
Norman Rockwell Museum
9 Glendale Road
Stockbridge
MA 01262
USA
Website: nrm.org

OTTO ROTHMAYER
Villa Rothmayer
U Páté baterie 896/50
162 00 Prague 6 - Břevnov
Czech Republic
Website: en.muzeumprahy.cz/villa-
rothmayer
Note: Tours by appointment only.

JEAN-JACQUES ROUSSEAU
Les Charmettes
890, chemin des Charmettes
73000 Chambéry
France
Website: chambery.fr/302-les-
charmettes-maison-de-jean-jacques-
rousseau.htm

PETER PAUL RUBENS
Rubenshuis
Wapper 9–11
2000 Antwerp
Belgium
Website: rubenshuis.be/en

JOHN RUSKIN
Brantwood
East of Lake
Coniston
Cumbria
LA21 8AD
UK
Website: brantwood.org.uk

ELIEL SAARINEN
Saarinen House
Cranbrook Center for Collections and
Research
39221 Woodward Avenue
Bloomfield Hills
MI 48303-0801
USA
Website: center.cranbrook.edu/visit/
saarinen-house

VITA SACKVILLE-WEST
Sissinghurst Castle
Biddenden Road
Near Cranbrook
Kent
TN17 2AB
Website: nationaltrust.org.uk/
sissinghurst-castle-garden
Note: The garden is open to visitors,
along with the tower, library, gatehouse,
and south cottage.

YVES SAINT LAURENT
Villa Oasis
Jardin Majorelle
Rue Yves Saint Laurent
Marrakech
Morocco
Note: The house is shown only by
private tour.

NIKI DE SAINT PHALLE
Giardino dei Tarocchi
Pescia Fiorentina
Capalbio
Provincia di Grosseto (58100)
Italy
Website: ilgiardinodeitarocchi.it/en

AUGUSTUS SAINT-GAUDENS
Aspet
139 Saint Gaudens Road
Cornish
NH 03745, USA
Website: nps.gov/saga

ARY SCHEFFER
Museé de la Vie Romantique
Hotel Scheffer-Renan
16, rue Chaptal
75009 Paris
France
Website: museevieromantique.paris.fr/
en

FRIEDRICH SCHILLER
Schillers Wohnhaus
Schillerstraße 12
99423 Weimar
Germany
Website: klassik-stiftung.de/en/
schiller-residence

RUDOLPH M. SCHINDLER
Schindler House
835 North Kings Road
West Hollywood
CA 90069
USA
Website: makcenter.org/visit

FRANK SINATRA
Sinatra House (Twin Palms)
1145 East Vía Colusa
Palm Springs
CA 92262
USA
Website: sinatrahouse.com
Note: The house is available for private
tours and rental.

JOHN SOANE
Sir John Soane's Museum
13 Lincoln's Inn Fields
London
WC2A 3BP
UK
Website: soane.org

PAOLO SOLERI
Cosanti
6433 East Doubletree Ranch Road
Paradise Valley
AZ 85253
USA
Website: arcosanti.org/visit/cosanti

JOAQUÍN SOROLLA BASTIDA
Museo Sorolla
Paseo General Martínez Campos no. 37
28010 Madrid
Spain
Website: museosorolla.mcu.es

GUSTAV STICKLEY
The Stickley Museum at Craftsman
Farms
2352 Route 10 West
Morris Plains
NJ 07950
USA
Website: stickleymuseum.org

ROBERT TATIN
Musée Robert Tatin
La Maison des Champs
La Frénouse
53230 Cossé-le-Vivien
France
Website: musee-robert-tatin.fr

PYOTR ILYICH TCHAIKOVSKY
Tchaikovsky House-Museum
Ulitsa Chaykovskogo 48
Klin
Moscow Oblast 141600
Russia
Website: tchaikovsky.house

ALFRED, LORD TENNYSON
Farringford
Bedbury Lane
Freshwater Bay
Isle of Wight
PO40 9PE
UK
Website: farringford.co.uk

DYLAN THOMAS
Dylan Thomas Boathouse & Writing
Shed
Dylan's Walk
Laugharne
Carmarthenshire
SA33 4SD
UK
Website: dylanthomasboathouse.com

MARK TWAIN
The Mark Twain House and Museum
351 Farmington Avenue
Hartford
CT 06105
USA
Website: marktwainhouse.org

JØRN UTZON
Can Lis
Avinguda Jorn Utzon 77
07691 Santanyí
Majorca
Spain
Website: canlis.dk/en
Note: Tours by appointment only.

SUZANNE VALADON
Atelier-Apartment, Musée de
Montmartre
12, rue Cortot
75018 Paris
France
Website: museedemontmartre.fr/en

MART VAN SCHIJNDEL
Van Schijndelhuis
Pieterskerkhof 8
3512 JR Utrecht
The Netherlands
Website: martvanschijndel.nl
Note: Tours by appointment only.

GIUSEPPE VERDI
Villa Verdi
Via Giuseppe Verdi 22
29010 Sant'Agata di Villanova sull'Arda
Italy
Website: villaverdi.org

GIANNI VERSACE
The Villa Casa Casuarina at the former
Versace Mansion
1116 Ocean Drive
Miami Beach
FL 33139
USA
Website: vmmiamibeach.com
Note: The villa operates as a hotel.

GUSTAV VIGELAND
Vigelandmuseet
Nobels gate 32
0268 Oslo
Norway
Website: vigeland.museum.no/en

VOLTAIRE
Château de Voltaire
Allée du Château
01210 Ferney-Voltaire
France
Website: chateau-ferney-voltaire.fr/en

OTTO WAGNER
Otto Wagner Villa I
Ernst Fuchs-MuseumHüttelbergstraße
26
1140 Vienna
Austria
Website: ernstfuchsmuseum.at

EMERY WALKER
Emery Walker's House
7 Hammersmith Terrace
London
W6 9TS
UK
Website: emerywalker.org.uk/house

GEORGE FREDERIC AND MARY WATTS
Limnerslease
Down Lane
Compton
Surrey
GU3 1DQ
UK
Website: wattsgallery.org.uk/about-us/
artists-village/limnerslease

EDITH WHARTON
The Mount
2 Plunkett Street
Lenox
MA 01240
USA
Website: edithwharton.org

VIRGINIA WOOLF
Monk's House
Rodmell
Lewes
East Sussex
BN7 3HF
UK
Website: nationaltrust.org.uk/monks-
house

FRANK LLOYD WRIGHT
Taliesin West
12621 North Frank Lloyd Wright
Boulevard
Scottsdale
AZ 85259
USA
Website: franklloydwright.org/taliesin-
west

RUSSEL WRIGHT
Dragon Rock House and Studio,
Manitoga
584 Route 9D
Garrison
NY 10542
USA
Website: visitmanitoga.org

N. C. WYETH
N. C. Wyeth House and Studio
1 Hoffman's Mill Road
Chadds Ford
PA 19317
USA
Website: brandywine.org/museum/
about/studios

ANDREA ZITTEL
A–Z West
Joshua Tree
California
USA
Website: zittel.org/work/a-z-west
Note: Tours by appointment only.
Visitors may not show up on A-Z West
grounds unannounced or without an
appointment under any circumstance.

ANDERS ZORN
Zorngården
Vasagatan 36
792 21 Mora
Sweden
Website: zorn.se/en/visit-us/zorn-house

ARTISTS BY CREATIVE DISCIPLINE

This book features the homes of 266 of the world's most creative people, including artists, architects, designers, musicians, and novelists. This directory is organized according to the creative discipline for which each person is best known. Of course, many of these people are (or were) multi-talented, so please see individual entries for a more detailed list of their creative abilities.

INDEX

PICTURE CREDITS

AUTHOR'S ACKNOWLEDGEMENTS

I'd like to thank the homeowners and caretakers of these spectacular homes; particularly the hardworking staff of the house museums, who generously provided information, insights, images, and in many cases access into their beautiful properties. Thanks also to my talented researcher, Monica Nelson, for digging into so many projects, and unearthing things I couldn't. I'm grateful to my excellent editors Clare Churly and Virginia McLeod for inspiring me, keeping me on track, and expertly guiding the book along, even as its scope shifted. I'm grateful to my family and friends, who are always an inspiration and a joy. And especially to my wife Barbara, who put up with missing weekends and stressed-out evenings, and always lovingly encourages me to follow my passion.

PUBLISHER'S ACKNOWLEDGEMENTS

The publisher would like to extend special thanks to Clare Churly for project-managing this title. Thanks also to Caitlin Arnell Argles, Emma Barton, Sarah Bell, Jane Birch, Vanessa Bird, Adela Cory, Lisa Delgado, Philipp Hubert, João Mota, Anthony Naughton, Monica Nelson, William Norwich, Angelika Pirkl, Rebecca Price, Michele Robecchi, and Gemma Robinson for their invaluable contributions to the book.

Phaidon Press Limited
2 Cooperage Yard
London E15 2QR

Phaidon Press Inc.
65 Bleecker Street
New York, NY 10012

phaidon.com

First published 2020
© 2020 Phaidon Press Limited

ISBN 978 1 8386 6131 1

A CIP catalogue record for this book is available from the British Library and the Library of Congress.

Commissioning Editor: Virginia McLeod
Project Editor: Clare Churly
Production Controllers: Adela Cory and Rebecca Price
Design: Philipp Hubert / Hubert & Fischer

Printed in China